EATING AND DRINKING IN
ROMAN BRITAIN

What were the eating and drinking habits of the inhabitants of
Britain during the Roman period? Drawing on evidence from a
large number of archaeological excavations, this fascinating new
study shows how varied these habits were in different regions and
amongst different communities and challenges the idea that there
was any one single way of being Roman or native. Integrating a
range of archaeological sources, including pottery, metalwork and
environmental evidence such as animal bone and seeds, this book
illuminates eating and drinking choices, providing invaluable insights into how those communities regarded their world. The book
contains sections on the nature of the different types of evidence
used and how they can be analysed. It will be a useful guide to all
archaeologists, and those who wish to learn about the strengths and
weaknesses of these materials and how best to use them.

HILARY COOL is a professional archaeologist who, for the past ten
years, has run her own business providing post-excavation services
to the professional sector. She is also a director of Barbican Research
Associates, a company specialising in writing up backlog sites. Her
publications include *The Roman Cemetery at Brougham, Cumbria*
(2004) and (with J. Price) *Roman Vessel Glass from Excavations at
Colchester* 1971–1985 (1995).

EATING AND DRINKING IN ROMAN BRITAIN

H. E. M. COOL

CAMBRIDGE
UNIVERSITY PRESS

CAMBRIDGE UNIVERSITY PRESS
Cambridge, New York, Melbourne, Madrid, Cape Town, Singapore, São Paulo

Cambridge University Press
The Edinburgh Building, Cambridge CB2 2RU, UK

Published in the United States of America by Cambridge University Press, New York

www.cambridge.org
Information on this title: www.cambridge.org/9780521003278

First published 2006

Printed in the United Kingdom at the University Press, Cambridge

A catalogue record for this publication is available from the British Library

ISBN-13 978-0-521-80276-5 hardback
ISBN-10 0-521-80276-8 hardback
ISBN-13 978-0-521-00327-8 paperback
ISBN-10 0-521-00327-X paperback

For Mike
who has patiently lived with me and the Romans for a very long time

Contents

Contents

Figures

Tables

Preface

I decided to write this book as it combined three of my great interests in life – food, drink and Roman Britain. Whilst few people would be surprised at the first two, a passion for the third would raise eyebrows in many archaeological circles. For much of my professional life just as real men didn't eat quiche, so real archaeologists didn't do Roman Britain. For Classical archaeologists, the province of *Britannia* was a distant excrescence, far from the 'proper' archaeology of the Mediterranean lands. Within British archaeology, it was seen as the preserve of arcane specialisms pursuing their own agendas far from where the theoretical action was. Whilst theory has now come to Roman Britain, it is still an uncomfortable place for many. Modern tastes wish to do away with anything that recalls colonialism, whilst rising nationalisms prefer not to engage with periods when Britain was self-evidently part of a wider world. Prehistory is still a safer, more comfortable and purer world for archaeologists to play in.

This is a great pity as Roman Britain is a very strange place, much stranger than the many popular books written about it would lead one to think. It is fully worthy of being studied in its own right, but that has to be done on its own terms. This involves knowing how to interpret all the data relating to it. The problem with Roman Britain is that there are just too many things. Too much pottery, too much metalwork, too many animal bones. People tend to be overwhelmed by the sheer volume. They deal with it by picking out the occasional morsel, and hoping the rest will go away. This book is offered as a kind of hitchhiker's guide to those who would like to explore this material, but who lose the will to live when faced with the reams of specialist reports that even a minor excavation can generate. It shows, I hope, how these reports can be used to explore different facets of the past. I have chosen to explore eating and drinking

because not only does it interest me but, as the celebrated gourmet and bon viveur Brillat-Savarin said 'Tell me what you eat, and I will tell you what you are'. Where better to start exploring Roman Britain?
Bon appetit!

Acknowledgements

A book like this depends on the work of the specialists who have sorted, identified, analysed and published the multitude of items on which it is based. Their names are mentioned in the footnotes, but I would like to put on record my thanks here, and my apologies too if I have misrepresented them.

Over the years I have benefited from discussions with many people. Those who have kindly answered questions specifically to do with this book include Richard Brewer, Peter Davenport, Brenda Dickinson, Jerry Evans, Andrew (Bone) Jones, Ruth Leary, Scott Martin, Quita Mould, Stephanie Ratkái, Paul Sealey and Vivien Swan. Special thanks are due to Ruth and Scott, who made the results of currently unpublished work available to me; and to Bone for reading the sections pertaining to fish. Jerry has been particularly generous with unpublished work and useful discussion. I'm sure he won't agree with what I've made of it all, but I hope he'll enjoy the result. Alex Smith and Oxford Archaeology kindly allowed me to refer to the results of the Claydon Pike excavations in advance of full publication and provided additional details.

Jaye Pont is thanked for her invaluable guidance in matters pertaining to illustration software, and I am grateful to the West Yorkshire Archaeological Service (via Chris Philo) and the Winchester Excavation Committee (via Professor Martin Biddle) for providing figs. 9.1 and 17.4.

I would like to thank Cambridge University Press for publishing the book, and the two editors who have overseen it, Jessica Kuper and Simon Whitmore. Simon is owed special thanks for his forbearance over its much delayed appearance. I am most grateful also to Sarah Parker, Joanna Breeze and Gwynneth Drabble for their work in preparing the book for publication.

Mike Baxter provided fig. 15.1 and read the final draft which was much improved by his comments. He has also provided constant encouragement and support during the book's prolonged gestation, and indeed for much longer than that. So, as is only right, this book is for him.

The final stages of preparing the manuscript have been enlivened by listening to the Test Match Special commentary of the thrilling 2005 England – Australia Ashes series. It has been most distracting – many thanks to the players of both teams and the commentators.

CHAPTER I

Apéritif

This is a book that takes that most common question 'What shall we have for dinner?' and uses it to explore the communities that lived in Britain during the first half of the first millennium AD (a period that will hereafter be called Roman Britain as a convenient shorthand). Subject-matter such as this has not always been thought very respectable. Certainly it has not been considered central to the story of Roman Britain. Yet in many ways there is no better way of understanding past societies. Eating and drinking are frequently about much more than sustaining life by the ingestion of sufficient calories. What you can and cannot eat, who you can and cannot eat it with, tends not to be so much a matter of personal choice, as the result of social conditioning. By studying the eating patterns of a society, you enter areas far beyond the mere nutritional. Eating and drinking rituals will quite frequently take you into the realms of religious beliefs, class, gender relationships, and ethnicity. Or, as Brillat-Savarin said more succinctly, 'Tell me what you eat, and I will tell you what you are'.[1]

The information that can be used for this study is entirely dependent on archaeological exploration. The scanty ancient sources that have trad-itionally underpinned the study of Roman Britain are virtually silent on the topic; and, when they do say anything relevant, can generally be shown to be unreliable witnesses. Archaeology, by contrast, produces data in almost embarrassing abundance. We have so much information that the problem is how best to use it, not just to explore eating habits, but also any other topic of interest. Most of these data are in the specialist contributions analysing and cataloguing the things found during excav-ation. These lurk behind the structural narratives of excavation reports like the submerged part of an iceberg, and are a seriously underused

[1] Brillat-Savarin 1826, 4th aphorism.

resource. I do not consider it an overstatement to say that they are where Roman Britain resides though, being a specialist myself, it might be considered that I am prejudiced. The patterns seen in the artefact and environmental reports often cut across preconceived notions of how life was lived in Britain during the earlier first millennium AD. It is my aim to bring this information to wider attention and, in doing so, demonstrate how it can be used.

If the specialist reports are so important, why are they so underused? The answer lies in the fact that this knowledge base developed as a service industry providing excavators with the information they needed to understand the structural narrative. It was generally very highly focused towards the provision of dating evidence because of the way Romano-British studies developed. There is a long history of studying the province stretching back to the antiquaries of the eighteenth century such as Stukely and Horsley. For many years the preferred approach was to use the archaeology as an illustration of the meagre historical record derived from the ancient sources. The role of the army, and the changing military dispositions, took centre stage. For this the overwhelming need was to be able to date sites, and to identify the different periods when particular forts were occupied. This led to a hierarchy of esteem with the finds that were either intrinsically dateable, or which could be dated, valued over those perceived as not providing this information. So, much attention was devoted to coins and inscriptions, which often come with their dates written on them. Dated typologies of pottery could be built up using the stratigraphic associations with these independently dated items, and the pottery could be used to date contexts without coins or inscriptions.

Over the past two or three decades, attention has shifted much more towards how provincial society developed. Ways of looking at the province have been much influenced by broader, theoretical approaches of the type loosely described as post-processual. Though these approaches look at much wider issues than the previous military – historical approach, what is still wanted by excavators is the dating that can be provided by the finds, and such information about the trade and exchange networks of the site as the material can provide.

The specialists who produce the reports naturally structure their work to the requirements of their 'client', the person writing up the excavations. The end result of this can easily be seen by glancing at most pottery reports. There will frequently be detailed considerations of the decorated and stamped samian sherds and the stamped mortaria, as these are perceived as best being able to give the types of dates needed. The rest of the pottery will often be dealt with in a more summary way. The most favoured route currently is to prepare fabric and vessel type series, then quantify and summarise the assemblage according to these criteria, as this will help to provide information about the trade and exchange networks.

Increasingly whilst providing this basic, but ultimately rather boring, information, wider aspects of what the data are telling us are buried in the better specialist reports. This has been going on for some time but much of the wider archaeological community seems unaware of it. This is probably because few people read excavation reports from cover to cover. They will gut them for such information that is directly relevant to what they are working on, and hope that the author of the excavation monograph will have extracted the 'best bits' of the specialist reports for the overview. In my experience of writing and publishing specialist reports for over a quarter of a century, this is a misguided hope. It is a rare report that explores the interactions between all aspects of the data. It is the aim of this book to explore such interactions to show what a richly textured picture of the past comes about when this is done.

It has to be admitted that the picture is still a very patchy one. In part this comes about because some areas and types of site have seen relatively little work. Until the advent of developer-funded archaeology, for example, rural sites other than villas were seriously neglected.[2] Some of the gaps result from inadequate specialist reporting. This can come about for various reasons. Sometimes it is because work on the specialist categories is seen as an optional extra. Funds are not invested in various categories, or it is decided not to report fully on the material. Sometimes they are inadequate because certain conventions of reporting have arisen. In some areas the reports appear to be written mainly for the handful of fellow specialists who work in the field, blithely ignoring the fact that the ultimate aim must be to enable the integration of their information with all the rest of the data from the site. It is hoped that excavators and specialists reading this book will come to appreciate the gains that result from a full integration of all the material, and will perhaps mend their ways if necessary.

This book can be regarded as being structured in three parts. The next four chapters introduce the sources of the evidence. The first three of these are strictly archaeological and look at the food itself, the packaging it came in, and the results of ingesting the food as demonstrated by skeletal

---

[2] Hingley 2000, 150–1, Table 10.3; James 2003, 5–6, Illus. 1.

Figure 1.1. Map showing the principal sites mentioned in the text.

Figure 1.2. Detailed insets 2 and 3 for fig. 1.1. Inset 2 shows principal rivers in the area and inset 3 the main Roman roads.

Figure 1.3. Detailed inset 4 for fig. 1.1 showing the main Roman roads.

remains. The biases inherent in these sources will be examined, and the ways in which the different types of finds are generally studied will be discussed. This first part concludes with a consideration of the written evidence (Chapter 5). Some of this is archaeological and directly relevant to Roman Britain, such as the accounts and shopping lists recovered from Vindolanda. Most of the ancient literary sources are not directly relevant to the province as they relate to the Mediterranean world, a very different social milieu. It is useful to look at them because they do provide a background to the lifestyles of at least some of the elite population in the province.

The second and third parts look at the data in two different ways. Chapters 6 to 15 look at general patterns seen in the ingredients available and favoured, and cooking techniques. It starts with basic information about the kitchen and utensils, and moves through the major food categories to finish with drink. This section takes as its model classic works in the culinary repertoire that explore the cuisine of particular parts of the world such as Elizabeth David's *French Provincial Cookery,* Marcella Hazan's *Essentials of Classic Italian Cooking* and Rosemary Brissenden's *South East Asian Food.* This section exploits data from a wide variety of sites. In the third section (Chapters 16–19) the focus shifts to particular sites at particular times to explore the tastes of different communities. These case studies demonstrate how different strands of information can be combined to show how life was changing.

The chronological scope of the book ranges from the late pre-Roman Iron Age, when the influence of Rome was being felt in the south-east, until the fifth century when a new social environment was developing. The geographical range is that part of Britain that had extended periods within the Roman province, i.e. the mainland to approximately the Antonine Wall on the Forth – Clyde isthmus.

Finally, a few words about conventions used are appropriate. The term 'finds' will be used as a convenient shorthand to represent both artefactual and ecofactual material. The book is heavily dependent on a very large number of specialist reports, but to keep the references within publishable bounds the full details of each one cannot be given. In the footnotes the convention has been adopted of citing the specialist by name and the editor or author of the monograph; thus 'Mould in Wilson 2002a'. In the references the details of the publication will be found under Wilson 2002a. The sources used for each table will be found in Appendix 1, and the locations of the main sites mentioned in the text are shown in figs. 1.1–1.3.

CHAPTER 2

The food itself

INTRODUCTION

The main direct sources of information about food come from animal bones and plant seeds. The types of meat and varieties of vegetables and fruit consumed will be considered later in the book. Here the various factors that govern the type of information that can be extracted from this material, and the biases that are inherent in its study, will be discussed. The opportunity will also be taken to consider the question of quantification. Knowing how much of a commodity has been found at a site is essential if comparisons of consumption patterns on different sites are to be made. Finally in this chapter, the nature of rubbish disposal will be considered.

ANIMAL BONES

The biases that affect animal bone assemblages can be divided into two broad categories relating to what can actually survive, and how what survives is excavated and subsequently studied.

What survives depends very much on the soil conditions in which the material was deposited. Bone does not survive well in acidic soils, and in extreme cases can disappear in its entirety.[1] The acidity of a soil is measured on the pH scale from 1 (extremely acid) to 14 (extremely alkaline), and below a value of 6 the mineral that makes up bone becomes extremely soluble. Soil acidity can vary greatly over small areas depending on husbandry, drift geology, and whether or not deposits are waterlogged. This is well demonstrated at Catterick where extensive excavations in and around the Roman town have produced conditions ranging from very good to so bad that no bone was recovered.[2] Even within a site there may

[1] Mays 1998: 17.   [2] Stallibrass in Wilson 2002b: 392.

be differential survival according to what type of feature the bones are deposited in. On a site with otherwise good preservation, it was possible to show that sheep and pig bones survived far better in pits than they did in ditch fills,[3] probably because they were not being exposed to the elements and to scavenging animals. Dogs can have a noticeable impact on a bone assemblage when they ingest the more succulent bones.[4] It is also suspected that the bones of different species may decay at differential rates,[5] though in the words of one eminent specialist 'the decay of buried bone is complex, and still not well understood'.[6] With all of these factors to keep in mind, it is not surprising that most animal bone reports devote some time to assessing the site formation processes that may have influenced the assemblage that survives.

One of the most important developments in archaeological methodology over the past quarter century has been the routine sieving of samples of deposits. The sample is generally disaggregated in water, and then passed through a series of sieves of increasingly fine mesh size. Such a process is vital if plant remains of the type discussed in the next section are to be recovered, and it is also very important for the study of animal bone. It has long been appreciated that hand collection on site results in a very biased assemblage favouring large fragments, often from large animals. To evaluate fish and bird consumption large-scale sieving is vital,[7] but it can also be important for some other types of meat. The consumption of suckling pig can only be evaluated if sites have been sieved, as the bones of this delicacy are rarely recovered by hand collection.[8]

As will be obvious from this, comparing assemblages from different sites to build up a picture of who was eating what and at what time, has to be done with some care. There would be little useful information gained if the assemblage from a site with good preservation that had been sieved was compared with one where only hand collection had been carried out, even if the preservation was equally good. An additional problem arises with quantification, because assemblages can only be directly compared if they have been counted in the same way.

Counting things that are habitually found in a broken state, like animal bone and pottery, is not simple. Counting fragments is unsatisfactory as the same amount of bone may end up being found in different numbers of fragments on two sites depending on butchery practice and

---

[3] Maltby 1981: 165 Table 2.   [4] O'Connor 2000: 22.
[5] King 1978: 210.   [6] O'Connor 2000: 25.
[7] Coy 1989: Table 2.   [8] O'Connor 1989: 17.

site formation processes. As a very simple example we can imagine a long bone from a steer. On site A this is removed during butchery as an intact bone and disposed of in a pit where it remains undisturbed until excavated. On site B a similar bone may be chopped into six pieces to remove the marrow and the pieces then thrown into a ditch. One of these may be removed by a dog and be further fragmented into four pieces by a combination of chewing and people walking on the fragments where the dog leaves them. In total there are ten fragments of this bone from site B. Simple fragment count would indicate that there was ten times the amount of bone on site B as on site A, but of course this would not be true.

Even though these problems have long been recognised, a considerable amount of fragment-count data exists in the animal bone literature. The commonly used Number of Identified Specimens (NISP) measure falls into this category. This has the added problem that the number of bones is not identical in all animals. Pigs have more teeth and toes than cattle, whilst goats can only be identified from a limited number of elements.[9]

To overcome this a variety of counting strategies have been devised by animal bone specialists.[10] One method is to calculate the minimum number of individuals represented; but any calculation of minimum numbers, be it for animal bone, pottery or any other category of find, is only useful for comparing the numbers of things of different sorts in a single assemblage. Minimum numbers have been shown to be very dependent on the size of an assemblage,[11] and so are not a useful measure when comparing different assemblages with each other.

A more useful measure is to count different elements of the skeleton based on identifying different diagnostic zones. This has the advantage that it not only allows comparison between assemblages, but also allows the investigation of what sort of consumption was going on at different sites. As a simple example, a site where the assemblage is dominated by bones from the heads and feet of cattle is likely to be an abattoir, as these are the elements often removed with the hide after the animal is slaughtered. The value of this method of quantification was shown in a study that incorporated a large number of animal bone assemblages from London. It was possible to show a pattern that could be interpreted as slaughter and hide removal taking place in the countryside, then transfer of the carcases to primary butchery sites within the city. At those the

---

[9] See O'Connor 2001: 54–7.   [10] O'Connor 2001: 57–67.   [11] Orton 1993.

removal and disposal of the vertebrae could be observed as the carcase was butchered into joints. Finally, another set of sites could be identified which were associated with a high proportion of bones relating to prime meat joints, presumably the waste from the kitchens where they were consumed.[12]

The number of assemblages quantified by the zonal method is, alas, limited; and this book makes use of many assemblages quantified in far from ideal ways. The method of quantification will be stated, and the various drawbacks should always be borne in mind.

Best would be MNI + Zoral

PLANT REMAINS

Most archaeological sites in Britain other than those with very acidic soil will produce debris from meat consumption in the form of bones. The recovery of the vegetable part of the diet tends to be much more erratic. Plant remains are generally recovered only if they have been deposited in a damp or waterlogged environment, if they have been burnt, or if they have been mineralised. Again, this is a source of evidence that is only recovered when systematic sampling and flotation is undertaken.

In waterlogged deposits the normal processes of decay are arrested because of the lack of oxygen. What tends to be preserved are the seeds, pips and stones. Whether a site produces any evidence like this clearly depends on the depositional circumstances. Mineralised remains are also reliant on the type of context, as mineralisation takes place when organic parts of seeds and stones are replaced by calcium phosphate through exposure to urine and lime.[13] Latrine pits are ideal sources for such remains.

Plant remains preserved by burning tend to be more widespread, as once burnt they are not subject to decay and can be recovered from most soil types. The level of burning has to be relatively gentle as otherwise they will be burnt to ash. Burnt plant remains relating to diet are normally in the form of seeds, as various processes involved in preparing them for consumption require the application of heat. Not all cereals result in clean grain when threshed. The glume wheats (emmer and spelt) break into separate spikelets where the grains are still enclosed and have to be released from the glume. This is generally done by parching (heating) and pounding the grain.[14] Malting grain to make beer also requires heat to

---

[12] Moreno Garcia *et al.* 1996; Orton 1996.   [13] Greig 1982: 49.   [14] Hillmann 1981.

be applied. Here the grain has to be germinated so that the proteins it contains are converted to enzymes, which in turn convert the starch into soluble sugars which can be fermented to produce beer. Germination has to be halted at a point that optimises the amount of enzyme in the grain, and this is done by the application of a gentle heat.[15]

As large quantities of grain will have been heated for cleaning and malting purposes, charred plant remains tend to be biased towards cereals, but other food stuffs can also be preserved as chance contaminants. The residues from cleaning crops (straw, chaff and weeds) were often regarded as a useful fuel, and some carbonised deposits found in kilns and corn driers are clearly fuel rather than accurately reflecting the quality of a processed crop.[16]

Various other events can lead to the preservation of foodstuffs by charring. Sometimes food stores are burnt down and, though the overall temperature of the fire would be sufficient to reduce most of the contents to ash, some material may well be merely charred if it was covered by ash at an early stage. This would have prevented oxygen reaching it and thus complete combustion. This is what clearly occurred at several venues at Colchester when it was destroyed during the Boudican rising in AD 60/1. Here fruit has been recorded, as well as fully processed grain.[17] Foodstuffs were also placed on funeral pyres and again, though much would have been fully consumed by the fire, some will survive as charred remains.[18] A particularly good example of this was associated with a burial in Southwark where dates, figs and almonds had been amongst the pyre goods, as well as barley and wheat.[19]

The types of food crop being grown can be investigated by using pollen analysis, though in general this is not as useful a resource as might be hoped. Typical analysed sequences tend to come from bogs, and are often far from cultivation sites. As the pollen of some species such as cereals does not travel over any great distance such sequences, though ideal for mapping general vegetation change through time, are of limited use for exploring the food crops produced.[20] In some circumstances, pollen analysis of samples gathered on archaeological sites can be of great value. It was from the pollen found in bedding trenches at Wollaston that it was possible to show that they had been used for vines, and to demonstrate conclusively for the first time that vineyards had been present in Roman

[15] Protz 1995: 10–11.   [16] van der Veen 1991: 305.
[17] Murphy in Crummy 1984: 40 and 108.   [18] Bouby and Marinval 2004: 77–8.
[19] Mackinder 2000: 12.   [20] Huntley 2000: 68.

Britain.[21] Another intriguing use of pollen analysis was to suggest the presence of honey in a pit at Castleford.[22]

RESIDUES

Traces of foodstuffs can be trapped in the walls of pottery vessels in which they were stored or cooked, and this is potentially a very important source of information. Animal fats and plant oils are preserved as lipids and, if the pottery fragment is crushed, these can be extracted or dissolved and their molecular chemistry analysed by the technique of gas chromatography. The results are compared with modern flora and fauna to identify what was in the vessel.[23] Unfortunately, despite the large amounts of Romano-British pottery that are found every year, such techniques have rarely been applied to it. Where analyses do exist, many were carried out in the early days of lipid analysis.[24] Developments in the technique mean that some early analyses are suspect,[25] and there is a great need for new programmes of analysis. Why the methodology has not been more widely applied to Roman pottery is an interesting question. Possibly it arises from the assumption that we know what vessels were being used for. This is actually far from true, as will be explored in the case of mortaria in Chapter 6.

WHEN IS RUBBISH NOT RUBBISH?

Archaeology deals with the detritus of people's lives, but alas rubbish disposal is not a simple thing. Earlier in this chapter we saw that the type of context in which rubbish was disposed can have an important bearing on the type of evidence that survives. There is also the question of what the rubbish relates to. An ideal world would be one where the rubbish generated by a household would be neatly deposited in rubbish pits close to the house. Though this does occasionally happen, there was obviously often a more organised rubbish-disposal system also in place, so that the rubbish from a variety of different sources was mixed together. To complicate this matter still further, it is appropriate to consider here the phenomenon of structured deposition. Up to the 1980s it is fair to say that rubbish was simply rubbish to most Roman archaeologists. The things

---

[21] Meadows 1996. [22] Bastow in Abramson *et al.* 1999: 173.
[23] Evershed *et al.* 2001. [24] For example Evans, John and Going in Going 1987: 91.
[25] Evershed *et al.* 2001: 332.

dug up were regarded as broken and worn-out items that that had simply been disposed of. This was merely to impose our own cultural standards on the past. We had refuse collectors who arrived to take the detritus away each week; what could be more obvious than sensible people such as the Romans would have done the same? Increasingly it came to be appreciated that what is and isn't rubbish is very much a construct of the society you live in. Works exploring this within an archaeological context were appearing in the late 1970s and early 1980s.[26] This made people look afresh at what previously had been considered as unproblematic rubbish deposits.[27] Coming from a different intellectual tradition, the eminent Romano-British archaeologist Ralph Merrifield was also drawing attention to the fact that 'rubbish pits' often contained unusually complete items and odd combinations of things. He suggested that these were deliberately deposited items, and the motivation behind such deposits lay in the realms of ritual and magic rather than simply rubbish disposal.[28]

As the data were re-examined, it became apparent that a phenomenon now referred to as structured deposition was taking place. This was where items were deliberately placed in pits or ditches, often to mark a change or cessation of use. This activity had its origins in the prehistoric period, but there is no doubt that it was widespread in Roman Britain as well.[29] This means that data need to undergo an additional layer of interrogation. Obviously, if they come from such a deposit, they may not relate to the daily eating practices of the inhabitants of the site, but instead may be special produce appropriate for a deity.

---

[26] For example Hodder 1982. [27] For example Hill 1989: 20.
[28] Merrifield 1987. [29] Fulford 2001.

CHAPTER 3

The packaging

INTRODUCTION

It is useful to think about packaging according to the material it is made of: whether it is an organic material such as wood, or an inorganic one such as pottery. If the latter, there are no problems of survival and the material may be found on any sort of site. If the former, waterlogged deposits or at least damp, anaerobic ones will be required to preserve them, so their survival will be an exception rather than the rule. It is likely that much packaging was made from organic materials. Grain would have been most conveniently transported in sacks, fruit in baskets. Fragments of these sorts of containers survive only rarely, and even when they do, it is not possible to say what they contained. Pottery containers occur on many sites and some even have graffiti or inscriptions that identify the contents. Such containers will dominate discussion in this chapter, but it should always be borne in mind that they will have only accounted for a fraction of the food packaging that would have been used. That said, the information that can be gleaned from the principal pottery containers – amphorae – is invaluable for exploring the long-distance trade in luxury foodstuffs such as wine and oil.

AMPHORAE

Amphorae were large pottery vessels used to transport primarily liquid contents such as wine, oil and fish sauce over long distances: other contents could include preserved fruits, and occasionally things that were not food.[1] They are studied primarily by considering the shape of the vessel, and the fabric it is made from. Various forms of information were also written on them, and these can be used to identify the contents. It has

---

[1] Borgard and Cavalier 2003.

long been clear that different shapes were used to transport different commodities (Fig. 3.1). Unfortunately, there is no one generally agreed typology for amphora shapes, and nomenclature is not simple. Amphorae can be identified according to both systematic typologies such as that of Heinrich Dressel, and according to a type specimen named after the site on which it was first identified. In this book the different types will be referred to by the Peacock and Williams[2] typology numbers, as that work provides cross references to the names given to a form in other typologies. Where appropriate, reference will also be made to the commonest name used for a type in the British literature.

Pottery fabrics reflect the place where the vessel was made because different inclusions in the clay may only be found in particular regions. Some fabrics may be identified easily in the hand specimen. A notable example of this is the fabric of the amphorae from the Campanian region of Italy, a notable source of good wine. It is very distinctive as it appears to be full of black sand (green augite crystals).[3] Other fabrics need to be studied by taking a thin section and studying it under the microscope. Studying otherwise undiagnostic body fragments in this way allows them to be assigned to the area they were made in. It does not always allow them to be assigned to a particular type as, if a region makes a variety of commodities transported in amphorae, the fabric of all of them is likely to be the same or very similar. This is a particular problem for amphorae from southern Spain which was a major exporter of both olive oil and salted fish products.

Identifying what was in a particular amphora form can be established by a combination of strands of evidence. Amphorae can have written information on the exterior in the form of stamps made before the vessel was fired, and painted inscriptions made after. Some of this information relates to the production of the amphora itself, but the painted inscriptions (known as *tituli picti*) relate to the contents giving the weight and the item being transported. Just occasionally, they also name the place of origin.[4] Unfortunately, painted inscriptions need good preservation conditions to survive. So, though it is likely that the majority of amphorae would have been labelled, such inscriptions are not common. Another useful source of information about contents come from shipwrecks, as vessels can be found with the contents intact. An interesting example of this was an amphora found in the Thames which had clearly been

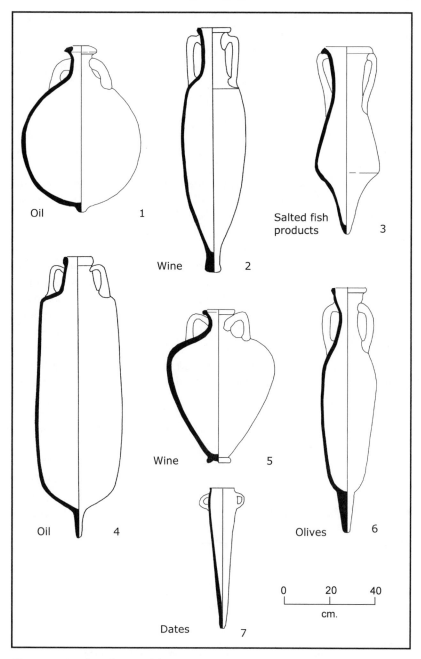

Figure 3.1. Amphora forms and their main contents. 1: Dressel 20 / PW25. 2: Dressel 2/4 / PW10. 3: PW18. 4: North African / PW35. 5: PW27. 6: London 555. 7: 'Carrot' / PW 12. (After Tyers 1996.) Scale 1 : 16.

transporting preserved olives from Spain as it still contained over 6,000 olive stones.[5]

It used to be considered that an important distinction was whether or not the inside of the vessel was coated with resin. Such coatings were known from the ancient sources to be a typical treatment for the inside of vessels involved in making and transporting wine.[6] Ongoing scientific work using such techniques as gas chromatography has detected such linings on amphorae used to transport olive oil and fish sauces,[7] and so the presence of a resin lining cannot now be taken as diagnostic that the contents were wine.

As with animal bone assemblages, there are problems with comparing the quantities of amphorae from different sites. They can be found virtually entire in shipwrecks and in burials, but on most sites amphorae are found as fragments. The specialists who study this material are divided on the best method of quantification. Some favour weight, some favour minimum numbers, and some still use sherd count. Only weight fulfils the criteria that allow comparisons across sites because measures of minimum numbers are very much dependent on the size of the assemblage, and sherd count on site formation processes. The value of usefully quantifying pottery assemblages may be appreciated by an inspection of Table 3.1.

Table 3.1 has been derived from sites that were occupied throughout the Roman period. and which have had all of their pottery quantified,

Table 3.1. *Amphorae as a proportion of total pottery assemblages at various types of sites.*

Site	Type	Weight (kg)	Amphora (%)
Bainesse	Military	253.6	27.8
Leicester	Urban	7621.3	18.1
Lincoln	Urban	318.0	11.7
Alchester	Small town – suburban	536.7	11.1
Kingscote	Rural	497.4	8.2
Ivy Chimneys	Rural religious	379.6	5.4
Asthall	Roadside	144.0	4.9
Chignal	Villa	253.3	2.3

[5] Sealey and Tyers 1989.   [6] Sealey 1985: 129.
[7] Paper presented at the 33rd International Symposium on Archaeometry, Amsterdam in 2002 by A. Redford C. Heron.

*Terra sigillata type of plain + decorated tableware made in Italy + Gaul. Gaulish ware = samian ware

** Mortaria: hemispherical or conical bowls, commonly w/ heavy flanges, coarse sand or grit embedded in interior or mixing food surface - used for pounding

The packaging   19

Table 3.2. *Size and capacities of some of the commoner amphora forms found on British sites.*

Type	Also known as	Contents	Average Capacity (litres)	Weight range (kg)	Date (centuries)
PW 25	Dressel 20	Oil	60–65	24.5–37.2	1st – 3rd
PW 34	North African	Oil	60	14.0–17.5	2nd – 4th
PW 10	Dressel 2–4	Wine	26–34	12–16.5	1st – 2nd
PW 27	Gallic	Wine	26–37	10–15	1st – 3rd
PW 16–19	Salazon	Fish sauce	14–18 and 27–33		1st – 2nd
PW 15	Haltern 70	*Defrutum*	30	15.5–20.5	1st

including other specialist wares such as mortaria and samian. The picture it is painting reflects the situation in the third century and earlier, as the supply of amphora-borne commodities to Britain declined markedly after that. By including the whole pottery assemblage it is possible to get a broad picture, and overcome the problem of residuality. The rows of the table have been ordered by how large a proportion of the assemblage amphorae form. As can be seen from the second column, this figure is a very good indication of what sort of settlement the assemblage is coming from. It suggests that amphora-borne commodities did not commonly reach all parts of society, unless the rural sites were regularly purchasing them in repackaged form.

The different types of amphorae varied in size and weight as may be seen in Table 3.2. Given the size of the large oil amphora of Dressel Type 20, it is always to be expected that these will dominate the amphora assemblage from any site; but the varying proportions of other types present do provide an insight into consumption patterns. One factor that does have to be considered is that the later amphorae may be lighter than the earlier ones, despite having a similar capacity. This is most marked in the olive oil amphorae, but is also noted for the wine amphorae. The implications of this will be considered later in relation to patterns of olive oil importation.[8]

OTHER CERAMIC VESSELS

Occasionally other ceramic vessels have graffiti on them that allow the contents to be identified such as the jar that appears to record it held 1,884

[8] See p. 63.

coriander seeds[9] found at Vindolanda, but in comparison to the amphorae, these are a very minor source of information.

WOODEN BARRELS

It is clear that large wooden barrels were also used for long distance transport, and various sculpted reliefs show them being hauled on wagons. The best preserved barrels have survived because they were reused to line wells and this naturally biases the sample to very large examples. Ones recovered from Silchester, for example, are estimated to have held approximately 900 litres of liquid, but smaller ones are also known. Oak barrels found in a third-century wreck at Guernsey had capacities of 85 and 35 litres.[10] Unlike amphorae, the brands and inscriptions found on barrels were not used to indicate origin or content. Where it is possible to identify the wood the large barrels are made from, it is often found to be from species that grow in the Alps or Pyrenees.[11] The assumption is that they were used to ship wine from Gaul or Spain. If so, and it seems reasonable, then it indicates bulk shipment on a different scale to that provided by amphorae. As can be seen from Table 3.2, the two commonest types of wine amphorae (PW Classes 10 and 27) found in Britain have been estimated to have capacities in the region of 30 litres.[12] The Silchester barrels would have held thirty times that amount.

---

[9] RIB II.8 no. 2503.1.   [10] Rule and Monaghan 1993: 99.
[11] RIB II.4, p. 1.   [12] Sealey 1985: 10 Table 2.

CHAPTER 4

The human remains

INTRODUCTION

How well or poorly nourished people are can lead to changes in the bones. So study of the skeleton can give indications about the food consumed. This chapter explores the sort of information that can be gathered. It will look at the biases in the record and at how rich and poor diets may manifest themselves. This information will then be used to explore the nutritional history of various late Roman communities.

Human bones suffer from the same limitations with respect to preservation as animal bones do. Any inhumation cemetery on acid soil will not preserve skeletons. An even more important bias is to do with chronology. Many communities in the earlier Roman period cremated their dead. Though it is now possible to gain much useful information from cremated remains regarding the age, sex, and pathological conditions of the deceased,[1] this is a relatively new departure in Romano-British studies. The bulk of the cremated dead have never been examined in this way. Most information comes from people who were inhumed. Inhumation became increasingly popular as time progressed, and much of our evidence stems from the third and fourth centuries. Inhumation was practised earlier, and some people were still being cremated in the fourth century; but we know far more about the nutritional health of the later Roman population than we do about that of the people of the later Iron Age and early Roman period.

EVIDENCE FOR RICH DIETS

Aetiology, or causes of observed changes in bones, often has more than one source; and the food eaten is just one of them. In the case of diffuse

[1] See for example McKinley in Barber and Bowsher 2000: 264–77.

idiopathic skeletal hyperostosis (DISH) it seems to be generally accepted that it is associated with obesity and diabetes.[2] The disease results in much new bone formation and the gradual and complete fusing of the spine. It generally affects those older than fifty, and males are more liable to suffer from it than females.

Gout has long been associated with a rich diet and during some points of its history sufferers have seen it as a mark of distinction.[3] The disease is associated with the production of excessive uric acid, and results in the erosion of joint surfaces, mainly in the hands, feet, elbows and knees. In 90% of cases the big toe is involved. Again, it generally affects people over fifty, but affects men twenty times as often as it affects women.[4] There is a genetic predisposition towards the condition, but it is also clear that the ingestion of high quantities of lead can be a factor in its onset. It has been suggested that for the Roman period one of the sources of lead poisoning might have been the consumption of the sweet syrup *defrutum*,[5] as this was made by boiling down grape must in lead cauldrons.[6] The syrup was used both in its own right, and as a preservative for such items as olives.[7] It would have been an imported delicacy, and to be expected in the diets of those prone to overindulging themselves. There is a problem, though, with associating fourth-century gout sufferers with the consumption of such products as the evidence suggests trade in them had ceased by then.[8]

Syrups and other sweet things could be expected to lead to caries in teeth, but not all caries noted are the result of a sweet diet. They can result if there is poor dental hygiene and food is trapped between teeth. In those cases the food can break down into soluble sugars, even though the diet was relatively sugar-free. This was demonstrated in the East Cemetery in London where the teeth of 310 individuals were studied and 7% were found to be carious. The teeth affected tended to be the ones at the back of the mouth which are most difficult to clean. Over 90% of the caries observed were mild and this too suggested a lack of sweet items in the diet.[9] Where caries are combined with other indications of a rich diet it seems reasonable to conclude the condition depended on the sort of food eaten, rather than merely poor dental hygiene. A good case illustrating this was found in the cemetery at Dover Street, Southwark where a woman

[2] Roberts and Manchester 1995: 120–1.   [3] Porter and Rousseau 1998: 71.
[4] Roberts and Manchester 1995: 122–3.   [5] Molleson in Farwell and Molleson 1993: 193.
[6] Columella XII.19.   [7] Sealey 1985: 63.
[8] See p. 68.   [9] Conheeney in Barber and Bowsher 2000: 283.

aged between 25 and 45 was diagnosed as showing incipient signs of DISH.[10] Only 16 of her teeth remained but 4 of these showed caries. She had been buried with a rite that involved packing the grave with chalk. Such graves appear to be a fashionable burial ritual for the elite in the late Roman period;[11] and so the supposition that this individual was wealthy enough to indulge in a rich diet, including sweet things, seems likely.

EVIDENCE FOR POOR DIETS

Again, it has to be said that the observed changes in bone which seem to suggest a poor diet can have more than one cause; and it may be that sometimes the signs of poor nutrition are the result of illness which did not allow a person to take nourishment from their food. There are two regularly observed conditions that may indicate that an individual was not well nourished when young. Both result in changes to the bones of the skull and teeth which remain present in the adult.

(1) Enamel hypoplasia is observed on teeth, and consists of defects in the enamel such as lines and pits. The stress that gives rise to them can be caused either by nutritional deficiencies or by illness.[12] It can manifest itself as a response to weaning. (2) Cribra orbitalia is a condition where pits form on the surface of the orbital roof of the skull. The generally accepted aetiology is anaemia caused by a deficiency of iron. The changes are thought to come about when the body attempts to produce more blood cells in the marrow to compensate for the lack of iron.[13] It may be noted that some osteologists are still unconvinced of this link.[14] Iron is found in such foods as red meat, legumes and shellfish. Anaemia can be caused by a diet deficient in iron. It can also be caused by illness, and as a result of an individual suffering from a heavy parasite burden.[15] Environmental reports often report the background presence of whipworm of a size appropriate to humans suggesting that some individuals would have suffered in this way.[16]

(3) Vitamin deficiencies can also be seen in the bones. Vitamin D is necessary for the mineralisation of bones, and a deficiency can lead

---

[10] MacKinder 2000: 45 burial 27. [11] Philpott 1991: 92.
[12] Roberts and Manchester 1995: 58. [13] Roberts and Manchester 1995: 167.
[14] Waldron in Davies *et al.* 2002: 153. [15] Molleson in Farwell and Molleson 1993: 178.
[16] See, for example, Jones and Hutchinson in McCarthy 1991: 70; Boyer in Connor and Buckley 1999: 344.

to rickets. Though some of this vitamin is acquired through the diet, 90% of an individual's needs can be created by the skin if exposed to sunlight.[17] Vitamin C is acquired from fresh fruit and vegetables. A deficiency will lead to scurvy, which may manifest itself in the skeleton in the form of the deposition of new bone. It is also likely to lead to periodontal disease because the gums swell and bleed.[18] Scurvy is not often diagnosed in ancient populations, but some authorities have suggested that periostitis may reflect a Vitamin C deficiency.[19] This condition results in plaque-like new bone formation.[20] The cause is not fully understood, and it could come about as a result of repeated minor traumas. It is frequently observed in shin bones; a part of the body often subject to casual knocks and blows. Vitamin C deficiency is probably under-diagnosed in the Romano-British population. In the medieval period scurvy was endemic during winter in northern Europe due to the scarcity of fresh fruit and vegetables,[21] and similar conditions must have applied in Britain during the Roman period.

A WELL-FED POPULATION?

There is now sufficient evidence to start exploring the nutritional health of the late Roman population. Wherever possible the data presented are of third- or fourth-century date, though it is not always possible to extract subsets of data of that date for the important cemetery at Poundbury. The people buried in the cemeteries considered would have lived in a variety of environments. Those from London, Cirencester, Colchester and Poundbury lived in large towns. The people from Dunstable and Alchester lived in small towns, and the other sites are rural ones. It is not possible to compare all aspects of the population across all of the sites, as the level of reporting varies, but a general picture can be built up.

It is clear that how tall people grow to be depends, in part, on how well nourished they are when growing. One way of exploring this is to look at the mean male height and the difference between the heights of the male and female populations (sexual dimorphism). Populations with a low availability of protein tend to have a low mean male height and a low degree of sexual dimorphism.[22] As a guide it has been proposed that 1.6 m

---

[17] Roberts and Manchester 1995: 173.   [18] Roberts and Manchester 1995: 171.
[19] Molleson in Farwell and Molleson 1993: 189.   [20] Roberts and Manchester 1995: 130.
[21] Waldron 1989: 57.   [22] Molleson in Farwell and Molleson 1993: 184.

Table 4.1. *Mean stature of adults in eight late Roman cemeteries.*

Site	Date (century)	Male (number)	Male (mean)	Female (number)	Female (mean)
London East	2nd–4th	unknown	1.69	unknown	1.58
Cirencester	3rd–4th	107	1.69	44	1.58
Dunstable	3rd–4th	33	1.68	24	1.60
Poundbury	4th	341	1.66	360	1.61
Alington Avenue	4th	29	1.66	15	1.58
Maiden Castle Road	4th	6	1.67	6	1.59
Colchester	4th	85	1.68	59	1.56
Bradley Hill	Late 4th	10	1.69	10	1.59

should be regarded as short and 1.7 m as tall.[23] Table 4.1 shows the mean heights of the adult populations in eight cemeteries. As can be seen, none of the mean male heights are particularly low and sexual dimorphism is generally well pronounced with the possible exception of Poundbury. On the whole the figures suggest that these populations did not suffer regular food shortages, and there was adequate protein in the diet of the young.

Table 4.2 shows the incidence of caries, enamel hypoplasia and cribra orbitalia. In general the caries rates are quite low reflecting the lack of sugary foods, but the incidence at Poundbury stands out as being exceptional. The author of the report suggested the reason for this might be the result of the number of elderly people in cemetery.[24] At the site 12% were aged over 55, and the caries rate rose with age. The other large cemeteries, though, also have noticeable elderly communities. At Butt Road, Colchester, 6% of the individuals to whom an age could be assigned were over 50, at Cirencester 7% were over 53, and in the East Cemetery in London 13% were over 45. All of these sites have markedly lower rates of caries, and so the argument based on the demography at Poundbury does not seem a convincing reason for the discrepancy seen there.

Molleson[25] also noted that susceptibility to caries in later life depended on the nutrition received during infancy and childhood; and it seems very likely that, at Poundbury, this is the reason for the unusually high caries

[23] Roberts and Manchester 1995: 26.   [24] Molleson in Farwell and Molleson 1993: 183.
[25] Molleson in Farwell and Molleson 1993: 184.

Table 4.2. *Incidence of dental caries, enamel hypoplasia and cribra orbitalia.*
The number columns refer either to total teeth or individuals for which the
percentage could be calculated. Blank fields indicate the numbers were not
given, but percentages were. The total population for Poundbury was 1442
individuals.

Site	Date	Caries Rate		Enamel hypoplasia		Cribra orbitalia	
	(century)	(%)	No.	(%)	No.	(%)	No.
London East	2nd–4th	7.3	2031	*c.* 10.0	294	>5.0	—
Cirencester	3rd–4th	5.1	3251	24.0	178	17.7	—
Dunstable	3rd–4th	3.8	1187	—	—	—	—
Chignall	3rd–4th	—	—	30.5	36	22.0	36
Poundbury	1st–4th	15.8	—	38.5	—	28.0	—
Alington Avenue	1st–4th	2.6	1954	—	—	2.7	109
Colchester	4th	3.9	3665	27.2	235	9.9	262
Alchester	4th	1.0	496	12.5	24	13.0	30

rate. The incidence of cribra orbitalia and enamel hypoplasia is also
noticeably higher at the site, possibly reflecting nutritional stress in
childhood. The lower sexual dimorphism seen in height at Poundbury
has been commented on, and this too may be part of this pattern. Why
the population at Poundbury should suffer in this way is unknown but
there is other evidence at the cemetery that young children failed to
thrive,[26] and it might be suspected that how they were fed had an impact
upon them.

The way in which the Poundbury population seems to differentiate
itself from the rest of the sites reminds us that Roman Britain was not a
homogenous mass. It was full of different groups leading different lifestyles which undoubtedly would have included different ways of feeding
themselves and their children. The figures for Poundbury are especially
interesting when compared to a small rural cemetery also outside
Dorchester (Maiden Castle Road). Only twenty-two individuals were
recovered but there were no examples of enamel hypoplasia recovered,
and caries was restricted to one tooth in one individual.[27] Is the difference
observed a simple one between a healthy country life and an unhealthy

---

[26] Molleson in Farwell and Molleson 1993: 176.   [27] Rogers in Smith *et al.* 1997: 156.

urban one; or are we perhaps looking at preferences at the level of the family unit?

Family burial plots within the Butt Road cemetery at Colchester have been suggested on the basis of similarity of burial ritual and genetic traits.[28] In the cemetery it was found cribra orbitalia and enamel hypoplasia tended to cluster in the proposed family plots,[29] and were not spread across the cemetery. In one complex, clearly reused over some time, individuals with enamel hypoplasia were found throughout the sequence.[30] Excluding the neonates and the individuals whose skeletons did not survive, thirty individuals were buried in this complex, ten of whom show the condition. This gives an incidence of 33% comparable to the Poundbury figures. The small cemetery at the Chignall villa also shows a high rate, and again one might hypothesise that these individuals would have been part of the same family group. Given the association of enamel hypoplasia with weaning, it is interesting to speculate that here we may have indications of particular child-rearing habits, not necessarily shared with the neighbouring families. Was it the tradition to wean them early, and perhaps onto inappropriate food? It is clear from the ancient authors that the weaning food of choice in the Mediterranean world was cereal based, and that some mothers started to wean children after as little as six weeks.[31] Modern advice is not to move babies onto solid foods until about six months and then to start with purees of fresh fruit and vegetables.

It is probable that more could be learnt about early infant-feeding habits, but at present the data are not always presented in such a way that the information can be extracted. The incidence of enamel hypoplasia is rarely presented according to the sex of the individual. It would be interesting to know if it affected both sexes equally, with the implication that the feeding regime for both boys and girls was the same. At Butt Road, Colchester, it did,[32] but more data are clearly needed.

It might be suspected that some at least of the population suffered from a lack of fresh food during the winter months. Given that it is thought that scurvy is under-diagnosed,[33] it is difficult to assess the level of the problem. If we take Vitamin C deficiency to be one of the causes of periostitis, then some people in urban populations probably did have

---

[28] Crummy, N. *et al.* 1993: 92.   [29] Crummy, N. *et al.* 1993: Figs. 2.42–2.43.
[30] Crummy, N. *et al.* 1993: 93.   [31] Garnsey 1999: 107.
[32] Pinter-Bellows in Crummy, N. *et al.* 1993: 88.   [33] Roberts and Manchester 1995: 173.

Table 4.3. *The incidence of DISH in sexed individuals over the age of 45 at Poundbury.*

	Male	Female	Total
With DISH	11	0	11
Without DISH	84	129	213
Total	95	129	224

inadequate access to fresh fruit and vegetables. At Cirencester the condition affected 10–12% of the individuals examined[34] and a similar figure has been noted for the East Cemetery in London.[35] Again some communities appear to have avoided it. At Butt Road, Colchester only 1% of the individuals were affected.[36]

Overindulgence in a rich diet can also be detected, generally in the elderly. Gout has been recorded at Cirencester,[37] Poundbury[38] and in the East Cemetery in London.[39] Given the nature of the disease it is unsurprising that the cases identified are those of males, and it is of little help in distinguishing different eating patterns between the sexes. DISH, by contrast, occurs both in males and females though not equally; in modern North American populations the ratio is 65 : 35. The condition is regularly observed in Romano-British populations, but unfortunately is not always quantified. When it is, an interesting pattern can emerge.

At Poundbury eleven cases were observed, all male.[40] The incidence in the older population is shown in Table 4.3. Assuming the ancient population was susceptible to the condition in the same proportion as the modern one, this pattern can be explored statistically via a modified form of the chi-square statistic, and this shows that the condition does seem to affect males disproportionately at Poundbury.[41] It could be taken as suggesting that males were far more likely to overeat than females. There is independent evidence that at least two of the males with DISH did indeed have a rich diet. Three of the skeletons with DISH formed part of

[34] Wells in McWhirr *et al.* 1982: 182.   [35] Conheeney in Barber and Bowsher 2000: 286.
[36] Pinter-Bellows in Crummy, N. *et al.* 1993: 77.   [37] Wells in McWhirr *et al.* 1982: 191.
[38] Molleson in Farwell and Molleson 1993: Table 43.
[39] Conheeney in Barber and Bowsher 2000: 286.
[40] Molleson in Farwell and Molleson 1993: 194, Tables 46 and 60.
[41] Cool and Baxter 2005.

a programme to investigate the food sources by stable-isotope analysis.[42] Two of the individuals clearly ate more foodstuffs derived from the sea than the bulk of the population. Interestingly one of the Poundbury gout sufferers also did. As will be seen in chapter 12, fish does not appear to have formed a major part of the diet of the bulk of the population, and there is some evidence to suggest this may have been an elite delicacy.

In other cemeteries DISH has been identified in female skeletons, sometimes where the burial rite suggests the individual was a member of the elite, as in the case of the woman buried at Southwark discussed above. It would be of some interest to quantify the incidence at other cemeteries in a similar way to that done in Table 4.3 as it might tell us whether the females of elite families had an equal access to rich delicacies. Poundbury stands out as unusual in many respects, and it would probably not be fair to condemn only the male element of the elite population as gluttons on its evidence.

The evidence would seem to suggest that for most of the populations examined, there was adequate nourishment though some parts of the communities such as young children may have been at risk. It is also clear that currently the evidence human bones provide for what different groups of people were eating is an underused resource. In some cases this is because of particular reporting conventions such as not distinguishing the sexes of the people with enamel hypoplasia. In others it is because techniques such as stable-isotope analysis are relatively new[43] and Romano-British skeletons have rarely been subjected to them. Certainly the latter technique with its ability to identify the eaters of marine food, most probably an elite preference, will be a most useful tool.

[42] Richards *et al.* 1998.   [43] Mays 1998: 182–90.

CHAPTER 5

Written evidence

INTRODUCTION

Direct written evidence for the food and drink of Roman Britain consists of the labels on packaging such as amphorae discussed in Chapter 3, and the information preserved on writing tablets found in the province. Indirect evidence comes from the ancient literary sources, many of which touch on matters of food and drink. This chapter will consider the sort of information captured in the writing tablets, and the ancient sources. The opportunity will also be taken to consider the nature of the well-developed food culture that the Roman elite at the centre of Empire clearly enjoyed, and whether some of the inhabitants of Britain were able to partake of it.

WRITING TABLETS

Two different forms of writing media were used in Roman Britain. Both were made of wood and thus require damp environments to survive. One has long been recognised and understood. These are the stylus tablets which consist of rectangular sheets of wood with narrow, raised borders around each edge. The recessed area was filled with black wax, and this could be written on with a stylus which removed the wax to reveal the pale wood below. When these tablets are found, the wax has generally disappeared but sometimes the stylus had scored deeply enough to leave traces of the writing on the wood. Many of these documents seem to recount legal or official transactions. Of these, one from London describing an enquiry into the ownership of a wood in Kent[1] is a good example, but personal letters are also known.[2] The contents of many tablets have not yet been read because the traces of writing consist of a palimpsest of

---

[1] Tomlin 1996.   [2] RIB II.4 no. 2443.7.

different messages. So far, no information about food and drink has been recovered on a stylus tablet, but that does not mean that they were not used for shopping lists, household inventories etc. It is possible that the current bias towards legal documents is the result of those tablets being used once only. More humble household ones may exist, but their messages are lost in the jumble of reuse.

The other form of writing tablet was written on using an ink pen. These tablets were thin sheets of wood about 1 to 3mm thick, and the size of a modern postcard. When found, the traces of the writing can quickly fade. The full significance of what these slips of wood were only became apparent when large numbers of them were found during excavations at Vindolanda in 1973–5; and conservators at the British Museum developed techniques to preserve both the tablets and the writing. Excavations at the site have continued to produce these ink tablets, and there is now a large corpus of information available.[3]

Similar ink tablets have also been found elsewhere, for example at Caerleon[4] and Carlisle;[5] but the Vindolanda tablets remain by far the largest group found anywhere in the empire. They are one of the greatest treasures ever to have been uncovered by archaeology in Britain. They relate to a relatively short period in the life of a fort that lies just to the south of Hadrian's Wall. The waterlogged conditions that allowed them to survive apply to the earliest phases of the fort from c. AD 90 to 130. Vindolanda was a frontier fort at the extreme edge of the empire. It was garrisoned at this time by auxiliary units who came originally from Batavia, the area in modern Belgium and the Netherlands at the mouths of the rivers Rhine and Scheldt.[6] It is important to realise that the documents relate to the lives not of native Britons, nor of 'Romans' from the heart of empire, but to a Germanic military unit. Native Britons appear only occasionally, and then are disparaged as *Brittunculi* (wretched Britons).[7] The governor of the province, and similar high-ranking people, are distant presences.[8]

All sorts of information is preserved. There are personal letters including an invitation to a birthday party, official military inventories and movement orders, household inventories, shopping lists and children's

---

[3] Bowman and Thomas 1994; 2003. The definitive publication is now the website http://vindolanda. csad.ox.ac.uk – last accessed August 2006 – where developments in photography and digital imaging that make revised readings possible are reported.

[4] Hassall and Tomlin 1986: 450–2.   [5] Tomlin 1998.   [6] Bowman 1993: 26.

[7] Bowman and Thomas 1994: 106 no. 164.   [8] Bowman and Thomas 1994: 200 no. 225.

writing exercises. The lists of provisions include items such as pepper[9] which is very hard to find in the archaeological record. They provide a unique window onto the northern frontier at the end of the first century, and a start has already been made in attempting to use them to explore the military diet.[10] It would be fascinating to compare the inventories with the bones and plant remains preserved on the site. The damp conditions that preserved the writing tablet has also preserved much other organic material. This, alas, is currently impossible because the definitive publications of the sites have not yet appeared and only tantalising summaries are available.[11] It is much to be hoped that the reports will, eventually, appear. It would be a tragedy if the writing tablets were to remain divorced from the rest of the material culture relating to life at Vindolanda.

ANCIENT SOURCES

There is a great deal of information about food and drink scattered through the texts that have survived from antiquity. This is of variable value when exploring what was consumed in Roman Britain, as it relates to the Mediterranean heartlands of the empire where different foodstuffs were available. It is probably most useful when providing information about the food known to have been imported via amphorae. The encyclopaedic *Naturalis Historia* (Natural History) of Pliny the Elder, who died in the eruption of Vesuvius in AD 79, provides an overview of the different wine-producing areas and the quality of the products. This allows us to get some insights into how the wine, whose origins we can identify from first-century amphorae, would have been regarded by the people who drank it. Treatises on farming such as Columella's *De Re Rustica* written in the 60s provide information about how wine was customarily made, and how produce could be preserved. Such texts help us to interpret finds such as the amphora found in the Thames full of olive stones;[12] for they indicate that far from being preserved in brine or olive oil, as would be the modern practice, the olives had been packed in a very sweet syrup made from grape juice.

    The doctors of antiquity viewed diet as an important medical tool. The works of such eminent practitioners as Galen, who wrote in the second half of the second century, and Dioscorides, who was a contemporary of Pliny the Elder, provide much useful information; not just on how food

[9] Bowman and Thomas 1994: 135 no. 184.   [10] Pearce 2002.
[11] Seaward in van Driel Murray *et al.* 1993: 91–119.   [12] Sealey and Tyers 1989.

and drink were used as treatments, but also how they were prepared. One of the most detailed descriptions of how *garum*, the fish sauce that will be discussed in Chapter 7, was made, comes from a work entitled *De Medicina et de Virtute Herbarum* (On medicine and the worth of plants) attributed to the third-century writer Gargilius Martialis.[13]

The only recipe book to survive in anything close to entirety is *De Re Coquinaria* (On Cookery) attributed to Apicius. Quite when the work was written, or who wrote it, is unknown.[14] The earliest manuscripts extant are of ninth century date, but the Latin they are written in dates to the later fourth century. The three legendary gourmets called Apicius lived much earlier; one during the first century BC, the second in the mid-first century AD and the third slightly later during the early second century. It is not known whether any of these individuals were directly connected with any parts of the work. Even if some parts of it can be attributed to one or the other of them, other parts were clearly written later as there are recipes named for the emperor Commodus who reigned in the mid-second century. It seems best to regard the book as a compilation to whom the name Apicius, synonymous with good living, became attached. It is a practical cookbook rather than a literary work; and was clearly aimed at an audience that was expected to know how to cook. The recipes give lists of ingredients but rarely quantities, and the cooking instructions can be very abbreviated. It can still be used as a practical guide, and forms a mainstay of many modern recipe books that attempt to recreate the dishes of antiquity.

It is clear that in the Ancient World there were many more recipe books in existence. Rome inherited and developed the culinary traditions of Greece, and with it the culinary literature. Much of this is now lost, with titles and fragments known only from passing references in the *Deipnosophistai* by Athenaeus. This work was written in the early third century AD in the style of discussions between dinner guests, and contains many excerpts from lost works. From these we can discover that by the third century BC, books were being written on particular aspects of cooking, and were providing recipes for regional specialities.[15] What survives is what medieval scribes chose to copy. Generally food, and matters pertaining to it, were not seen as matters suitable for serious study, so it is probable that a disproportionate number of works dealing with food did not survive. There is a fascinating chapter of recipes for cakes and

[13] Gozzini Giacosa 1992: 27; on the author see Curtis 1991: 11–12.
[14] Edwards 1984: ix–xiii; Gozzini Giacosa 1992: 7–8.   [15] Dalby 1996: 160.

doughnuts in *De Agricultura* (On Farming) written by the stern moralist Cato in the mid-second century BC.[16] One suspects that had he chosen to write instead *On Cakes*, not even his eminence would have preserved the work for posterity.

Recipes and references to food can often be found in literary works, and sometimes the recipes are detailed enough to be used directly in the kitchen. A poem attributed to Virgil called *Moretum*, after the dish of cheese pounded together with herbs and garlic, provides a recipe often reproduced almost verbatim in modern recipe books.[17] Literary works have to be used with some caution if they are to be pressed into service as evidence of how people of the Roman world actually ate. It is obvious, even from a superficial reading, that the dinner party given by Trimalchio as described by Petronius in the *Satyricon* is a satire on the nouveaux riches and, as such, is exaggerated for effect. In many other works, too, food is clearly being used as a metaphor; and Gowers has pointed out that despite the large number of texts dealing with meals that have survived, there is 'no straightforward, detailed description of a normal Roman meal'.[18] The types of dishes and the menus described are present for literary reasons. Rich food can stand for a bloated literary style, whilst a wholesome diet is the equivalent of literary restraint. What may appear to be a straightforward recipe for a sauce made with refined ingredients, can also be read as the poet's reflections on the type of satire that is needed for the age he is living in.[19]

That Latin literature of all sorts was so saturated with references to food is clearly an indication that the Roman world had what has been termed a differentiated cuisine.[20] This develops when a society is stratified culturally as well as politically. It has been suggested it requires access to a variety of foodstuffs, not just the locally available, a discerning and sizeable community of adventurous eaters, and a well-developed agricultural system. The habit of using literacy for a wide range of purposes, practical as well as literary and religious, is also important, as such a cuisine needs a body of recipes that can be developed by specialists. The cooks of the elite, and not just the elite themselves, need to be able to read. The Latin of Apicius's cookbook is relevant here. It is written in Vulgar Latin used by people of little formal education.[21] Clearly not everyone who lives in a society with a differentiated cuisine will eat exotic

---

[16] Cato: 72–84. For the character of the author see Holland 2003: 190–1.
[17] Dalby and Grainger 1996: 85–6.   [18] Gowers 1993: 7.   [19] Gowers 1993: 157.
[20] Goody 1982: 98–99.   [21] Dalby 1996: 179.

and elaborate dishes; but it could be expected that those at the higher end of society might, from time to time at least. To what extent did the higher levels of Roman cuisine spread to Britain?

Such a question can only really be discussed at the end of the book, but there is one aspect that can be considered here and that is the level of literacy in the province. Was it confined to a small subset of the population, or was it more widespread? There are three different strands of evidence that can be considered. They are provided by graffiti, styli and curse tablets.

Graffiti survives scratched on fragments of pottery and tiles. On pottery vessels the words scratched are generally personal names indicating ownership of the vessel; and it is noticeable that finewares, especially plain samian vessels, were so labelled. An interesting study has shown that the incidence of graffiti seemed to be dependent on site type, with forts and their *vici* having a higher level than small towns and rural sites. It was suggested that this probably reflected levels of literacy, with the implication it failed to penetrate the countryside to any great extent.[22] The alternative explanation that it was at the bigger sites that there was a greater possibility of personal possessions being stolen or borrowed was considered but rejected.

Styli for use with wax writing tablets were most commonly made of iron. In the past they were not particularly common finds. The current practice of routinely X-radiographing iron finds from excavations has greatly improved the recovery rates. X-radiography reveals the object hidden in the rusty corrosion, and it has to be suspected that previously some of the corroded fragments identified as nails were probably styli. When the types of sites on which styli are found are examined it is found that they are present at all levels of the settlement hierarchy, including rural sites.[23] It is always possible that the inhabitants of rural sites were using styli for some function other than writing, but the evidence of the curse tablets seems to support the idea that at least some part of the rural population was literate.

Curse tablets are inscriptions scratched onto pieces of lead or lead alloy. The messages are petitions to the deities; generally in the form of offering the god some reward if they exact revenge on the person who has done the petitioner wrong. Lead is a soft metal, and messages can be written on it with an implement like a stylus without great difficulty. In comparison

[22] Evans 1987.   [23] Cool and Baxter 2002: 375.

to the rest of the empire, the Romano-British population seem to have been particularly fond of denouncing their fellows in this way. They have been found at a variety of temples across the province. The greatest number that have been read so far were recovered from the Sacred Spring in the great Temple complex at Bath, and belonged to the later second to fourth centuries. Study of the handwriting has suggested that the tablets were not written by scribes, but very probably by the individual making the petition.[24] This led the epigrapher who studied the tablets to conclude that a respectable number of people at Bath could read and write. Bath was a spa town and so it might be suggested it would have attracted a disproportionate number of upper-class, literate visitors. The same cannot be said of the rural hilltop temple at Uley where an equally large number of tablets have been found. Fewer of these have yet been read, but again it seems that different hands are represented.[25]

The styli and the curse tablets suggest that literacy spread into the rural, presumably British, population. They do not indicate that it was confined to the forts and major towns, where it might have been restricted to an incomer group. The apparent conflict with the graffiti evidence may be because security was a more important issue in the towns and especially the forts. Being literate does not necessarily mean that you can read and write fluently; but it does fulfil our need for cooks to have a practical literacy as far as recipes went. Obviously few houses will have had a shelf of cookbooks, but the possibility that some did cannot be excluded; and this may have been amongst the Romano-British elite living in their comfortable villas, as well as in the senatorial and equestrian households of commanding officers and administrators.

[24] Tomlin in Cunliffe 1988: 101.   [25] Tomlin in Woodward and Leech 1993: 117.

CHAPTER 6

Kitchen and dining basics: techniques and utensils

INTRODUCTION

The next eleven chapters explore the utensils and ingredients we have evidence for, and what the general patterns in the data are. This chapter concentrates on the objects used to prepare and cook food, the types of heat sources available, and how the food was served. By examining the types of sites things are found on, it is possible to start developing a picture of how cooking practices varied over time, and between different groups of the population. These objects also provide a salutary warning against assuming that vessels of similar shape will necessarily have the same function in different cultural milieus.

POTS AND PANS

In many areas of Roman Britain, though not in all, pottery vessels were central to cooking. As will be discussed in Chapter 16, this in itself marks a major change with what had been common practice in the Iron Age. Unfortunately, despite the tons of pottery excavated and published each year, this is not as helpful a source of information as it could be. The concentration on using it to date sites means that considerations of what it was actually used for are often overlooked. Vessels that are regularly used to cook food on hearths and over open fires can be expected to develop coatings of sooty deposits. Vessels used as kettles to heat water can be expected to build up deposits of limescale in hard water areas. However, it is a rare report that systematically records this. Table 6.1 has been prepared to show what types of vessels are regularly sooted and/or burnt. The sites have been selected because the information was recorded, rather than because they provide a representative sample; though they do span a range of rural, small urban and military sites.

Table 6.1. *Incidence of sooting, burning and limescale on different categories of pottery vessels.*

		Beaker	Flagon	Dish	Bowl	Mor-taria	Jar	Lid
Baldock	Number	53	41	55	159	56	268	10
	Sooted %	0	2	4	8	4	9	0
	Burnt %	2	2	4	6	21	9	30
	Lime %	—	—	—	—	—	6	—
Dalton Parlours	Number	0	0	12	16	14	18	1
	Sooted %	—	—	17	6	14	39	0
	Burnt %	—	—	0	6	0	0	0
	Lime %	—	—	—	—	—	3	—
West Yorkshire	Number	0	0	9	14	10	70	0
	Sooted %	—	—	22	7	0	33	—
	Burnt %	—	—	11	0	30	1	—
Warrington	Number	37	20	47	131	86	296	9
	Sooted %	3	0	2	0	0	2	0
	Burnt %	5	5	11	5	12	4	22
Segontium	Number	27	27	68	195	67	394	68
	Sooted %	0	0	2	1	0	2	1
	Burnt %	7	0	19	8	21	6	8
Menai Straits	Number	4	0	12	10	4	24	0
	Sooted %	0	—	50	30	0	33	—
	Burnt %	0	—	33	0	25	8	—
Caersws	Number	22	26	18	99	14	212	39
	Sooted %	0	0	11	3	0	9	3
	Burnt %	0	0	22	2	7	3	3

It tends to be the jars followed by the bowls and dishes that are sooted and burnt, whilst the phenomenon is only occasionally noted on flagons and beakers. In the few studies of this phenomenon that have been published, a similar distribution of sooting or burning is reported;[1] and it seems reasonable to conclude that the jar was the principal cooking vessel. Generally the shapes chosen were ovoid with the greatest girth towards the shoulder, and with an everted rim to allow a lid to be securely held during cooking. The recurrent dish and bowl forms that show sooting and burning have straight, slightly outbent sides, occasionally with a small horizontal rim.

One of the very few detailed examinations of sooting has shown there is a significant difference between the heavily sooted rims, and the much less commonly sooted and burnt bases.[2] This would imply that the bodies and bases of the vessels were firmly bedded in the hearth, perhaps in the accumulated ash, with only the upper parts open to direct heat. The shapes of the vessels and this type of heat would be ideal for stewing or slow baking; and the ubiquity of cooking jars on most sites suggests that stewing would have been one of the principal cooking techniques.

Occasionally the pottery suggests other cooking methods associated with particular ethnic or regional groups. About AD 200 the kilns at the legionary fortress at York started to produce vessels which have strong similarities to shapes being made at that time in north Africa.[3] Given that the African emperor Septimius Severus was in residence at York between the years AD 208 to 211, and Africans are known to have been present in the army; it seems reasonable to conclude that these were vessels being made for a north African clientele, with cooking requirements that were not satisfied by the normal range of shapes available. One of the new forms was a bowl with a convex base which was designed to be used over a brazier. This was a type of cooking that is known to have been favoured in north Africa at the time, with the braziers also being made of pottery. Experimental work comparing a stew cooked in a jar on a hearth, and in a casserole on a brazier, has shown that the texture of the latter is much drier than that cooked in a jar.[4] The casseroles were used on other sites in the north of Britain where African soldiers were present, but in York itself did not find favour amongst the civilian population; presumably the

---

[1] Hammerson in Hinton 1988: 247–9; Evans 1993: 105 Table 1.   [2] Evans 1995: Table 5.3.
[3] Swan 1992: 8, fig. nos 16–25; Monaghan 1997: 872–3, 999 form BA.
[4] Croom 2001: 44–5.

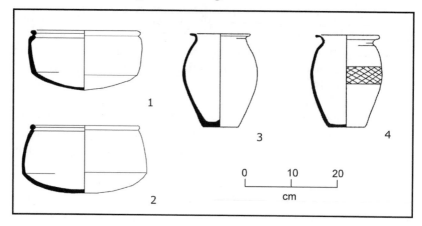

Figure 6.1. Early third-century 'north African' casseroles and cooking jars from York. (After Perrin 1981: fig. 35.452 (2); Perrin 1990: fig. 114.1225 (1); Monaghan 1997: figs. 385.3777, 3789 (3, 4).) Scale 1 : 8.

resulting stew was not found to have the correct texture. They seem to have been a short-lived fashion of a transient ethnic group.

One problem with assuming that these casseroles were used in exactly the same way as in north Africa is that fragments of the braziers have rarely been identified in Britain. It is possible that the braziers, being less well fired than the casseroles, have not survived in a recognisable form;[5] but it is worth considering whether or not it was the size of the vessel that was important. The casseroles come in a range of sizes, but are generally large. Fig. 6.1 shows two typical examples (nos. 1 and 2) compared with typical examples of the cooking jars (nos. 3 and 4) in use amongst the general population of York at the time. The casseroles would have held a greater quantity than the jar, possibly suggesting that what was important was the communal form of dining that they allowed and encouraged. A casserole such as this can be placed centrally amongst a group of diners who can help themselves to the contents. Such an action would not be so easy with the standard cooking jar, where the contents were probably decanted into individual bowls or plates prior to serving.

Another vessel type possibly associated with particular ethnic groups is the tripod bowl, which stands on three feet to lift the base above the direct heat (fig. 6.2). These are never a common part of any pottery assemblage,

[5] Viviene Swan *pers. com.*

Figure 6.2. Tripod cooking bowls. (After Zienkiewicz 1986: fig. 19 (1); Rush *et al.* 2000: fig. 50 (2); Davies *et al.* 1994: fig. 65 (3); Frere 1972: figs. 106–7 (4–5).) Scale 1 : 8.

but do occur on military and urban sites of the first century.[6] At that time such bowls were the typical cooking pot of the south of France;[7] and where they occur on Romano-British sites it is tempting to see them as providing evidence of the presence of individuals from that region. Certainly at the places they are found, it would not be unusual to have individuals from those areas. There appears to have been sufficient demand in some areas[8] for the form to be made by the local industries, hinting at the cosmopolitan nature of society in some of the larger cities.

Specialised pottery cooking utensils also seem to have developed within sections of the native population apparently without any external promptings from immigrant groups. An interesting example of this is what have been termed 'chapatti discs'. These are flat, thick discs of fired clay with a wide range of diameters from c. 14 cm to nearly half a metre. They are burnt on the underside and have carbonised deposits on the upper side around the edges. The suggestion that these are bake stones for something like a flat bread with or without a topping seems very probable. They have a very limited distribution centred on the Oxfordshire – Warwickshire region, and are noticeably more common on the rural than on the urban sites there. They start to appear in the later first century but appear

[6] Colchester – Symonds and Wade 1999: 470; Verulamium – Wilson in Frere 1972: 282 no. 231, 284 no. 234; London – Davies *et al.* 1994: 75, fig. 65 no. 379, 130 fig. III no. 708; Castleford – Rush *et al.* 2000: 109 nos. 135–6; Caerleon – Greep in Zienkiewicz 1986: 60 no. 1.18, fig 19; Malton – Wenham and Heywood 1997: 86 no. 237.
[7] Tuffreau-Libre 1992: 76.
[8] Colchester, London, Malton: see note 6.

Figure 6.3. A selection of mortaria showing size ranges. 1–2: Cream coarse pottery. 3: samian: 4: colour-coated. 5: Crambeck. (After Miller *et al.* 1986: no. 1.73 (1); Symonds and Wade 1999: figs. 4.13, 4.20 (2, 4); Cool 2004b: fig. 4.127 (3); Monaghan 1997: fig. 377.3399 (5).) Scale 1 : 8.

commonest in the late Roman period.[9] They are absent from Iron Age pottery assemblages in the area, and so are clearly a Roman-period innovation to cook something that only appears to have been appreciated within a small subset of a local community.

In the Classical Roman kitchen envisaged by the recipes of Apicius, mortars were needed to grind a variety of ingredients to produce either a puree that could be poured, or a more solid mass which was then shaped by hand. Amongst the finds from most Romano-British sites there are utensils that seem ideally suited to perform this function. The commonest are coarse pottery mortaria. These are cream-coloured shallow bowls with a pronounced rim, which normally has a wide pouring spout at one point, and grit embedded in the interior surface (Fig. 6.3 nos. 1–2).

Mortaria were also made in samian pottery which was normally only used for tablewares (Fig. 6.3 no. 3). They differ from the cream examples in having a pouring spout that emerges through the upper wall taking the shape of a lion's or bat's head, rather than having an open channel on the rim. It was a very late addition to the range with the commonest type (Dressel 45) emerging about AD 170 amongst the Central Gaulish

[9] Jeremy Evans unpublished, see also Booth *et al.* 2001: 261.

products, and continuing to be made in the third century by the East Gaulish industries.[10] There was sufficient demand for the form to be copied by the British colour-coated industries (see Fig. 6.3 no. 4).[11] This production started in the mid-third century, when imports of samian had almost disappeared, and continued well into the fourth. On these, the spouts were not considered to be an essential feature. Sometimes the wall is imperfectly perforated, and in others no spout is present. Indeed, on some there is only a painted representation of a spout.

Nothing like mortaria had been used in Britain prior to the conquest, other than on a very small number of elite sites.[12] The form is very much one that is associated with life after that event. Some were imported from the continent; but industries producing them were rapidly established in Britain, and there was a thriving trade in mortaria throughout the Roman period.[13] A similar pattern may be seen in stone mortars. These were used in much smaller quantities than the pottery ones, but again rapidly started to be made in Britain after the conquest.[14]

Strangely enough, though mortaria tend to occupy a privileged place in pottery studies with reports specially devoted to them, the function they served is rarely considered. Presumably it is taken as being self-evidently for the preparation of food, with the implication that this was being done in a 'Roman' manner.[15] Interestingly, in the early days of mortaria study this equation was doubted, and one suggestion was that the bowls were used in cheese making with the grits forming a rough surface that would provide a reservoir of bacteria to aid the curding of a cream cheese.[16]

At a superficial level, it is very tempting to equate the ubiquity of pottery mortaria in Britain with the adoption of a Roman cuisine. Some helpfully even have graffiti specifically stating that they are mixing bowls (*pelves*) or mortars (*mortaria*).[17] There are good reasons for doubting that the presence of such vessels always implies cooking methods that would have been recognisable to cooks from the Mediterranean heartlands. A variety of uses is suggested when size, distribution and wear characteristics are considered.

Fig. 6.4 compares the internal diameter of over 600 pottery and 50 stone mortars. It makes no claim to be a random sample, but is probably

[10] Bird 1993: 8.
[11] Tyers 1996: fig 217 no. 84; Young 1977: 127; Forms 97–100; Fulford 1975: 68 Type 79.
[12] See p. 166.   [13] Tyers 1996: 116, figs. 103–4.   [14] Cool 2005.
[15] See for example Tyers 1996: 116.   [16] Oswald 1943: 46.
[17] RIB II.6 2496.3, 2797.4; RIB II.7 2501.18.

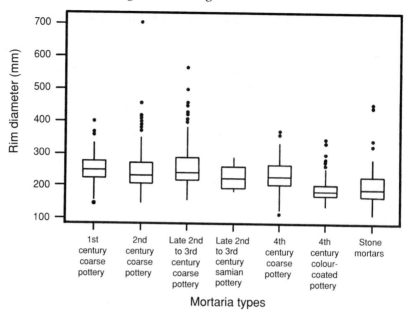

Figure 6.4. Boxplot showing the internal diameters of pottery mortaria and stone mortars by date. (The boxes enclose the inter-quartile range, dots represent outliers.)

representative. The pottery vessels are presented according to typological date and fabric. The coarse pottery mortaria maintain a fairly uniform average size across the centuries, though it is noticeable that there appear to be more small vessels in the late Roman period. Diameters as small as 112 mm and 120 mm have been recorded for some from the late fourth-century Crambeck industries of Yorkshire (see Fig. 6.3 no. 5).[18] The large examples tend to be of the late first to mid-third centuries, and are apparently missing in the late third and fourth centuries. These must have been used in a different way from most mortaria as they are far too heavy to hold, and it has long been suggested that they had some specialised culinary or commercial use.[19] Samian mortaria are similar in size to the average coarse pottery ones, but the colour-coated copies are noticeably smaller. This, together with the evidence of the small fourth-century coarse pottery ones, suggests that by that time, some mortaria were being used for a specialised function.

[18] Monaghan 1997: 937 no. 3398; Evans in Wilson 2002b: 334 no. M60B.
[19] Hartley 1973: 41; Richardson in Miller *et al.* 1986: 110.

Coarse pottery mortaria are far from being an ubiquitous element of material culture across the empire, and Britain appears to stand apart as being an unusually heavy consumer of them.[20] That they were not a vital part of Roman cookery is shown by their rarity in Italy as demonstrated by the fact that a recent exhibition of the evidence of food and flavours at Pompeii did not feel the need to include any examples within the wide range of vessel types on display.[21] This might hint that mortaria are not being used in Britain simply as kitchen utensils to produce Romanised food. This hypothesis is strengthened when the distribution of these vessels is considered. Whilst it is conceivable that a new cuisine might have been adopted in the towns and the more prosperous rural sites of the south of England, it becomes much harder to imagine this happening in the rural, native sites of the north. The people who lived in these appear to have had virtually no use at all for Roman material culture. Yet even here mortaria sherds are found, often from an early date and frequently forming a disproportionately large part of the pottery assemblage.[22]

The best way of establishing what the vessels were used for would be a detailed study combining residue analysis and detailed study of the wear and sooting patterns. So far, mortaria do not seem to have been subject to modern residue analysis, and it is difficult to establish wear patterns in any rigorous way. It can be established that the interiors often show considerable wear, and that there are consistent indications that the vessels may have been used in cooking as sooting and burning are regularly recorded (see Table 6.1).

The combination of the various strands of the evidence suggests that these bowls may have had a variety of different functions, changing both with time, and with the social group that they were being used in. Within early rural communities there is the distinct possibility that some may not have been used in the kitchen at all. A noticeable phenomenon on rural sites of the first to second centuries is that the inhabitants seem disproportionately interested in acquiring large decorated samian and glass bowls which clearly were not being used in cooking.[23] Presumably such bowls served a role in those societies that may have been different to the roles they served in urban or military life. Perhaps on these sites mortaria were regarded simply as large bowls.

It is also seems likely that the bright red mortaria made in samian and other colour-coated pottery may have served a different purpose than the

---

[20] Hartley 1998: 209.   [21] Stefani 2005.
[22] Cool 2004a: Table 2.   [23] Cool and Baxter 1999: 93.

Table 6.2. *A comparison of the functional categories in selected late second- to third-century samian assemblages.*

Site	Dishes	Bowls	Cups	Mortaria	Quantification
Catterick Bridge	34	51	24	6	Min. nos.
Catterick, Bainesse	117	217	112	9	Min. nos.
Alchester, site B	76	164	138	9	Min. nos.
Alchester, site C	14	27	13	1	Min. nos.
Lincoln, the Park	1269	380	552	62	EVE

coarse pottery cream forms. Samian pottery is a tableware not a kitchen-ware. The low incidence of the form as shown in Table 6.2 suggests it was never used in large numbers. Presumably this was not a form that each individual might require in the same way they needed cups and bowls. The spouts, where present, would have been practical for decanting dry ground powders or liquid, but not a thick puree. Samian mortaria possess grits like the coarse pottery ones. Sometimes grits show evidence of having been worn down, but this is not always the case.[24] It is questionable whether they were always used, or perceived of, in a similar way to the other mortaria. At the third-century cemetery at Brougham, samian mortaria were included as grave goods, but coarse pottery ones were only represented amongst the unstratified deposits assumed to be derived from graveside ceremonies.[25] This suggests the mourners per-ceived them in very different ways. It may be that mortaria began to serve new functions in the later Roman period, perhaps explaining the decrease in size noticeable in some late coarse pottery ones. What these various functions were, will only become clearer when as much attention is devoted to wear patterns as is currently devoted to fabric.

Mortaria have been examined at some length because they provide a cautionary tale of how it can be far too easy to equate a type of vessel with a description in the ancient sources. Once different variants of the vessel are examined together with the information derived from the contexts in which they are found, such an equation becomes much more problematic. Next, we move onto a different type of problem; one where there is a mismatch between our perception of function and the perceptions of those who actually used them.

[24] Dickinson in Monaghan 1997: 947.   [25] Evans in Cool 2004b: 355.

Evaluating the role of metal vessels in cooking is less easy than considering the role of pottery. Partly this is due to survival. Once broken, most pottery vessels are good for nothing more than the rubbish dump. Damaged metal ones, by contrast, can either be mended or recycled. Consequently metal vessel fragments are rare as site finds. Most metal vessels that are recovered whole were deliberately deposited; either as grave goods, or as offerings in religious or magical rites. There is also the problem already alluded to that what may look like cooking vessels to the modern eye, clearly had far different functions as far as their users were concerned. The classic example is the handled open dish or bowl then known as a *trulleum* which has distinct similarities to the modern saucepan. The shallow hemispherical form, often with an elaborate handle terminating in a ram or lion head (see Fig. 6.5 no. 2), was part of a set with a jug.[26] Far from being a cooking implement, these sets were for washing hands; both domestically and in religious ceremonies. They were an integral part of sacrifice, and are often depicted on the sides of altars. An example from Birrens has a ram head *trulleum* carved on one side and the instruments of sacrifice on the other (Fig. 6.5 no. 4). It is also noticeable that the deeper form is often found in clearly religious contexts such as the sacred spring at Bath (Fig. 6.5 no. 1), and so it might be suspected that these too had a part to play in libations where offerings were poured out for the deity. Shallow-handled metal dishes (Fig. 6.5 no. 3) were part of the bathing regime and are sometimes termed bath-saucers.[27] Though some of these vessels could have been put to culinary use, such a function should not be unthinkingly assumed.

Other types of metal vessels do seem to have had a culinary function, but one that seems to have been very specialised. Frying pans with folding handles were in use during the third to fourth centuries.[28] The evidence currently suggests that these were favoured by the civilian population, and predominantly by those living in the countryside. Despite the assumption often made that these would be an ideal piece of military equipment,[29] the contexts of the known examples from Britain suggest that this was not the case, the identification of the only possible example from a military site being doubtful as it comes from an unusually early context.[30] Fragments from them are very rare, and it is reasonable to conclude they were not common. Like the 'chapatti discs' discussed earlier in this chapter, iron

[26] Nuber 1972.   [27] den Boesterd 1956: 13–5; Koster 1997: 84.
[28] Manning 1985: 105; Keevil 1992.   [29] Alcock 2001: 107.
[30] Scott in Evans and Metcalf 1992: 168 no. 32.

Figure 6.5. Metal vessels used in sacrifice (nos. 1–2) and bathing (no. 3) with altar depicting *trulleum* (no. 4). (After Cunliffe 1988: fig. 8.24 (1); Havis and Brooks 2004: figs. 147–8 (2–3); Keppie and Arnold 1984: pl. 1 (4).) Vessels – Scale 1 : 8.

frying pans were probably designed for a very particular dish favoured by a small subset of the population.

One metal vessel form that seems self-evidently designed for cooking is the cauldron, but even here there are problems with associating it with everyday cooking practices. Cauldrons are known from both late Iron Age and Roman contexts,[31] and their continuing use is also shown by the iron suspension chains. There is a continuity in the development of these running from the late Iron Age through to the later fourth century and beyond.[32] The survival of the cauldrons themselves is often due to the fact that they had been used as containers for votive hoards and were deliberately deposited in lakes and pools. The suspension hooks and chains again also tend to be found because they had been placed in special hoards or as grave goods.[33] Fragmentary parts of both cauldrons and suspension gear are strikingly rare on domestic sites. Even when they do occur, it is noticeable that they often form parts of deposits that were special in some

[31] Piggott 1952–53: 13.   [32] Manning 1983.   [33] Manning 1983: 136–42.

way. The pair of cauldron hooks found at Danebury, for example, were clearly part of a structured deposit.[34]

The amount of wear and patching seen on some[35] clearly indicates they had seen practical use as cauldrons, but their pattern of deposition argues against them being everyday, utilitarian items. Whilst in the later Iron Age the scarcity of fragments on domestic sites may reflect nothing more than the fact that metal finds in general tend to be rare then, the same cannot be said for Roman-period ones. In the later Iron Age metal was clearly carefully curated and recycled. In the Roman period, whilst recycling was practised, metal is present in much higher quantities in the archaeological record. If cauldrons and their suspension gear were standard cooking equipment, fragments ought to be more visible in the archaeological record and they are not. They are considerably rarer than those from the various types of metal vessels associated with drinking and dining.[36]

In a fascinating survey of cauldron use reviewing the early medieval Welsh and Irish myths, early Welsh Law and the archaeological incidence of cauldrons, it was noted that cauldrons appear special from the late Bronze Age to the medieval period.[37] The myths clearly relate cauldron use to the realm of the gods and the otherworld, and the contexts in which they are deposited indicate this as well. Cauldrons may well have been used for cooking, but in very particular contexts and situations. The food cooked in them would probably have been special, and may not always have been intended for human consumption.

All the evidence we currently have points to them belonging to the ritual rather than the everyday realm, and their use may have been restricted to very narrow parts of the community. During the Roman period, cauldrons and suspension gear tend to be found in hoards and so it is difficult to know who was using them. Before and after that period, they are found forming part of the grave goods of individuals who were clearly high-ranking members of their communities. In the later Iron Age, for example, a tripod, suspension chain and cauldron was placed in an obviously elite burial at Stanfordbury[38] and a cauldron in another at Baldock.[39] Seven centuries or so later a cauldron with its very long and elaborate suspension chain was found in the Sutton Hoo ship burial.[40] The amount of skill required on the part of the smith to forge the

---

[34] Cunliffe and Poole 1991: 353 nos. 2.299–300.
[35] Piggott 1952–53: 28 no. C.1.
[36] See Table 15.3. [37] Green 1998: 75.
[38] Stead 1967: 55.
[39] Stead and Rigby 1986: 55 no. 6.
[40] Bruce-Mitford 1972: 39 figs. 16–7.

elaborate chains, not forgetting the amount of metal needed to make them, would have made cauldrons an excellent vehicle for elite display. Given their association with the otherworld, however, it is probable that they were buried with these individuals not merely as a symbol of conspicuous consumption, but because these people were believed to have a special relationship with that world either as king or priest.

UTENSILS

One of the great advantages the Roman cooks had over their late Iron Age predecessors was that iron became a much more commonly used material, and a wide range of knives and cleavers became available.[41] As we shall see in Chapter 9, this had an effect on butchery practice, but it must undoubtedly have made a cook's life easier to have a range of knives for different purposes; and the ubiquity of knife-blade fragments in site assemblages suggests that these would have been available to all strata of society for much of the Roman period. This may have changed in the later fourth century as there are some grounds for thinking that attitudes towards iron were changing and this may have been because it was becoming scarcer.[42]

Spoons of non-ferrous metals and bone are not uncommon as site finds, but their sizes and their associations strongly suggest that these were items for use in the dining room rather than as kitchen utensils. Metal spoons frequently form parts of services of tableware throughout the Roman period.[43] Spatulas and spoons of wood that would have been ideal cooking utensils are occasionally recovered from damp environments and were probably common.[44] Iron flesh-hooks were often combined with a ladle at the other end. Where these have come from good dated contexts, a later second- to fourth-century date is suggested.[45] They seem relatively common on rural sites and in small towns, especially in the south-east north of the Thames. They are occasionally found on sites with military associations, but appear curiously absent on major urban sites. Again this may suggest they are linked with particular cooking and dining practices.

[41] Manning 1985: 108–23.   [42] Cool 2000a: 52.
[43] Painter 2001: 69, fig. 7; Painter 1977a: 30–32.
[44] Padley and Winterbottom in McCarthy 1991(fascicule 3): 205 nos. 783–4.
[45] Carlisle – Padley in McCarthy 1991: fascicule 2, 133 no. 333; Kelvedon – Rodwell 1988: 76 no. 81, fig. 59; Scole – Rogerson 1977: 144 no. 14, fig. 61; Catterick – Mould in Wilson 2002a: 120 no. 45, fig. 290.

SOURCES OF HEAT

It is clear that the principal heat source throughout the Iron Age was the hearth, centrally positioned in the roundhouses. This form of architecture continued to be used well into Roman period in many areas.[46] Hearths were also used even when the architecture takes on a more traditionally Romanised form. In the late-first-century strip buildings at Leadenhall Court, London, for example, it is noticeable that most are supplied with hearths rather than ovens.[47] One reason for this may well have been the perceived danger of having ovens within timber buildings. This is graphically demonstrated at this site, where one building had been provided with an attached room that had an oven which eventually needed to be rebuilt because of destruction by fire.[48] The same fear of fire getting out of control was the impetus for the positioning of the bread ovens in forts. They are built into the backs of ramparts giving space for any fires to be brought under control before they spread.[49]

In some kitchens both hearths and ovens were present, sometimes with hearths at both ground level and on raised platforms. This would have provided a range of heat sources, and the possibility of a wide range of cooking practices.[50] Some of these ovens may have been fairly sophisticated as it has been suggested that a pottery pipe found at Gestingthorpe was part of some form of hood or chimney to remove fumes. Residues suggested olive oil, pork and wine had contributed to the condensates that had been trapped in its sooty linings.[51]

Kitchens where a range of heat sources have been recognised are often part of large houses which were clearly the residences of members of the upper classes; and it has to be questioned to what extent oven cooking would have been practised by all ranks of society. A wood-fired oven is very versatile, providing a range of temperatures as it cools down but it does require a considerable supply of fuel.[52] This was not necessarily cheap or easily available, especially in the towns, as a large part of the country had been deforested by the Roman period.[53] In Colchester, where many domestic buildings have been excavated, it has been noted that most of the ovens are early, possibly hinting of a move to the use of braziers.[54]

[46] E.g. Jarrett and Wrathmell 1981: 90 fig 43 – early second century.   [47] See fig. 17.2B.
[48] Milne and Wardle 1996: 40 fig. 41.   [49] Johnson 1983: 200–2.
[50] Colchester – Crummy 1984: 54; Crummy 1992: 101; Caerleon – Zienkiewicz 1993: 52–4.
[51] Evans (John) Elbeih, and Biek in Draper 1985: 99.   [52] Hartley 1954: 39–41.
[53] Dark and Dark 1997: 31.   [54] Crummy 1984: 25.

These would require less fuel but of course would be more limited in their range of products.

Hearths, however, can be very versatile cooking installations. We have already seen how they would be ideal for heating the contents of the cooking jars. With the aid of gridirons; pots can also be raised above the direct heat of the fire;[55] and food can also be baked using the process known to the Romans as *sub testu*. Here the item to be baked is placed on the hearth and a cover, previously heated, is placed over it. The whole ensemble is then buried in hot ash.[56] Its efficiency is demonstrated by the fact that the creation of a miniature oven inside a heat source has survived into the present. Hartley described it as hearthstone cooking, and David suggests a version of it for baking bread in an electric oven.[57] Special covers known as a *clibanus* or *testum* were manufactured in the Roman world. An increasing number have been identified from Britain,[58] but they are still rare – possibly because fragments are being misidentified as tile. Many of the large bowls could have been used in this way, and the flanges often noted on the sooted examples would have been particularly useful in manipulating the hot cover at the end of cooking.

The precise fuel used would probably depend on the type of installation and the area of the country. In addition to wood and charcoal, peat and coal were options in some parts of the country; the latter being exploited rapidly after the conquest and being found on a range of site types throughout the Roman period.[59]

Given the continued popularity of hearths, the virtual absence of fire-dogs in the Roman period is interesting. These were a feature of late Iron Age elite graves together with other evidence of the important role that feasting played during the funeral ceremonies, and presumably during the life of the deceased.[60] They do not appear to have had any practical use other than holding the logs of the fire together, as they do have any attachments for spit roasting.[61] They are occasionally found in elite burials of the immediate post-conquest period;[62] but thereafter they appear to disappear with the exception of the example from the later second-century deposit at Welshpool.[63]

[55] Manning 1985: 100.   [56] Cubberley *et al.* 1988.

[57] Hartley 1954: 47; David 1977: 303.

[58] Williams and Evans 1991; see also Evans in Wilson 2002b: 201; Compton, Evans, Sell and White in E. Evans 2000: 303–5.

[59] Dearne and Branigan 1995.   [60] Stead 1967: Table 1.

[61] Saunders 1978: 19–20.   [62] Foster in Niblett 1999: 150 no. 13, fig. 58.

[63] Boon 1961: 27 no. 7.

The differing trajectories of cauldrons and their suspension gear and fire dogs during the Roman period is quite informative. Possession of both showed that you could command access to scarce resources of material and craftsmanship. Both had been thought of as important parts of the burial rituals of the late pre-Roman elite in the south-east, sometimes as at Baldock and Standfordbury occurring together in the same grave.[64] The continued use of cauldrons, compared to the disappearance of firedogs, underlines the fact that the former were indeed special. They were part of the ritual life of the people. Firedogs, by contrast, would appear to be a fashion item. Perhaps it was the increased availability of iron that sealed their fate. Once anything ceases to be scarce, elites have a tendency to abandon it and to seek new items whose possession acts as a mark of distinction.[65]

FROM KITCHEN TO DINING ROOM

Throughout much of the Iron Age there do not appear to have been separate categories of cooking and tablewares. The differentiation starts to appear in the south-east in the century or so before the Roman invasion,[66] but it is not until the Roman period that it starts to be more widely seen.

A good place to start to explore what it was thought appropriate to eat and drink out of, is a group of graves of wealthy, native individuals buried in the later first to early second centuries with what appears to be a meal and its serving vessels. In some cases this is made explicit because bones clearly from joints of meat were also included. In one cremation burial at Winchester[67] dated towards the end of the first century, for example, bones from a young pig were found on a shale tray together with an iron knife and a spoon. Graves like this will be discussed in more detail in Chapter 17; here it is sufficient to note that they regularly contain place settings. These consist of a pottery cup and a shallow bowl, both of sizes suitable for each person to have an individual serving. Interestingly, though such graves frequently have place settings for four people, this only extends to the vessels. Other eating implements such as spoons or knives are either absent or present only as single items suggesting it was not seen as vital that everyone had their own. This contrasts with the picture derived from broadly contemporary hoards of silver plate. In that found in the House of the *Menander* at Pompeii, there were sufficient

---

[64] Stead and Rigby 1986: 55–60 nos. 6–8, Stead 1967: 55.
[65] Bourdieu 1986: 247.   [66] See pp. 155–7.   [67] Biddle 1967: 230–45.

spoons for each diner represented by the dishes and cups to have had their own.[68] The rarity of cutlery in these graves would suggest that food was normally eaten with the fingers and with the aid of bread to mop up the juices.

The emphasis on individual servings seen in these graves is supported by the distribution of graffiti cut into pottery vessels. Graffiti of all types occur on vessels including makers' names, indications of how much a vessel contained and occasionally what was in it. On cups, beakers and dishes, personal names indicating individual ownership are by far the dominant type.[69]

A number of studies have shown that the increase in the proportion of the classes of vessels associated with individual place settings (cup, dishes and bowls) in an assemblage and the decline in the proportion of jars can be seen as the defining feature of a Romanised assemblage.[70] The preference for individual settings was not uniform across the country. Detailed study of well-dated assemblages in the north of Britain has shown that in the second century there was a noticeable division between the rural sites which favoured jars, and the military and urban sites where the proportion of dishes and bowls was much higher. This division that can still be seen in the late fourth century, though by that time jar use has risen on other types of sites as well.[71] Something similar can be seen on a group of sites in the Midlands,[72] where the inhabitants of the rural sites are certainly using far more jars than dishes and bowls.

The lower amounts of tablewares on the rural sites would definitely imply that food was being served in a different way. There is always the temptation to suggest that the levels of tablewares on rural sites are depressed because many of them were being made in other materials such as wood that have not survived. There are, however, a considerable number of waterlogged assemblages where organic material survives, and it cannot be said that wooden or leather vessels are at all common in them. A jar-dominated assemblage probably implies that the common dining regime was communal, with everyone helping themselves from a single dish. As already noted, the standard cooking jar is not a very practical vessel to use for this. Wide-mouthed jars would have been more suitable; and it has been observed that the proportion of these in rural assemblages in South and West Yorkshire rises steadily from the late

---

[68] Painter 2001. [69] Evans 1987: 201.
[70] Millett 1979: 37–9; Evans 1993; Evans in Booth *et al.* 2001: 368–74.
[71] Evans 1993: figs. 7 and 13. [72] Evans in Booth *et al.* 2001: fig. 7.56.

second century.[73] As the author of that study has noted, pottery reports do not often distinguish between narrow-necked and wide-necked jars. Where this is done, it can be seen that wide-necked jars are generally at a very low level where the bowl – dish category remains high.[74] Exploring the incidence of wide-mouthed jars compared to that of dishes and bowls might well be a very fruitful way of exploring how people ate. As will be discussed in Chapter 16, the difference between eating from a communal pot and having one's own plate is quite a fundamental one.

[73] Leary in Brown *et al.* forthcoming.
[74] Evans in Booth *et al.* 2001: Table 7.31.

CHAPTER 7

The store cupboard

INTRODUCTION

In most kitchens there is a cupboard or shelf where the cook stores basic ingredients for which there is a regular need but which, for various reasons, do not have to be regularly brought in as fresh produce. Most modern British kitchens will have salt, sugar, cooking oil, and possibly a range of proprietary sauces such as tomato ketchup or brown sauce. This chapter looks at this category of food in the Romano-British kitchen.

SALT

Sodium is vital for life as without it cells become dehydrated. As sodium is continually lost through bodily functions such as sweating, it has to replaced by what we eat. People who mainly exist on a carnivorous diet can acquire the sodium they need from meat and blood. People who eat a diet with a higher proportion of plant food need to add salt (sodium chloride) to their diet.[1]

During the late Iron Age and Roman period, salt was needed in large quantities, both as a condiment and to preserve food. It was produced by evaporation. Many salterns were to be found in areas such as the Fenland, and the coasts of Essex, Kent and the southern counties. The manufacturing process involved trapping seawater, which has a salt content of about 3%, in shallow ponds and tanks. As the water gradually evaporated by the action of the sun and wind, a brine was produced. When the salt level had risen sufficiently so that it formed a supersaturated solution (at least 26%), the salt could be made to precipitate by heating the brine. It was placed in large vessels made of briquetage, a type of poorly fired handmade pottery. These were supported on stands and

[1] Kurlansky 2002: 9–10.

bonfires lit beneath them. The saltern sites tend to be recognised because of the large quantities of briquetage present. This was a seasonal activity, limited to the months when there was high sunlight, low rainfall and good winds.[2]

Salt could also be produced away from the coast at the brine springs of Cheshire and Worcestershire. These produced brine that was already supersaturated, so no preliminary evaporation was needed. A litre of seawater will yield 0.031 kg salt, whereas the same amount of brine from the Droitwich springs produces 0.294 kg.[3] Briquetage has been found in large quantities on these sites suggesting clay vessels were used, but the Cheshire industry also used lead evaporating pans.[4] Possibly salt would have been another source for the lead poisoning that is sometimes noted in skeletons.[5]

Both the coastal and the inland industries were already well established during the Iron Age, and the trade can traced via the briquetage known as Very Coarse Pottery (VCP) as the salt was clearly moved in the containers it was made in.[6] Even before Britain became part of the empire, salt was being produced in large quantities. The capacities of various brine settling tanks dated to the early first century AD at Droitwich have been calculated, and it is estimated that the smallest found would have produced 1.56 tonnes of salt at a time and the largest 4.17.[7] Seven of these tanks were excavated, and it is very likely that the complex contained more beyond the boundaries of the excavations. Excavated evidence of salt production at Middlewich belongs to the post-conquest period;[8] but given the place was known as *Salinae* in the Roman period,[9] one might suspect a similarly large production centre was already in place by the time the Army arrived in the area.

It is often asserted that salt was an Imperial monopoly, and that this may have meant that access to it was difficult for some parts of the population.[10] However, there is no evidence of how the industry was organised in Britain, and the pattern of widespread, dispersed production is at odds with the model of a commodity held under monopolistic control. It was also very cheap. The Vindolanda tablets appear to record a price of 12 asses for 85 pounds of salt whereas 60.5 pounds of bacon /lard cost 8 *denarii* and 2 *asses*.[11] There were 16 *asses* to the *denarius* so, pound

---

[2] Bradley 1975: 21 fig. 10; Gurney 1986: 141 fig. 89. [3] Woodiwiss 1992: 4.
[4] Penney and Shotter 1996; Shotter 2005: 43–5. [5] See p. 22.
[6] Morris 1994; Nevell 2005. [7] Woodiwiss 1992: 13.
[8] Bestwick 1975: 67. [9] Rivett and Smith 1979: 451.
[10] E.g. Jackson and Potter 1996: 688–9; Alcock 2001: 72.
[11] Bowman and Thomas 1996: 306–7.

for pound, bacon was approximately 15 times the price of salt. Again this argues against it being a source of revenue for the state. It is interesting to speculate whether the view of state control that has arisen was unconsciously adopted from the experience of British rule in India. There salt was a state monopoly, effectively policed, and this became an issue around which the Independence movement coalesced.[12]

Unlike the situation in the Iron Age, for much of the Roman period salt generally becomes invisible once it leaves the production sites. There are a few finds of briquetage from sites other than salterns, hinting that salt may occasionally have been transported in the evaporation vessel,[13] but this does not appear to have been usual. It has been suggested that the large storage jars in North Kent shelly ware which are ubiquitous on London sites of the later first and second centuries could have been salt containers, as the area they are coming from had many salterns.[14] Pottery jars would have been an ideal transport medium for salt as they would have kept the contents dry. A very common and widespread cooking ware made in Dorset (BB1) came from an area with many salterns.[15] Perhaps some of the common BB1 jars found all over the country started life as salt packaging. Even if they did not, the very obvious supply routes that they map[16] can be taken as a picture of how salt could have travelled from one end of the province to the other.

FISH SAUCE

Another source of salt in the diet was the condiment known as *garum*. This was a fish sauce made by alternating layers of oily fish, herbs and flavourings, and salt in a vat; and then leaving it in the sun until the contents had fermented and the sauce formed.[17] The end result was a liquid that could be variously called *garum*, *liquamen*, or *muria*; and a sediment called *allec*. The literary sources tend to use the names of the liquid indiscriminately, so if there was any real difference between them, this has now been lost. Whatever it was called, it was a very pungent seasoning. To modern eyes the large number of Roman recipes that call for it to be used, including sweet confections,[18] are startling. An appreciation of how it would have worked in cooking can be gained from considering how the sauce

[12] Kurlansky 2002: 334–53.   [13] Richardson in Miller *et al.* 1986: 131.2.
[14] Davies *et al.* 1994: 101–2; Miles 1975.   [15] Tyers 1996: 182–6; Farrar 1975.
[16] Allen and Fulford 1996.   [17] Curtis 1991: 6–15.
[18] Apicius: 4.ii.35 – a dish of pears cooked in honey and raisin wine.

nahm pla functions in Thai cuisine, as this is made in the same way as *garum*,[19] and can be looked on as its modern equivalent. An authority on Thai cooking describes it thus:

Fish sauce is an unusual condiment: it smells and tastes extremely pungent, yet when combined with other ingredients it melds into the whole, supports other flavours and is unobtrusive.[20]

In the recipes he gives, the food for one individual per meal could require 1 to 2 tablespoons of *nahm pla* (15–30 ml). By chance we have from Vindolanda an account that notes 1.5 *sextarii* (0.8 litres) of *muria* was used in the commanding officer's household on 24 June in the period AD 97 to 103.[21] Given the Thai rate of use, that amount would have seasoned food for between 25 and 50 people. We don't know how many people would have eaten in the *praetorium* that day, but the lower end of the estimate is a possibility given the day was a festival. This document is also useful in that it shows fish sauce may not have been a universal ingredient; but rather something used in food for special days. There is no mention of it for the days on either side of the festival.

The principal source for the fish sauce coming to Britain was the Iberian peninsula.[22] It was shipped in a variety of well-recognised amphora forms which could contain both fish sauce and pickled fish (see fig. 3.1 no. 3).[23] These have been recognised in Iron Age contexts in southern Britain which pre-date the conquest,[24] generally on sites which show evidence of other elite imports from the Roman world. At Braughing, for example, as well as other amphora-borne commodities,[25] there were also glass vessels which are very uncommon before the conquest. It is sometimes suggested that the late Iron Age sites where this Roman material appears in quantity, may have been centres for Roman traders.[26] If that is correct, then the presence of fish-sauce amphorae could not be used as evidence that the local elite inhabitants were altering their cooking practices. The presence of such an amphora in a probable pyre debris deposit at the pre-conquest cemetery at King Harry Lane, Verulamium,[27] however, would seem to suggest that

[19] Thompson 2002: 154.   [20] Thompson 2002: 156.
[21] Bowman and Thomas 1994: 153 no. 190.
[22] Curtis 1991: 46–64; Martin-Kilcher 2003: 69–70, footnote 4.
[23] Peacock and Williams 1986: Classes 16–22.
[24] Peacock in Partridge 1981: Table VII; Williams and Peacock 1994: 32.
[25] Williams in Potter and Trow 1988: Table 13.   [26] Potter and Trow 1988: 158–9.
[27] Williams in Stead and Rigby 1989: Table 7 burial 206, fig. 128.

Table 7.1. *A comparison of dated amphora assemblages (+ means present but less than 0.5% of assemblage; − means absent).*

	Date	Oil (%)	Wine (%)	Fish (%)	Other (%)	Total (kg)
Kingsholm	Neronian	42	37	12	9	97.60
Exeter	c. 55–80	61	15	21	3	67.40
Wroxeter	c 57–79	57	19	21	3	88.31
London, Billingsgate	c. 70–150	69	23	7	1	115.8
Wanborough	Mid 1st – mid 2nd C	97	−	3	−	10.67
Carlisle	Late 1st – early 2nd C	100	−	−	−	39.60
Gloucester	2nd C	68	25	−	+	4.76
Wroxeter	2nd C	88	6	4	2	21.36
Bainesse	2nd C	98	2	−	−	34.43
Carlisle	2nd C	98	2	−	−	31.80
South Shields	2nd C	100	+	−	+	31.16
Lincoln	Mid 2nd – mid 3rd C	83	17	−	−	11.31
Alchester	Mid 2nd – mid 3rd C	100	.	−	−	16.03
London, NFW	c. AD 200 – 250	82	18	−	−	30.60
London, Shadwell	3rd C	73	27	−	−	8.07
Caister	3rd and 4th C	62	38	−	−	18.42
Newcastle upon Tyne	3rd and 4th C	82	18	−	−	31.34

such ingredients were reaching the native population, as there is nothing in the deposit to mark the deceased as different in any way from the rest of the community.

The evidence for the consumption of fish sauce and other pickled fish products becomes much more common after the conquest. Table 7.1 shows amphora assemblages derived from dated contexts on a number of civilian and military sites. Fragments from fish sauce amphorae form a sizeable proportion of the early military assemblages (Kingsholm, Exeter and Wroxeter). They are present in civilian urban assemblages but at a lower level (Wanborough, Gloucester and Wroxeter). It is noticeable that they are less regularly part of second century assemblages, and appear to be absent from later ones.

Properly quantified amphora data are still not common, but there is a considerable amount of data which can be examined from the point of view of presence/absence. Table 7.2 shows data such as this, also from dated contexts.

Table 7.2. *The presence (+) / absence (.) of amphora types in dated assemblages.*

Site	Date	Type	Oil	Wine	Fish	Other
Longthorpe	c. 45–60	Military	+	+	+	+
Nanstallon	55–80	Military	+	.	.	.
Castleford	71–86	Military	+	+	+	+
York	71–100	Military	+	+	+	+
Segontium	Late 1st – early 2nd C	Military	+	+	+	+
Canterbury	50–80	Urban	+	+	.	.
London	75–90	Urban	+	+	+	.
Dorchester	Late 1st – early 2nd C	Urban	+	+	+	+
Cirencester	Early – mid 2nd C	Urban	+	+	+	.
Chelmsford	Late 1st – mid 2nd C	Urban	+	.	.	.
Towcester	Late 1st – mid 2nd C	Small town	+	.	+	.
Castleford	c. 140–180	Vicus	+	+	+	+
Wilcote	2nd C	Roadside	+	+	.	.
Cramond	Later 2nd – early 3rd C	Military	+	.	.	.
Greta Bridge	Later 2nd – late 3rd C	Vicus	+	+	.	.

Again the pattern shows presence at both military and urban civilian sites up to the mid-second century, and thereafter an absence. This absence is a curious one as the Iberian fish-products industry continued to export its products in quantity to other northern provinces into the third century, and in declining quantities it is still recorded in the fourth century.[28] It is always possible that the later ones are being overlooked in amphora assemblages; but the evidence currently suggests that Iberian fish sauce was not being used in either military or civilian contexts by the later second century. It is possible that fish sauce continued to be used, but came from different areas. Brittany, for example, has extensive installations that have been linked to its production in the second and third centuries.[29] There is also some evidence that it was being produced in Britain itself. Deposits of local fish bones plausibly interpreted as the debris from *garum* production have been recovered from a third-century context on the waterfront in London and from an undated deposit in York.[30] Large quantities of sand eels from late Roman waterfront contexts at Lincoln might also have been associated with *garum*

[28] Curtis 1991: 59; Martin-Kilcher 2003: 77–8.   [29] Sanquer and Galliou 1972.
[30] Bateman and Locker 1982; Jones in O'Connor 1988: 126–30.

production[31] Unfortunately these northern industries are not associated with distinctive, durable packaging and so their products cannot be traced on consumer sites.

It is noticeable that fragments from fish sauce amphorae tend to be restricted to military and urban sites. Whether this pattern can be used to suggest that this ingredient did not find favour with the rural population is open to question. As can be seen from Table 3.2, even the smaller of these amphorae contain between 14 and 18 litres. Given the Thai rate of use this is far more than even a large household would have had need of. Decanting into smaller containers must have been standard. A shopping list dated to AD 85–92 found at Vindolanda, for example, requests eight *sextarii* of *muria*,[32] approximately a quarter of one of the smaller amphorae.

Overall, the picture we have of fish sauce in Britain is that its use was far from universal. Even in an elite household like that of Cerialis at Vindolanda, it may have been mainly used on high days and holidays. Urban populations developed a taste for it but not necessarily rural ones; and there is every indication that its use declined by the late second century. Its use in late Roman Britain seems rare.

OLIVE OIL

In the Roman world olive oil was used not just as a cooking ingredient. It was also a vital part of the bathing regime, and was used as the base for perfumes and as fuel for lamps. Fragments of the very distinctive large spherical Spanish olive oil amphorae (see Fig. 3.1 no. 1) start to appear in south-central and south-eastern England, and very occasionally further north, up to fifty years prior to the conquest.[33] In the absence of bath-houses and the appropriate types of lamps in late Iron Age Britain, it may be assumed that it was imported for culinary purposes. This suggests that that in some sectors of native society, cooking practices were changing prior to the conquest. Where it is possible to track the introduction of the different amphora-borne commodities in the Iron Age, it appears that olive oil was adopted before fish sauce.[34]

After the conquest, olive oil amphora fragments are found widely and continue to be found into the third century (see Tables 7.1 and 7.2). At that point it becomes more difficult to establish the level of supply due to

---

[31] Dobney *et al.* 1995: 54.   [32] Bowman and Thomas 1994: 278 no. 302.
[33] Williams and Peacock 1983: 266–7; Fitzpatrick 2003: 17, fig. 8.
[34] Peacock in Partridge 1981: Table VII.

changes in the Mediterranean olive oil industry. During the third century the Spanish olive producers, who had dominated the market, were overtaken by producers in north Africa. They marketed their oil in a different type of amphora (see fig. 3.1 no. 4) which, though it held about the same amount as the Spanish globular amphora, was considerably lighter. As can be seen from the figures in Table 3.2, the same volume of oil might be represented by either 10 kg of north African amphorae or 20 kg of Spanish amphorae. If the level of supply had been maintained, the quantities of north African fragments should have been about half that of the Spanish ones. This is not the pattern that is observed. At York 591 kg of Dressel 20 fragments have been found in comparison to only 13.4 kg of north African ones.[35] Even allowing for the fact that the period of when Spanish supply could be expected was slightly longer (York was founded *c.* AD 71); there is a serious mismatch between these figures. Spanish imports didn't cease entirely in the later Roman period but were transported in smaller amphorae.[36] At York these only add another kilogram to the late olive oil amphora assemblage. The pattern seems to be that though the import of olive oil continued, it was at a much lower level.

Various reasons for this have been advanced;[37] but whatever they were, it would have had an impact on cooking practice as much of the oil imported into Britain would have been used in the kitchen. Lamp use declined markedly after the first century in Britain and so the use of oil as a fuel would have been negligible by the second century;[38] and the only non-culinary use was as oil for the baths.

Given the pattern of supply, it could be hypothesised that the greatest penetration into different parts of society could be expected during the second century. Dressel 20 fragments are not uncommon on rural sites during that period; both in the southern lowland,[39] and in northern and western areas where the level of Romanised material culture is generally low.[40] Were these being used for their contents, or were they brought onto the sites empty as very large containers, in the manner that oil drums can get reused for other purposes?[41] It may be significant that glass bottles, common from the later first to the early to mid-third centuries, are often

[35] Williams in Perrin 1990: Table 22; Williams in Monaghan 1997: Table 175.
[36] Carreras Montfort and Williams 2003.
[37] Williams and Carreras 1995: 238–40.   [38] Eckardt 2002: 58.
[39] Williams in Rickett 1995: 98; Waugh in Going and Hunn 1999: 96; Williams in Green 1987: Mf3. C1 Table XXVI.
[40] Jones in Cowell and Philpott 2000: Table 4.3; Evans in Roberts *et al.* 2001: Table 8.
[41] Evans in Longley *et al.* 1998: 213.

the only type of glass vessel present on rural sites.[42] In the very rare circumstances where the contents of these has survived and been analysed, it has been olive oil.[43] Whether or not the use of olive oil spread down into small, marginal rural communities in the second century could only really be answered by a programme of residue analysis on types of pottery used in cooking. Olive oil is one of the foodstuffs that can be detected by lipid analysis. One of the relatively few published analyses which relates to Roman pottery detected oil and albumen in the burnt residue on an early to mid-second-century dish at Chelmsford, possibly indicative of an accident relating to the cooking of a *patina* made with oil and eggs.[44]

SPICES AND FLAVOURINGS

It is not unusual for the recipes in Apicius to call for several different herbs and spices, and to conclude with the injunction 'sprinkle with pepper and serve'. We know from many written sources that a considerable number of different spices were available at the heart of empire.[45] Judging the extent they were in use in Britain is difficult, as many will have been used in a ground form, and so will not be recovered. Another problem is that the routine environmental analysis of waterlogged deposits, which would provide the best information, is a relatively recent phenomenon. Until very recently, for example, the only evidence there was for the use of black pepper in the province consisted of a reference to the purchase of it to the value of 2 *denarii* in one of the Vindolanda writing tablets, and pepper grinders such as those from the late fourth-century Hoxne hoard.[46] Now the extensive environmental sampling undertaken as part of excavations in London in the 1990s has produced examples of mineralised black peppercorns from three sites,[47] So it is to be expected that the pattern presented here will be augmented considerably in the next few years as more environmental reports become available.

Table 7.3 has been prepared to show the presence of various spices in a selection of waterlogged deposits. Those from Castleford, Vindolanda, Ribchester and Leicester come from aggregated samples taken across the sites. The Bearsden sample is from a ditch believed to have received

---

[42] Cool and Baxter 1999: 84.   [43] Stefani 2005: 89 no. 105.
[44] Evans, John in Going 1987: 91; see for example Apicius IV.ii.17.   [45] Miller 1969.
[46] Bowman and Thomas 1994: 135 no. 184; Bland and Johns 1993: 25–6.
[47] Gray in Drummond-Murray *et al.* 2002: 246 Table 121. The example from Bath (Durrani 2004) was a misidentification (Peter Davenport *pers. com.*)

Table 7.3. *The presence (+) / absence (.) of various spices in waterlogged deposits.*

	Date	Type	Coriander	Poppy seed	Celery	Dill	Summer savory	Mustard	Fennel
Castleford	Late C1	Military	+	+	+	.	.	+	.
Caerleon	85–100	Military	+	.	.	+	.	.	.
Vindolanda	85–120	Military	+	+	+	+	.	+	.
Ribchester	70–150	Military	+	+	+	+	.	.	.
Bearsden	142–58	Military	+	+	+	.	.	.	.
Leicester	120–200	Urban	+	.	.	.	.	.	.
London	Late C2	Urban	+	+	+	+	.	.	+
York	Late C2–C3	Military	+	+	.	+	+	.	.
Dragonby	C2–C3	Rural	+	.	+	.	+	.	.
Bancroft	C3–C4	Villa	+	.	+	.	+	+	.
South Shields	Early C4	*Vicus*	+	.	+	.	.	.	.

the discharge from the bath-house latrines, and thus represents faecal remains. The London sample comes from a pit filled with kitchen waste; and those from Caerleon, York, Dragonby and South Shields are well fills. The Bancroft sample is particularly interesting as it is a chance accumulation reflecting what was growing in the villa gardens. Though all of the flavourings in the table could be grown in Britain, and are occasionally recorded in prehistoric contexts;[48] they appear to be additions to the diet particularly associated with the Roman period. Coriander is ubiquitous, and has been found in many other analyses from Roman sites. Interestingly, it is a very common ingredient in Apicius, occurring in 18% of the recipes. The next commonest spice in the table, poppy seed, does not occur in the recipes, but was recommended by ancient dieticians as an addition to bread.[49] A cautionary note has to be sounded about automatically assuming all poppy seeds recovered were for culinary use. Those from charred grain assemblages are likely to be weeds of cultivation;[50] but culinary or medicinal use is indicated by mineralised examples from cesspits such as one in the legionary fortress at Colchester.[51] Given the associations, it is likely that those noted in Table 7.3 were culinary as well.

An interesting feature of the table is that summer savory only appears in the later deposits, and is missing from the early military samples. This may be chance, but it also appears to be absent from other early military samples such as at Carlisle,[52] though it does occur in London in a late first-century context.[53] It is possible that it was a later addition to the range of ingredients. It was certainly in use in the Classical Roman kitchen as it occurs in 6% of the recipes in Apicius.

At present, judged against the wealth of spices and flavourings known to have been in use in Roman cuisine, the British evidence is meagre. Lovage for example, a very popular ingredient featuring in a third of the recipes in Apicius, is known only from a reference to it in a shopping list from Vindolanda.[54] The poverty of the British evidence is likely to change in the coming years as the results of more environmental reports are published. Comparing the list of herbs and spices reported so far from the environmental sampling at Vindolanda (see Table 7.3) with the list derived from the writing tablets is instructive, as they show there was a

[48] Willcox 1977: 273.   [49] Dioscurides *Materia Medica*: IV.64.
[50] Letts in Smith *et al.* 1997: 268.   [51] Murphy in Crummy 1992: 283.
[52] Goodwin and Huntley in McCarthy 1991: fascicule 1 54–60.
[53] Davis in Milne and Wardle 1996: Table 2.
[54] Bowman and Thomas 1994: 175 no. 204.

much wider range in use there than the interim environmental report so far hints at. The tablets mention anise, caraway, cumin, lovage, mustard seed, thyme and pepper,[55] and only mustard occurs in both the tablets and from the sampling. The environmental list derives from samples taken during the excavations of the 1970s and 1980s and nothing is yet known of what has been recovered during the more recent excavations. When this is finally published it will be fascinating to see how the environmental and written evidence compare.

SWEET THINGS

Honey was the principal sweetener of antiquity, but was also considered a potent drug by ancient medical authorities.[56] Given the bad reputation it now enjoys, it is ironic that the same doctors also considered sugar to be a beneficial medicine.[57] Sugar was a rare and exotic item, but honey was common with much discussion in the ancient literature over which varieties were best. Unfortunately, archaeologically honey is virtually invisible. It had no distinctive, durable packaging, and the hives for the bees would have been made of organic materials that do not survive. We know that at Vindolanda it was brought in large quantities as an account dated to the end of the first century refers to purchasing one or more *modii* of it (a *modius* was 8.6 litres).[58] An equally large quantity is recorded on a sherd from a storage jar found in a second-century pit at Southwark. This has a graffito recording that the contents were 24 *librae* of honey (*c.* 8.4 litres).[59] Two other tablets from Vindolanda mention it apparently in connection with medical supplies.[60] It is also possible that there is evidence of honey, in the form of a concentration of *salix* pollen, from a mid-second-century pit at the Castleford.[61] Other than that, we have little evidence of what must have been a widely available ingredient.

Another sweet ingredient was the syrup made from boiling down grape must.[62] These syrups were given different names (*defrutum, sapa* and *caroenum*) depending on the reduction required for each.[63] Such products were made in Spain and southern Gaul, and shipped in distinctive amphorae.[64] The dates of these overlap, with the Spanish ones dating

[55] Bowman and Thomas 1994: 135 no. 184, 175 no. 204; 2003: 40 no. 588, 44 no. 591.
[56] Scarborough 1995: 22 footnote 110.   [57] Discurides *Materia Medica* II. 104.
[58] Bowman and Thomas 1994: 157 no. 191.   [59] RIB II.8 no. 2503.3.
[60] Bowman and Thomas 2003: 44–7 nos. 591–2.
[61] Bastow in Abramson *et al.* 1999: 173.   [62] See p. 22.   [63] Sealey 1985: 63.
[64] Peacock and Williams 1986: Classes 15 and 59.

from the first century BC to the late first century AD[65] whilst the Gallic form continued in use into at least the early second century. Later forms that might have transported the syrups have not been identified.

In Tables 7.1 and 7.2 the *defrutum* amphorae appear as part of the category 'other', as they only ever form a very small part of the amphorae assemblage. It is noticeable that *defrutum* is only represented in the first-century assemblages. In the second-century ones, the category is represented by amphorae that transported fruit. This chronological pattern is also noticeable elsewhere. At Southwark they regularly occur in the first-century assemblages, but are very rare in those of the early to mid-second century.[66] Therefore, though the Gallic sources appear to have continued to export syrups into the second century, the amphora evidence suggests they were not being imported in any quantity to Britain by then. There are some indications that the syrups may have continued to arrive but in different packaging. Olives were often preserved in these syrups and the amphorae transported both the preserved olives and syrups on their own. Though the evidence for the amphorae disappears in the first century, olives continue to be found up to the early fourth century implying a continuing supply, possibly transported in Spanish olive oil amphorae.[67] Given the decline in Spanish olive oil imports, it seems likely that these syrups would have disappeared from the British diet by the third century at the latest. They were always only a minor element of the diet for a small number of people.

---

[65] Carreras Montfort 2003: 88.

[66] Symonds in Drummond-Murray *et al.* 2002: Tables 44, 49, 54, 57, 61, 65.

[67] Sealey and Tyers 1989: 68–9, see also p. 123.

CHAPTER 8

Staples

INTRODUCTION

A staple food may be defined as something that forms the most important part, or a principal part, of the diet.[1] Judged by the literary sources, cereal foods performed this role in antiquity. Cato specifies the quantity of wheat and bread suitable for a household, and relegates all other food-stuffs to the role of relishes. Vegetius, writing about supplying the army in the field, lists grain together with wine and salt, as the provisions whose shortages should be prevented at all times.[2] Considering the quantities of quernstones found, and the evidence of the charred grain deposits, it seems very likely that the inhabitants of Roman Britain viewed foods derived from grain in a similar way. This chapter explores what those foods might have been, and how they were prepared. It also attempts to explore how the consumption of different grains might have been regarded, as within the Roman world there was a hierarchy of esteem relating to this.

THE GRAINS THEMSELVES

Three different types of wheat are found in the charred grain assemblages of Roman Britain – emmer (*Triticium diococcum*), spelt (*Triticium spelta*) and bread wheat (*Triticium aestivum*). Emmer had been grown in Britain since the Neolithic period. Spelt appears to have been an introduction of the first millennium BC, and was well established by the late Iron Age. Bread wheat, which is less disease resistant, occurs sporadically from the Neolithic period onwards, but it is not until the post-Roman period that it appears to have become a popular crop.[3] The different types needed

---

[1] Davidson 1999: 751.   [2] Cato 56, 58; Vegetius III.3.   [3] Jones 1981: 106–7.

different threshing regimes, and had different cooking properties which were well known to the cookery writers of antiquity.

Emmer and spelt are glume wheats. When threshed the head of the wheat breaks up into separate spikelets where the grain is still enclosed in the glume surrounding it. The spikelets have to be broken up to release the grain. This can be done by heating the spikelets (parching), and then pounding them to release the grain. Bread wheat by contrast is free threshing, with the grain being released from the glume in the initial stage.[4] The glume wheats can also be prepared simply by pounding, though it is harder work.[5] This method might have been preferred if the aim was to make leavened bread, as too intense a heat during parching could destroy the enzymes in the grain necessary if the bread is to rise. Glume wheats can be transported to the point of consumption in separated spikelet form, and the final preparation prior to milling can be done there. The presence of carbonised or mineralised glumes, even when no grains are present, can be a useful indication of the consumption of these types of wheat. At Leicester their consistent presence in an extensive sampling programme showed that spelt wheat was being prepared and consumed in the town throughout the Roman period.[6] Given that bread wheat does not have to be parched, it might be suspected that it is under-represented in the carbonised deposits, and it may have been more widely used than they indicate.

These wheats produce flours of different qualities. To make leavened bread, it is necessary for the grain to contain the insoluble proteins glutenin, gliadin and aglobulin that form gluten when wetted. As one old baking manual describes, the gluten may be thought of as the little balloons that hold the gas formed by yeast, and provide the open texture of leavened bread.[7] Spelt and bread wheat contain these proteins, and will produce a well-risen loaf. Emmer, by contrast, produces bread that does not rise so well. It has a heavy texture, but it does produce better porridge than spelt and bread wheat.[8] Emmer is also better for making cakes, and Cato seems to appreciate this as his recipe for fried honey-soaked dough-nuts (*globi*) calls for emmer.[9] An account from Vindolanda also itemises a variety of wheats by different names, suggesting that the cooks in the *praetorium* appreciated the difference and had need of a variety.[10]

---

[4] Hillman 1981: fig. 4.   [5] Braun 1995: 36.
[6] Monkton in Connor and Buckley 1999: 353.   [7] Banfield 1937: 7.
[8] Dickson and Dickson 2000: 120.   [9] Cato 79.
[10] Bowman and Thomas 1994: 157 no. 191; Pearce 2002: 934, Table 2.

The other principal grain recovered is barley. This is a free-threshing grain which lacks sufficient of the proteins to form gluten to produce a good loaf. Bread made from it is flat, grey and goes dry quickly, though it can be mixed with wheat to form a better quality loaf.[11] It makes good griddle cakes, and it may have been such a food that formed the last meal of Lindow man.[12] Other grains such as oats and rye are recovered, but they tend to form small parts of the assemblages. It is often open to question as to whether they had been deliberately grown, or were just present as weeds.

CLEANING AND MILLING

Although grain could be stored over a long period, flour could not. Wholemeal flour retains traces of endosperm, so there would have been a need to grind flour on a regular basis.[13] For this reason many consumers would have acquired grain rather than flour or meal, and would have ground it themselves. Cleaning the grain crop was a chore shared by both the producers and the consumers. Depending on whether the grain was free-threshing or not, the crop may have been shipped as clean grain or as spikelets. Certain weed and chaff elements could be removed by sieving, but others had to be picked out by hand as they were of similar size to the grain itself. A vivid example of the consumer having to do this was revealed in a granary at the fort at South Shields, which had been burnt in the late third or early fourth century. The grain being stored was dehusked spelt and bread wheat in approximately equal quantities. The samples from close to the entrance consistently had more glume bases and weed seeds in them than those in the body of the granary. This was plausibly interpreted as soldiers collecting their allocations, and then cleaning them in the better light by the entrance before going back to their barracks. It was noticed that the weed seeds were dominated by corncockle, something that is poisonous to both men and animals, and which needs to be carefully picked out.[14]

In the majority of cases converting the grain to flour or meal would have been done in the home with hand querns. The normal quern of the later Iron Age was the beehive quern. This had a domed upper stone with a narrow feed pipe through which a spindle passed. The spindle lodged

---

[11] David 1977: 62.   [12] Holden 1995: 79.   [13] Banfield 1937: 19–20.
[14] van der Veen in Bidwell and Speak 1994: 243–58.

Figure 8.1. Beehive (no. 1) and lava (no. 2) querns. Scale 1 : 16.

in a socket in the lower stone. Handles were normally inserted into a socket in the side, and were inclined or horizontal (Fig. 8.1 no. 1). These were heavy stones. The grain was fed through the feed pipe on the upper stone, and wear patterns suggest they may have been used in an oscillating, back and forth motion.[15] The grain was mashed between the upper and lower stone with a tearing, crushing action.

When the army arrived in Britain it brought with it a much more effective type of hand quern made of lava from the Mayen area of Germany (Fig. 8.1 no. 2) These were disc-shaped with an inclined grinding face between upper and lower stones. The upper stone was held in position by means of a rynd across the base of the feed pipe, through which the spindle passed. This allowed the space between the two faces to be adjusted and ensured that in the area at the edge (the skirt), the two stones fitted together well, important if the meal was to be finely ground.[16] Being made of lava, these stones were much lighter than the beehive querns, and the ability to adjust the space between the stones meant the grain was sheared and ground between the dressed faces rather than crushed. The handle was vertical which would have facilitated a rotary action, though some wear patterns suggest they, too, may sometimes have

[15] Wright in Wilson 2002a: 268.   [16] Welfare in Bidwell 1985: 157.

been used with a back and forth motion.[17] The new, improved, flatter designs were adopted by quarries in Britain, and examples made in British rock types such as the Millstone Grit from the Pennines were appearing by late in the first century AD.[18] These Romano-British flat querns did not signal the automatic decline of the beehive quern. The industry producing the examples made in the very distinctive Hertfordshire Puddingstone seems primarily to be a Romano-British one,[19] and the bases of four beehive querns were found *in situ* in a probably third-century building at the Dalton Parlours villa, showing they were still in use then.[20]

Grinding grain by hand mill is hard work. Ethnographic observation in Algeria has shown that a skilled housewife could produce 3 kg of flour in an hour and a half; often having to regrind the coarsest fraction. This figure is broadly comparable with the rate of 1.8 kg per hour noted in India.[21] In Algeria it was considered to be a long and arduous task which was painful on the shoulders. By good fortune, an account on a writing tablet from Carlisle has survived which provides the allowance of wheat and barley given out to a cavalry unit. Taking these figures we can calculate how long it would have taken to prepare the grain for eating.[22] The allowances appear to cover three-day rations and, as is normal in antiquity, they are expressed by volume. Each *turma* was issued with wheat at a rate of 5 or 6 *modii* a day. The 500-strong unit was divided into 16 *turmae* or squadrons, and depending whether or not the officers rations were included, this would have been for about 30 – 33 men. A litre of sifted spelt flour weighs *c.* 0.45 kg. Working at a conversion of 0.55 litres to one *sextarius*,[23] a *modius* would be *c.* 4 kg. Assuming that the people doing the grinding were as skilled as the Algerian housewives, converting the wheat to flour would have occupied each *turma* 10 to 12 person-hours a day.

Given the time and discomfort involved in hand grinding, it is not surprising that alternatives were sought. A hand quern cannot easily be operated if it is more than c. 0.5 m in diameter, but stones with diameters of 0.6 m or more are found in quernstone assemblages. These were for powered mills, either driven by water, man or animal power. This was an innovation associated with the Roman period, and the development of the flatter rotary querns. Their use seems to be concentrated in urban and

---

[17] Wright in Wilson 2002a: 270.   [18] Welfare in Bidwell 1985: 157.
[19] King 1987: 70.   [20] Tindall in Wrathmell and Nicholson 1990: 43.
[21] Jansen 2001: 209; Alcock 2001: 25.   [22] Tomlin 1998: 36 no. 1.
[23] RIB II.2 no. 2415.56.

military centres and in villas; they do not seem to be much in evidence in the smaller rural settlements.[24] Very occasionally parts of the hour-glass-shaped stones that would have been used in donkey mills are found. Two, made from lava derived from central France, have long been known from London and Corfe Mullen. A third, not made of lava, has recently come to light from the fort at Clyro.[25] Donkey mills such as these were used in commercial bakeries in the Mediterranean area.[26] It is probably of significance that the latest find of such a stone from Britain was found at a military site. As the calculations in the previous paragraph show, considerable amounts of time would have been taken up grinding corn for soldiers' rations, and some form of mechanisation would have been attractive when the troops were in their base camps. Powered mills in other military settings are certainly suggested by large flat stones over 0.6 m with ownership marks specifying which century they belonged to.[27]

Some people would have been lucky enough to be able to buy meal and flour, but for most households milling would have been a lengthy, arduous chore. The lower stones of hand querns have to be securely bedded so that they do not move when the upper stone is rotated. Where quernstones have remained *in situ*, they are bedded into the floor.[28] Naturally a bias to querns in this situation is to be expected from archaeological evidence; but this position might be expected to have been the norm, rather than popular museum reconstructions which have the querns placed at a convenient waist-height on a wooden surface. Both ethnographic and experimental observations point to the bedding of the querns being most effective at ground level,[29] with the operator consequently having to sit or squat alongside. In the light of this, the fact that at the Poundbury cemetery nearly three times more women than men showed modifications to their skeleton associated with squatting, is probably a very good indicator that grinding corn was woman's work.

BREAD OR PORRIDGE?

Depending on the type of quern used, the amount of regrinding, and the amount of sieving, it would have been possible to produce different grades

[24] Wright in Wilson 2002a: 280. [25] Williams-Thorpe and Thorpe 1988: Anon 2002: fig. 17.
[26] E.g. those from Pompeii – Stefani 2005: 67.
[27] RIB II.4 nos. 2449.2, 2449.19, possibly also 2449.3 and 2449.18.
[28] Frere 1972: 78; Tindall in Wrathmell and Nicolson 1990: 43; Price 2000: 99.
[29] See note 21.

of meal as well as finer flour. The traditional early Roman staple had been *puls*, a porridge made with emmer, but from the second century BC this had increasingly been augmented by bread.[30] Given the regular presence of spelt in the carbonised grain deposits, it seems likely that bread was preferred in Britain during the Roman period as well. Apart from the evidence of the digested remains of wholemeal wheat bread in what appears to be an outflow of a mid-second-century latrine at the fort at Bearsden,[31] there is little direct evidence of this, though the information derived from skeletons is suggestive. The wear on the teeth is indicative of a diet where it was necessary to chew most of the food.[32] The teeth often show heavy wear, and there is a lack of oclusal caries consistent with the eating of relatively coarse-grained wholemeal bread. The wear on the teeth comes about not just because of the glassy phytoliths from the grain casing, but also from tiny fragments of stone from the querns. The teeth are in a constant state of eruption to cope with this,[33] and the wear prevents oclusal caries developing. A diet where cereal is consumed in a soft form like porridge does not result in this type of wear.

With wholemeal stone-ground flour, the leaven for the bread would form naturally if it was mixed with water and left. Wild yeasts in the atmosphere combine with the sugars released from the grain to produce a fermentation. If a wooden bread trough was used for the mixing, such as the one found in London,[34] it would be likely to have been impregnated with the yeasts aiding fermentation.[35] Once the initial fermentation had happened, more flour could be added, the dough left to rise again, and then more flour and salt added to build up the final dough which was baked after a final rising. Keeping back a piece of the original dough would enable the baker to start the next batch of bread without undertaking the initial fermentation. This, at least, is the theory: though in practice the procedure may not be found to be quite so simple, as Jeffrey Steingarten's entertaining account shows. Baking bread from scratch in this way is a long-drawn-out affair; five to seven days from initial mixing to finished loaf.[36] The result would depend on the skill of the baker, and

[30] Tchernia 1986: 59; Braun 1995: 37.
[31] Knights *et al.* 1983: 143.
[32] Farwell and Molleson 1993: 182–3.
[33] Roberts and Manchester 1995: 53.
[34] Unpublished. High Street Londinium exhibition 2001, Museum of London.
[35] Hartley 1954: 501.
[36] See Steingarten 1998: 15–27; and David 1977: 296 for a less enthusiastic view.

the degree to which bran had been sifted out of the flour, as bran tends to make bread heavy.

In addition to this type of sourdough bread, yeast may have been derived from brewing beer. Pliny the Elder[37] noted that in Spain and Gaul they used the froth from brewing beer as a leaven, and it resulted in a lighter bread. Given the evidence for beer drinking and making in Roman Britain, it seems probable the British bakers would have been familiar with this more reliable source of leaven. Seventeenth- and eighteenth-century authors noted that the important thing to do when using ale barm was to wash it well by mixing it with water, allowing it to stand and then pouring off the water. This was to remove the bitterness, but they were dealing with hopped bitter beer as opposed to the unhopped ale of the Roman period, so it is not clear whether a similar cleansing period would be needed. If not, then the production of bread would have been much quicker than the process involved with sourdough bread, as Hannah Glass, writing in the mid-eighteenth century, implies ale balm will raise a loaf in two hours.[38]

Not all bread would have been baked in ovens, given the cost implications of the fuel.[39] One form of specialised vessel for baking bread may have been the shallow dishes in Pompeian-Red ware. The name reflects the colour of the vessels, rather than implying that they all originated at Pompeii.[40] These have a red slip internally which extends over the rim and part way down the exterior; this may have served as a non-stick coating. They are regularly found sooted as if they have been on an open hearth,[41] and at Pompeii several have been found with shallow loaves still in them.[42] The dishes come with matching lids which would have covered the contents whilst on the fire. This was a first to early second-century fashion, and the ware tends to be restricted to military sites and major urban centres, suggesting it was a cooking method restricted to a small part of the non-British community. However, there is an intriguing presence of these dishes and lids in pre-conquest contexts at Sheepen, an elite tribal centre close to Colchester.[43] This suggests that as well as ingredients such as oil and wine, cooking practices, and possibly cooks themselves, may have been imported.

[37] Pliny, 18.68.   [38] David 1977: 89–99.
[39] See p. 51.   [40] Tyers 1996: 156–9.
[41] Davies *et al.* 1994: 131.   [42] Green 1979: 130.
[43] Hawkes and Hull 1947: 221 Form 17A; Peacock 1977: 158.

WHITE BREAD, BROWN BREAD AND BARLEY CAKES

In societies with a differentiated cuisine, the form in which the staple food is taken often reflects the hierarchy inherent in a class system; and the poorer classes may well strive to emulate the elite. In a society whose staple is bread, the whiteness of the bread is often a matter of concern. White bread needs flour which has been carefully prepared, and sifted to remove as much of the bran as possible. There is much waste involved in preparing a flour like this; and also a great deal of effort. It fulfils all the requirements of being an item for, literally, conspicuous consumption. The rich eat white bread; the masses brown, and aspire to white even though brown bread is a far more nutritious food. The bran, that is carefully sifted out to make white flour, contains not only fibre but also many important fats, minerals and vitamins. The Roman medical writers clearly appreciated this, and recommended bread made from wholemeal flour, an appreciation that was not to be revived until the nineteenth century.[44]

Many different breads are known from the ancient literary sources, and discussions of them clearly consider not just their nutritional value, but also the esteem they are held in.[45] It seems very likely that the differences between white and brown bread with regard to social status would have been appreciated in Roman Britain; but from our current evidence it is difficult to explore this. Skeletal evidence would be useful if the wear state of teeth and their caries rate was compared to the perceived status of the individual as indicated by their grave goods and the nature of the burial. Do people in elite graves show evidence that they might have been eating white bread made with more refined flours? Unfortunately the records of individual skeletons as currently published are rarely detailed enough for this to be possible; but it might be an area to explore in the future.

One area that can be explored is the differences between those who ate wheat bread and those who ate barley bannocks. To Roman eyes wheat ruled supreme; barley was something you fed horses, or used as a punishment ration in the army.[46] In the north of Britain, though, barley appears to have been the preferred grain in civilian contexts;[47] whereas in civilian contexts in the south and Midlands, spelt wheat predominated.[48] There is

---

[44] White 1995: footnote 7; David 1977: 49.
[45] Garnsey 1999: 121; Flemming 2000: 480.
[46] Braun 1995: 33–4; Garnsey 1999: 119–20.
[47] Huntley in Wilson 2002a: 443–5.
[48] E.g. Murphy in Leach 1982: 288; Murphy in Crummy 1992: 281; Monkton in Connor and Buckley 1999: 353; Gray in Drummond-Murray *et al.* 2002: 245–6.

not necessarily any ecological reason for this; spelt is a hardy crop resistant to the cold as well as to pests.[49] Barley will not make good bread but it does make good griddle cakes, which are much easier to make and bake than wheat bread. Mixed to either a dough or a batter with skim milk, they can rapidly be cooked on a bake stone on the hearth.[50] There is an obvious visual difference between such griddle cakes and a raised loaf, even if the latter has not risen very much. It would have been obvious to any visitors to the north that the natives were eating a different food and one that, to some, was not thought fit for human consumption. One wonders if it gave rise to similar disdainful sentiments as Dr Johnson's celebrated definition of oats as 'A grain, which in England is generally given to horses, but in Scotland appears to support the people'.

There is a certain amount of evidence that even if this was the initial reaction, barley was preferred as a staple by some elements of the military. In some forts wheat was clearly preferred,[51] but in others barley dominates. In the case of Ribchester this may indicate nothing more than the fact it was a cavalry fort,[52] and large quantities of barley were needed for the horses. Elsewhere barley occurs stored in large quantities where the garrison was an infantry unit, as at Birdoswald.[53] Infantry units would have needed animal feed for officers' mounts, but the quantities do suggest that it may well have been for human consumption. Samples dominated by barley have been recovered from the forts at Newcastle upon Tyne and Catterick[54] at times when the units in the garrison may have been mixed infantry and cavalry. Though these may be reflecting animal feed, it was specifically noted that the grain from Catterick was a fully processed, cleaned crop, and it was doubted that this degree of care would have been exercised if it had been for animal consumption.

Whether the adoption of barley as a staple by certain units was just a case of adopting local food is open to question. It may be that their preference for barley bannocks was connected with the traditional cuisine of the area the unit was raised in. There is good evidence that at Catterick the garrison may have recently arrived from the Danubian territories.[55] At Birdoswald the unit had originally come from the same area. Though it had been long stationed in Britain, there is some evidence that it had kept

[49] Jones 1981: 106.   [50] David 1977: 535–6.
[51] Knights *et al.* 1983: 143; Nye in Casey *et al.* 1993: 83; van der Veen in Bidwell and Speak 1994: 249.
[52] Huntley and Hillam in Buxton and Howard-Davis 2000: 351.
[53] Huntley in Wilmott 1997: 141–4.
[54] Huntley and Daniell in Snape and Bidwell 2002: 239; Huntley in Wilson 2002a: 439.
[55] Wilson 2002a: 452.

some contacts with its homelands.[56] It should not automatically be assumed that soldiers from such a unit would necessarily have shared the cultural prejudices of a unit raised in Italy.

There is a certain amount of evidence that wheat bread may have been seen as something to adopt in emulation of Roman ways by some elements in native society. On two comparable rural sites in West Yorkshire there were noticeably different wheat to barley ratios. The one with a high wheat to barley ratio was the one that had more pottery finewares, amphora fragments and an imported lava quern.[57] The Dalton Parlours villa in the same county has also produced a high wheat to barley ratio.[58] There are thus grounds for thinking that in this area part of the Roman 'package' that was adopted by the native elite population could have included a change in the form of their staple food. This does not always appear to have been the case,[59] but it does suggest that examining the botanical remains from rural sites against a background of the evidence of the material culture found on them might be a fruitful avenue of research; and cast light on changing attitudes to food.

[56] Wilmott 1997: 407.
[57] Swillington Common and Parlington Hollins – Roberts *et al.* 2001: 158–62, 248.
[58] Murray in Wrathmell and Nicholson 1990: Table 27.
[59] See, for example, Longley *et al.* 1998: 243.

CHAPTER 9

Meat

INTRODUCTION

Domesticated animals can be kept for reasons other than to provide food. In addition to meat and milk, cattle (or more specifically oxen) were important beasts of burden; pulling carts and farm machinery. Sheep provide wool in addition to meat and milk; and it is only pigs that are solely raised for meat. Judging from the butchery marks seen on cattle and sheep bones, their role in providing meat was important. Nearly all the meat consumed in late Iron Age and Roman Britain came from cattle, sheep and pigs; and virtually all our information about this comes from the animal bone evidence. Using the animal bones to map consumption patterns is fraught with difficulties, some of which have been outlined in Chapter 2, but certain broad patterns do emerge; and it is clear that the meat eaten by different communities depended on spatial, chronological and social factors.

BEEF, LAMB OR PORK?

The study of animal bone from Romano-British sites only became standard practice in the 1970s; prior to that it was not unusual for them to be ignored and discarded.[1] As the number of such studies grew, it became apparent that the proportions of cattle, sheep and pigs present varied in a systematic way on different types of site. The proportions of cattle and pig bones were higher on the more Romanised sites (military establishments, major towns and villas), and sheep bones formed a larger proportion of the assemblages on the native sites, continuing a pattern that had been dominant in the later Iron Age.[2] The sort of differences may be seen in

---

[1] See for example Meddens in Ellis 2000: 316; Stallibrass in Wilson 2002a: 392.
[2] King 1978; 1999: 178–80.

Table 9.1. *A comparison of later first- to mid-second-century animal bone assemblages (NB: the Castleford fort assemblage is restricted to the later first century).*

Site	Type	Cattle (%)	Sheep (%)	Pig (%)	Total	Quantification method
Castleford	Fort	64	26	10	14155	NISP
Ribchester	Fort	63	25	11	2473	Zones
Castleford	Vicus	59	28	13	3648	NISP
Wroxeter	Urban	53	29	18	1548	NISP
Leicester	Urban	44	39	17	2039	Zones
Wilcote	Roadside rural	38	52	9	3116	Zones

Table 9.2. *The relationship between deadweight and meat yield with the possible implications for bone weights using an example from Colchester.*

	Cattle	Sheep	Pig
Average weight (kg)	363.00	35.00	79.00
Amount wasted (%)	50	45	25
Meat yield (kg)	181.50	19.25	59.25
Amount wasted (kg)	181.50	15.75	19.75
Colchester bone weight (kg)	30.70	4.26	4.69
Colchester bone weight (%)	77	11	12
Meat represented (kg)	30.70	5.21	14.07
Meat (%)	61	10	28

Table 9.1 where a number of assemblages of later first to mid-second-century date are shown. The rural site of Wilcote stands out as the only one where sheep are dominant. The urban sites, though interestingly not the military ones, stand apart with their higher proportion of pigs.

Tables such as this are useful for showing these systematic patterns, but it has to be remembered that the animal bones from different species, no matter how comparably quantified, are not directly equivalent in terms of meat yield. The different sizes of the animals, and the different amounts of waste they generate when butchered, have to be considered. Table 9.2 illustrates this. The first four rows show data derived from a nineteenth-century military manual providing advice to officers in charge of supply.

About half of the carcase of a cow and a sheep are discarded, but only a quarter of that of a pig. Rows three and four show the meat and waste yield. The next four rows explore the implications of this using a second- and third-century assemblage from a city-centre site in Colchester that had been quantified by weight.

It is freely admitted that extrapolating meat yield from bone weight in this way requires the making of some rather large assumptions, not the least of which is that the Romano-British population had the same attitude as a Victorian military officer to the parts of the animal that were edible. It does, however, highlight the fact that merely looking at the proportions of bones is unlikely to reflect the diet adequately. By weight of bone fragments sheep and pig meat look to form about the same amount of the diet at Colchester. Taking waste into consideration, nearly three times the amount of pork than of lamb may have been consumed. Such calculations have to be borne in mind when looking at animal bone assemblages with apparently very low proportions of pig bones. Even on those sites pork and its by-products may have been more commonly consumed than the figures suggest.

We know that eating pork and bacon was a distinctly Roman trait from both the literary sources and the bone assemblages of central Italy. These show a pattern that is dominated by pig with low cattle and sheep levels. The pattern of cattle and pork consumption that marks military and urban sites in Britain is thus not a 'Roman' one, but has much more in common with that of the northern Gaulish and German provinces. It has been plausibly argued by King that what we are seeing is a 'militarisation' rather than a 'Romanisation' of the diet.[3] He suggests that pork may have been thought of as being a high-status food, citing the higher proportion of pig bones in assemblages from legionary forts. Certainly there are some other indications from Britain that seem to support this.

Within the military domain there are several instances where pork consumption can be directly related to senior members of units. At Vindolanda a variety of pork products (pork fat, young pig and ham) are mentioned in the accounts relating to the *praetorium* and the household of the commanding officer. The only other meat products mentioned are venison and a prodigious number of chicken and geese; and certainly the venison would have been an uncommon food.[4] At Caerleon

---

[3] King 1999: 189.
[4] Bowman and Thomas 1994: 153 nos. 190 and 191; 2003, 23 no. 581. See also p. 100.

a similar suite of food is associated with a senior officer's house. There, the replacement of the timber fortress with one built in stone *c.* AD 85–100, sealed a well in a large courtyard house. This had been backfilled with debris including kitchen refuse. Amongst the mammal bone, cattle was in the majority but the number of pig bones was high, and there was also a relatively high presence of game and domestic fowl.[5] In the third-century military cemetery at Brougham, where there was a wide range of animal offerings on the pyre, pork was conspicuous by its rarity. Where it did occur, it was associated with individuals who appeared to be amongst the highest social class buried there.[6]

In civilian contexts the bone evidence associated with the palace at Fishbourne is particularly striking. Pig appears to be the commonest meat animal during the occupation of the palace. The specialist who studied this group argued that because of the different size of the animals, beef would still have been the commonest meat.[7] In the light of the evidence presented in Table 9.2, this conclusion is open to question. Clearly pork was a common meat on the tables of what was one of the royal families of Roman Britain. Finally the evidence from a mid-second-century pit at Bishopsgate in London can be considered. There an animal bone assemblage high in pig bones, together with game and domestic fowl, was found with many pottery food preparation vessels and amphorae.[8] The bone assemblage has distinct similarities to that in the well in the officer's house at Caerleon. Many of the vessels were complete or near complete, and the suspicion has to be that this is an instance of structured deposition. If so, then the food offerings may well have been regarded as special fare.

On many rural sites pig bones remain a relatively small part of the assemblage throughout the period under consideration. Even when pork was regularly being eaten in towns, the rural settlements surrounding them often show much lower levels of consumption.[9] On rural sites with a long continuous history stretching through the late Iron Age to the late Roman period such as Dragonby, a change in the diet can be seen occurring during the Roman period, but it consists of a rise in cattle at the expense of sheep. Pig levels remain consistently low.[10] It is on sites where elements of the native elite were clearly adopting many other new

---

[5] Hamilton-Dyer in Zienkiewicz 1993: Table 2 well 2.
[6] Bond and Worley in Cool 2004b: 328.   [7] Grant in Cunliffe 1971: 378–9.
[8] Tyers 1984.   [9] Levitan in Down 1989: 260; Reilly in Smith *et al.* 1997: 273.
[10] Harman in May 1996: fig. 8.2.

ways that a taste for pork develops. At the Dalton Parlours villa, for example, pig levels rise from 5% in the contexts associated with the roundhouses to 18% in those associated with the villa.[11]

Even allowing for the fact that the bones may not be accurately mapping meat consumption because of the differing proportion of waste they represent, it does appear that pig meat was not much favoured by most native elements of society. The animal bone evidence is matched by the evidence that is starting to emerge from lipid analysis of pottery. A large programme of analysis of sherds from four Iron Age sites in southern England showed that lipids associated with pork were strikingly absent from them.[12] It is interesting to speculate why pigs were avoided, given that it is such a useful meat animal, fecund and quickly maturing. In a review of animal exploitation in Iron Age Wessex, it was suggested that it may have been for environmental reasons, due to the absence of suitable woodland for them to forage in.[13] Though the lack of this may have been a problem if there had been a desire to keep them in herds, there would have been no reason not to keep them in more confined conditions. The cottage pig, raised by poorer labourers in restricted space to provide both a meat source and some income, has often been a feature of both rural and urban societies.[14] The presence of neonate pig bones in towns such as Lincoln, Silchester and Dorchester[15] suggest that pigs were being bred in towns, presumably in confined conditions. The reasons for the low level of consumption in the Iron Age and the rural Romano-British population must surely lie more in the cultural than the environmental realm. Whether this lay in the area of religious taboo, as in the case of the Jewish and Muslim prohibition on the consumption of pork, or was because the pig was a special animal, only consumed on special days, can only be guessed at. In some cases it might be suspected that the latter was the reason as it is noticeable that pork joints are sometimes included as grave offerings, by communities that are not consuming much of the meat in normal life.[16]

[11] Berg in Wrathmell and Nicholson 1990: Tables 13 and 18.
[12] Copley *et al.* 2005: fig. 3.   [13] Maltby 1994: 9.
[14] Malcolmson and Mastoris 1998: 45–65 ; Luard 1986: 150.
[15] Dobney *et al.* 1995: 44; Hamilton-Dyer in Fulford *et al.* 1997: 134; Maltby in Woodward *et al.* 1993: 326.
[16] Maltby in Davies *et al.* 2002: 169.

TOUGH BUT TASTY?

What meat tastes like, and how tough it is, depends on many factors including how old the animal was, the breed it came from, what it lived on and how long it was hung for. Unfortunately archaeological evidence provides little useful information about most of this, though it can normally say how old the beast was.

It is clear that the supply of beef to Romano-British towns was well organised, and that there must have been specialist butchers and slaughtermen involved with this. The evidence comes from large dumps of primary butchers' waste with a high proportion of bones from skulls, shoulder blades and feet. At Lincoln in the later fourth century, sufficient of this sort of debris was available for it to be used as parts of the dumps constructed at the river waterfront when it was being consolidated and extended.[17] Elsewhere, large dumps have been found that seem to reflect the place where the slaughtering and butchery was taking place. Sometimes this was centrally located as at Dorchester and Cirencester, and sometimes it lay just beyond the walls as at Chichester.[18] These primary deposits are a good place to start examining the age of the beef regularly consumed.

Age is generally calculated using the eruption and wear on teeth, and the fusion of the epiphyses at the end of the long bones. This means an estimate of the age distribution can be gained up to the age of four years. After that the beast is mature, and it becomes difficult to know how old it is. A striking feature of the primary butchery waste deposits is that the majority of the beasts were mature, i.e. older than four years. Modern practice in Britain is for prime beef to come from steers aged eighteen to twenty-four months. At this point they are well grown, and the additional cost of feeding them until they are fully mature will not be balanced by the additional yield in meat. The age of the cattle being slaughtered in the Romano-British towns suggests that they had a working life, either to produce milk or to be beasts of burden, prior to being eaten. This would suggest that most beef eaten in the towns would probably have been rather tough, and would probably have needed prolonged cooking to make it tender. It is not surprising that cooking jars, ideal for long slow cooking, are so common.

---

[17] Dobney *et al.* 1995: 10.
[18] Maltby in Woodward *et al.* 1993: 317–21; Maltby in Holbrook 1998: 358–3; Levitan in Down 1989: 245–9.

In modern parlance, veal comes from calves less than six months old. This would have been a much more tender meat, but it is rare to get evidence of it in towns. This may in part be due to problems of survival as immature bones are less well calcified. At Dorchester it was noted that evidence for calves was disproportionately gathered from cesspits where the preservation was good, and it was suggested that calves may have been processed differently to the mature animals.[19] It is noticeable that in the extensive deposits of bones from Wroxeter thought to be secondary waste, (i.e. that from the butcher as he sells on to the customer), evidence of veal was rare despite being derived from pits where preservation was good.[20] There is also clear evidence for the presence of veal calves in urban environments at other periods.[21] So, though depositional conditions may have had some effect, they do not seem sufficient to explain the rarity of calves in towns. It seems reasonable to conclude that veal would have been only an occasional luxury in Romano-British towns.

On rural sites, by contrast, a wider range of ages is recorded. As these will have been the production sites, this is unsurprising; illness and fatalities could be expected, and not all the beasts will have been for human consumption. Occasionally though there is clear evidence for the consumption of veal, as at the roadside settlement at Asthall.[22] Elsewhere there is sometimes a slight amount of evidence for an annual cull of younger beasts.[23] There are thus hints in the evidence that though beef may not have been the preferred meat on rural sites, the quality may have been better there than in the towns.

Distinct breeds of domestic animal are a relatively recent innovation in Britain, associated with the various agricultural improvements of the eighteenth century. The nearest breed to the Celtic Shorthorn type, that was common in the late Iron Age and Romano-British period, is probably the Dexter. This was a product of selective breeding from Irish hill cattle in the eighteenth century. It is currently used as both a dairy cow and for beef production. Other modern breeds that may have some similarities with the Roman beasts are the Kerry and the Welsh Black, both marketed these days as beef cattle. If it is appropriate to extrapolate back from these breeds to Roman cattle, it may be noted that nowadays all these are thought to produce very good tasting meat, which attracts

[19] Maltby in Woodward *et al.* 1993: 320.   [20] Meddens in Ellis 2000: 322.
[21] O'Connor 1988: 86.   [22] Powell, Clark and Searjeantson in Booth 1997: 142.
[23] Harmen in May 1996: 155.

a premium price. So, providing it was cooked with care, the beef could well have been tasty.

Up to now the evidence of the sheep bones has been discussed as if it was unproblematic. The reality is that what is being counted as sheep in most bone reports, are actually bones that could come from sheep or goats, as it is difficult in faunal analysis to distinguish between the bones of the two. Where efforts to distinguish between them have been made, sheep are commoner than goats. It is generally considered that in the Iron Age goats were rarely exploited as meat, and the pattern remained fundamentally the same in the Roman period.[24]

Goats were certainly present amongst the herds of Roman Britain, as can be seen from the large numbers available for sacrifice at the temple at Uley.[25] There is also the evidence of the leather to consider. Properly tanned leather was one of the great technical innovations of the Roman period, and an increasing number of assemblages preserved in damp environments have been studied. From these, it is clear that goatskin was often preferred over other leathers for such things as tents.[26] It is possible that these skins were imported, or that they have been wrongly identified and the leather actually comes from particularly hairy sheep;[27] but as it stands, the evidence suggests that the beasts were present in some numbers. Other direct evidence of them comes from tiles. In tile yards, when the tiles were laid out to dry, it wasn't unusual for animals and humans to walk over them leaving an impression on the surface. Where these marks have been studied in detail, goats are sometimes found to be almost as common as sheep.[28]

There is some evidence that goat meat may have been preferred when it was young.[29] Certainly in urban sites such as Colchester, Dorchester and at Southwark, where an attempt has been made to distinguish between sheep and goats, the latter that are identified are overwhelmingly juveniles, of an age where kid would be an appropriate description.[30] Sheep meat by contrast was clearly eaten at all stages of development from suckling lamb to mature mutton. The taste of sheep meat changes and intensifies with the age of the beast. In Victorian times, when the taste of mature mutton was much appreciated, it was derived from animals of three to five years. Modern British tastes now favour lamb of less than one

[24] Maltby 1981: 159–60.
[25] Levitan in Woodward and Leach 1993: 258, 266. Further discussed on pp. 211–13.
[26] Van Driel Murray *et al.* 1993: 56–7.   [27] Van Driel Murray in Cool and Philo 1998: 334.
[28] Cram and Fulford 1979: 205.   [29] Levitan in Woodward and Leach 1993: 301.
[30] Luff 1993, 66; Maltby in Woodward *et al.* 1993: 321 Table 56; Ainsley in Drummond-Murray *et al.* 2002: 266.

year.[31] In many bone assemblages there is evidence that most of the sheep meat eaten was from animals less than two years old. This can be noted both in assemblages from large urban centres,[32] where the beasts will have been deliberately brought in for consumption, as well as at rural settlements, which might be thought of as production centres.[33] This pattern suggests the sheep flocks were being managed with a principal aim being to produce supplies of prime young meat. In most assemblages there is evidence of some animals old enough to be regarded as stronger tasting mutton, and the taste for this may be a feature the later Roman period. Half of the sheep bones in the third-century butchers' waste in the *macellum* at Wroxeter could be regarded as mutton,[34] whilst in a number of urban assemblages where a comparison can be made between the early and later Roman period, an increase in the proportion of older beasts can be noted.[35] Whether this marks a change in taste, as has happened in modern Britain, or whether it reflects an increase in the importance of wool production, and a change in herd management because of this, is an open question.

It has been observed that there was regional and chronological variation in the size of sheep in the Roman period, and this may reflect a mixture of the native small sheep and some introduced larger sheep breeds.[36] The taste of sheep meat across the country will thus not have been uniform, even if the age was comparable. One feature of the meat that may be noted is that it is likely to have been leaner than is normal currently. Modern breeds descended from the types of native sheep that would have dominated in the early first millennium, such as the Welsh Black Mountain and the Soay, are always noted as being a lean meat.

As is to be expected, pigs were generally slaughtered when they were about twelve to eighteen months old and provided prime meat. Given that pigs develop rapidly, the slaughter of a beast before this age is not a rational economic decision. There was a market for suckling pig; and where it is possible to relate this to a particular type of occupation, it is often found to be associated with high-status occupation, and there are

[31] Davidson 1999: 441, 525.
[32] Luff 1993: 70; Maltby in Woodward *et al.* 1993: 323–4; Gidney in Connor and Buckley 1999: fig. 164.
[33] Locker in Neal *et al.* 1990: Table 1; Hamshaw-Thomas and Bermingham in Hands 1993: 171; Stallibrass in Jackson and Potter 1996: 592; Powell and Clark in Booth *et al.* 2001: 402.
[34] Meddens in Ellis 2000: 325.
[35] Levitan in Down 1989: 251; Maltby in Woodward *et al.* 1993: 323–4; Dobney *et al.* 1995: 39.
[36] Maltby in Woodward *et al.* 1993: 324.

grounds for thinking it was regarded as a luxury delicacy. At Fishbourne the consumption of this type of meat went up markedly during the palace phase of occupation, compared with what had been consumed before. It is also present in the special deposit at Bishopsgate, London, where several unusual meats were present.[37]

CUTS OF MEAT AND PRESERVATION

One of the notable changes that marks the transition from the Iron Age to the Roman period can be seen in butchery practice. The Iron Age population used knives to prepare the carcase: Roman butchers used cleavers.[38] Cleavers allowed very intensive butchery to be carried out on cattle carcases, maximising the utilisation of the meat. It is clear that this change was not restricted to the military and urban population, but spread to the rural one as well, presumably because of the much greater availability of iron. By the later second century, for example, this technique was not only being used in a major urban centre such as Cirencester,[39] but also in much smaller settlements in the surrounding region.[40]

The fragmentation seen in the cattle bones in the butchers' waste in the *macellum* at Wroxeter provides a good example of the type of butchery that can be expected.[41] Scapulae were especially strongly represented, as well as the pelvis and ribs. Long bones show a considerable amount of fragmentation consistent with extracting the marrow. The type of butchery seen on the scapulae is typical of a pattern often seen on this bone. The central spine was chopped off, and there was trimming and chopping around the glenoid cavity (part of the joint with the forelimb). This sort of trimming would be appropriate if it was intended to salt the shoulder for preservation, as it would allow the brine to penetrate the muscle mass.[42] Shoulders often seem to have been preserved in some way. A frequently observed modification consists of a hole punched through the scapula which has been plausibly interpreted as allowing the shoulder to be hung up so it could be dried or smoked.[43] The scapulae with these holes can also show knife marks, interpreted as the result of cutting the

[37] Grant in Cunliffe 1971: 383; Tyers 1984: 374.   [38] Maltby 1985: 20.
[39] Maltby in Holbrook 1998: 358.
[40] Hanshawe-Thomas and Bermingham in Hands 1993: 174; Powell, Clarke and Searjeantson in Booth 1997: 146.
[41] Meddens in Ellis 2000: 322–4.   [42] Dobney *et al.* 1995: 27.
[43] O'Connor 1988: 83.

Figure 9.1. Cattle scapula from Castleford showing typical puncture and knife marks from carving suggesting the meat had been preserved on the bone. (Photo: P. Gwilliam, copyright Archaeological Services WYAS – Abramson *et al.* 1999.

dried meat off (fig. 9.1).[44] The scapulae with suspension holes have most frequently been recorded in military contexts,[45] but are also present on urban and rural sites.[46] Smoking and/or air drying would not be a particularly efficient way of preserving shoulders of beef,[47] salting would be better for long-term preservation. It may well be, therefore, that the shoulders were being smoked because the taste of smoked beef was enjoyed; rather than because there was a need to preserve fresh food for later consumption. A taste for tongue is also indicated by the heavy fragmentation of the mandibles.

Fragmentation of long bones is frequently observed, sometimes there are rubbish deposits that consist just of that sort of waste. Some specialists argue that they are the end product of a process that was intended primarily to produce broth or grease, as marrow can be extracted without such intense fragmentation.[48] The ancient world certainly esteemed marrow as a delicacy, and as a useful food in the armoury of a doctor. Dioscurides ranks the marrow of different animals and provides instructions as to how it should be prepared.[49] It seems likely that the opportunity to extract the marrow was taken, even if the fragments were later exploited to make glue. The idea that these bones were being used to make soup or broth in large quantities seems less likely in a Roman context. Making such stocks and broths is very much a phenomenon that arose during the nineteenth century with attempts to relieve the poor.[50]

Sheep and pigs also regularly show butchery marks, but for these smaller beasts it is a case of dividing the carcass up into manageable joints left on the bone, rather than the filleting regularly seen on the cattle carcasses.

EATING HORSE – THE GREAT TABOO?

A notable feature of most bone reports is that though horse bones are identified, they very rarely show any signs of dismemberment or butchery. The horse is a large animal and if they had been eaten regularly, the distinctive chop marks of butchery should be present. When marks are seen on the bones, these tend to be knife cuts which can plausibly be

---

[44] Note 40; Berg in Abramson *et al.* 1999: 233.
[45] Morris in Ward 1988: 25; Hamilton-Dyer in Zienkiewicz 1993: 134; Izard in Wilmott 1997: 369.
[46] Maltby in Woodward *et al.* 1993: 319; Hanshawe-Thomas and Bermingham in Hands 1993: 174.
[47] Davidson 1999: 256, 728.   [48] See Berg in Abramson *et al.* 1999: 235 for discussion.
[49] Dioscurides II.95.   [50] Stokes 1996: 42.

associated with skinning.[51] It is sometimes asserted that horsemeat was being eaten, but the evidence in the form of butchery marks is often not presented in a way that can be independently assessed.[52] That horse was not a regular food item will not surprise a modern British reader, as to most of the population it is not an acceptable meat animal. Our aversion stems to a great degree from a thousand years or more of Christian prohibition, based on the perceived connection with paganism and barbarity. Many other religions also ban the practice.[53] Interestingly, one of the few cases in Roman Britain where the regular consumption of horsemeat can be convincingly shown occurs at a temple site.[54] Whether horse was, or was not, eaten may also have had a ritual or religious basis in Roman Britain. It has been suggested that the early Iron Age coin series from southern Britain show that the horse was viewed as a special animal; possibly associated with ideas of who had authority over the land.[55] If it was indeed looked on in this way, it is easy to see why horsemeat would not normally enter the food chain. Ideas of who owned land might have changed under Roman rule, but changing fundamental cultural beliefs about what could be eaten would not have been so easy.

[51] Berg in Abramson *et al.* 1999: 236.   [52] E.g. Bullock and Allen in Smith *et al.* 1997: 198.
[53] Gade 2000.   [54] Luff in Turner 1999: 206, fig. 132.
[55] Creighton 2000: 22–6.

CHAPTER 10

Dairy products

INTRODUCTION

Dairy products are a problem for archaeology because they leave little direct trace other than residues. Though we know from the literary sources that a range of cheeses and other milk products were consumed and enjoyed in the Mediterranean heartlands,[1] our knowledge of what was available in Britain is fairly minimal. Caesar referred to the tribes of the interior living on milk and meat, but as he also maintained they wore skins,[2] this seems more likely to belong to the realms of describing a generalised barbarian, than to the accurate reporting of eating practice. This chapter will outline what we do know about dairy products in Britain, but given the dearth of information it will be rather short. Given the results starting to emerge from residue analysis of prehistoric pottery,[3] it might be anticipated that a much longer one would be possible were Roman pottery ever to be analysed in a similar way.

MILK

The previous chapter has shown that milk-producing animals in the form of cattle, sheep and goats were present in some numbers in Roman Britain. To what extent they were exploited for milk is unknown. It is clear that in general cattle were not being managed primarily as dairy animals. In a dairy herd, most male calves are surplus to requirements so they are fattened and slaughtered as veal. This can often be seen in post-medieval animal bone assemblages,[4] but is not observable in the Roman ones. Cows could have been milked while suckling their young, though

---

[1] Alcock 2001: 57–60; Dalby 2000: 253.
[2] Caesar V.14.   [3] Copley *et al.* 2005.
[4] O'Connor 1988: 86; Luff 1993: 57–8.

the yield would be lower. Modern Dexter cattle are promoted as both house cows, and suckler cows for raising both their own calf and another.[5]

The skeletal evidence would also argue against widespread consumption of cow's milk. Tuberculosis is a disease that is spread from cattle to humans largely by the drinking of infected milk. It is noticeable that in Britain it was a common disease by the seventeenth century,[6] corresponding with the post-medieval rise of dairy herds as seen in the animal bone assemblages. The disease causes changes in the bones, but these are only seen rarely in late Roman skeletons.[7] A possible 3 cases were seen at Poundbury out of a population of over 1,400 burials; while at the East Cemetery in London there were possibly 2 cases out of 550 individuals.[8] These are the individuals that lived long enough with the disease for the skeleton to be affected. Others could have died of it before that happened; but at present the evidence does not suggest tuberculosis was a major problem in late Roman Britain.

The goat is a very likely candidate for having been a dairy animal, given the evidence we have for their presence, and the fact that they did not seem to have been a favoured meat when adult. The kill-off pattern for sheep suggested that in the earlier Roman period they were being bred primarily for their meat. As there appears to be more evidence for mutton in the later Roman period, older beasts may have became more common, possibly with a greater exploitation of sheep milk.

BUTTER AND CHEESE

Raw milk is not necessarily either a pleasant or safe drink in societies without refrigeration. It is better to convert it to butter or cheese to ensure long-term storage. In both cases there is an initial ripening to allow bacteria to sour the milk. Butter is produced from cream that is churned to form an emulsion. The equipment for this is traditionally made of organic materials, thus generally leaving no archaeological trace. It is noticeable that recipes for baked goods in the ancient literary sources call for cheese where modern practice would be to use butter.[9] The same sources indicate butter was considered a salve rather than a foodstuff in the Mediterranean world.[10] How it was regarded in the north is unknown.

---

[5] http://www.dextercattle.co.uk/breed.shtml – last accessed August 2006.
[6] Roberts and Manchester 1995: 136–7.   [7] Stirland and Waldron 1990.
[8] Farwell and Mollesson 1993: 185; Conheeney in Barber and Bowsher 2000: 287.
[9] Leon 1943: 215–6.   [10] E.g. Columella V.12.5.

Given the paucity of evidence for butter, it is really very irritating that the one account or shopping list from Vindolanda that might mention it, is so badly damaged that the reading cannot be secure.[11]

Cheese is made from ripened milk, kept warm during the initial stages to allow the bacteria to grow. Curdling may be encouraged by the addition of an agent like rennet. This separates the curds from the whey. The precise type of cheese produced depends on how the curds are treated. In a soft cheese they may just be drained. In harder cheeses they will be broken up by cutting or shredding to aid drainage. They are then placed in a form that needs to be perforated, as whey will still be draining from the cheese. Once the cheese is stiff enough to be removed from the form, modern practice would be to salt it. It can then be matured, which often involves it being infected by particular organisms to produce a distinctive taste or smell.[12]

Archaeologically, it might be possible to recognise cheese making at two stages; the point where the milk is kept warm initially, and the point at which it is drained and/or formed. Given that the milk has to be heated, a pottery or metal vessel would be expected, rather than one made of wood. Similar durable materials might be used for the strainers and forms, though cloth would have been adequate for the first, and wood for the second. For the heating stage it is worth bearing in mind that mortaria may have been used. The regular observance of sooting on them would be consistent with a vessel kept on or near a hearth; and an irregular interior is also thought to be helpful in the development of curds.[13] What is needed for these vessels is a rigorous programme of wear and lipid analysis.

For the draining and pressing stage, there are pottery vessels that would have been suitable. The strainers are normally wide bowls with perforated bases. A cylindrical form with a perforated base which has internal concentric ridges is also found, and this is normally given the name of cheese press (fig. 10.1). Residue analysis of a strainer bowl at Poundbury did show evidence for milk products,[14] so it seems reasonable to suspect that they could have been used in cheese production.

Like mortaria, strainers and cheese presses are a post-conquest introduction; unlike mortaria they are rare. This can easily be seen by looking at studies that provide a form series, the presses and strainers if present

---

[11] Bowman and Thomas 1994: 175 no. 204.
[12] Davidson 1999: 159–61.   [13] Oswald 1943: 45–6.
[14] Evans and Card in Green 1987: Table LV; see also fig. 88.36.

Figure 10.1. Military cheese presses and strainers from Longthorpe and Holt. (After Dannell and Wild 1987: fig. 41 (1, 3–5) and Grimes 1930: fig. 72 (2 and 6).) Scale 1 : 8.

tend to be placed in the miscellaneous category at the end.[15] There is evidence that strainers and presses were introduced by the military. One of the products of the kilns associated with the military works depot outside the fortress at Longthorpe were cheese presses, together with the occasional, rather unusual form of strainer bowl.[16] These kilns are dated to the 50s, and are a very early example of the army producing the vessels it had need of. Production of strainers and presses can also be seen at other military kiln sites such as at Holt, which served the fortress at Chester, and at York.[17] Not all military units seem to have felt the need for such vessels. At Colchester cheese presses tend to be a second-century phenomenon, and there are none associated with the fortress assemblages.[18] It is possible that we are looking at a particular style of cheese making, linked to particular units or regions. Consideration of the various ways British cheeses were traditionally drained, cut and formed shows that cheese makers could have quite precise requirements.[19] It is quite probable that those of antiquity had similar preferences.

The use of presses and strainers clearly moved beyond the military in the civilian population, both urban and rural. They were, for example, a product made in small numbers throughout the life of the South Yorkshire pottery industry.[20] Though some of these products were initially destined for a military market, the late Roman production was essentially destined for the local, native community. They continued to be in demand into the fourth century as cheese presses were made in Crambeck ware.[21]

[15] E.g. Monaghan 1997: 1022; Bell and Evans in Wilson 2002b: 396.
[16] Dannell in Dannell and Wild 1987: 151–3.
[17] Grimes 1930: 168 nos. 206–9; Monaghan 1997: 1022 nos. 4116, 4119, 4120.
[18] Bidwell and Croom in Symonds and Wade 1999: 476 type 199.   [19] Hartley 1954: 486–91.
[20] Buckland *et al.* 1980: 161.   [21] Monaghan 1997: 1022 no. 4118.

Cheeses made using these pottery vessels must always have been a minority, possibly specialist, product. Fragments from a strainer or a cheese press are very distinctive, so their rarity seems to be real and not just the result of them being overlooked during analysis. Most cheese made in Britain would appear to have been made with utensils made of organic materials, presumably continuing traditions established in the Iron Age.

CHAPTER II

Poultry and eggs

INTRODUCTION

This chapter will explore the consumption of poultry, regarded here as domesticated birds kept in farmyards, and their eggs. With these categories of foodstuff, we return to an area where direct evidence survives. It requires there to have been a systematic sampling programme for that evidence to be recovered in a reliable way, especially in the case of eggshell. These birds, especially domestic fowl, were not only sources of food, they also had a symbolic role in religion. There is some evidence too, that they were more likely to be eaten by certain sectors of the community, than by others. The pattern of their consumption is a very useful tool for exploring Romano-British society, and is likely to become even more valuable as the results of routine sampling become available.

THE BIRDS

The domestic birds kept in Roman Britain were chickens, ducks and geese. In the Mediterranean world during the Roman period, pigeons and doves were deliberately reared as food animals, just as they were to be in Britain during the medieval period.[1] Though these birds appear to have been introduced into Roman Britain, there is little evidence that they were a common food item.[2] The first evidence for the domestic fowl (*Gallus gallus*) in Britain occurs in late Iron Age contexts; and it was deliberately bred for food, cock fighting and religious purposes.[3] The ducks and geese present on Romano-British sites were a mixture of domestic and wild animals.[4] Here no attempt will be made to differentiate between the two.

---

[1] Johnston 2000: 563. [2] Parker 1988: 202.
[3] Maltby 1997: 402; for cock fighting see Luff 1993: 90.
[4] See for example O'Connor 1988: 100 Table 27; Hamilton-Dyer in Zienkiewicz 1993: 135 Table 2.

Table 11.1. *A comparison of the recovery of different types of poultry at selected urban sites.*

	Fowl (%)	Duck (%)	Goose (%)	Total	Quantification method
Colchester Culver St	63.0	30.5	6.5	1578	NISP
Colchester Gilberd	83.5	13.0	3.5	1382	NISP
Dorchester	84.0	15.0	1.0	1572	Fragment
Leicester	85.0	8.0	7.0	428	Zones
Southwark	82.0	18.0	—	462	Weight (g)

Table 11.1 shows the proportions of bones belonging to the three different types of birds on five urban sites which have produced relatively large assemblages. The methods of quantification vary, but the pattern is the same. In all, domestic fowl dominate. Apart from Culver Street, where special circumstances may have applied, ducks and geese are much rarer. This general pattern between the species is the one normally observed, but it is clear that chicken was not regularly eaten on all types of site. In an interesting study, Maltby assessed the contribution of chicken to the diet by looking at the proportions of domestic fowl, sheep and goats in the bone assemblages of a large number of different sites, using NISP measures. He was able to show that there was a noticeable urban – rural divide with the sites with the highest proportion of chicken being the large towns. Chicken was moderately well represented on military and villa sites, but tended to be rare or absent on rural sites.[5] The consumption of chicken could thus be seen as one of the ways in which Roman manners and tastes were adopted in some environments, but not in others.

The sizes of the bones of domestic fowl recovered show that they were of a variety of sizes, and it is possible that some male birds were deliberately castrated to produce large plump capons.[6] Where butchery marks are noted the recurrent pattern is for them to show that the feet and the wing tips were cut off.[7] Very little other carcase modification is recorded, so the assumption would be that these birds were often cooked whole, rather than jointed.

There are some indications that poultry in general may have been a high-status foodstuff. Chicken, ducks and geese were present in the

[5] Maltby 1997.   [6] Luff 1993: 97; Maltby in Woodward *et al.* 1993: 332.
[7] Maltby in Woodward *et al.* 1993: 331; Hamilton-Dyer in Fulford *et al.* 1997: 133.

Table 11.2. *A comparison of sheep/pig and poultry bone fragments from Culver Street, Colchester and Fishbourne.*

	Date	Sheep/Pig (%)	Poultry (%)	Total
Culver St	60–150	76	24	1782
	150–400	63	37	2075
Fishbourne	Pre-palace	70	30	1173
	Palace	61	39	882

kitchen-waste deposit associated with a senior officer at Caerleon during the late first century.[8] Large quantities of chicken and the occasional goose are recorded on one of the Vindolanda tablets that seems to be an account of poultry consumed in the *praetorium* in the period AD 102–4.[9] It is tantalisingly incomplete, but the implication is that chicken was an acceptable dish even when the governor of the province was dining. Domestic fowl, including capons, and goose bones were also present in the special deposit at Bishopsgate along with other high-status food items.[10]

The way in which poultry was regarded can be explored by looking at groups of bones where the status of the site is known to have changed. In the case of the Culver Street assemblage summarised in Table 11.1, it is noticeable that the high levels of ducks and geese are associated with the mid-second-century occupation and later. At that site there is a rebuilding programme in the early to mid-second century, resulting in more substantial houses, including ones with mosaic floors, being built.[11] It can be suggested that the later occupation on the site may well be of higher status than the earlier occupation. Maltby used the proportions of sheep : goat : domestic fowl to map the differing consumption of chicken. Here a slightly different approach is taken, and the total of the poultry bones is compared to the combined total of pig and sheep (Table 11.2). For the Colchester data the quantification is by NISP. Data from Fishbourne are also included comparing the pre-palace bone with that associated with the palace. The latter is old data published at the beginning of animal bone studies. The pig/sheep numbers approximate to a NISP measurement.

[8] Hamilton-Dyer in Zienkiewicz 1993: Table 2.   [9] Bowman and Thomas 2003: 23 no. 581.
[10] Tyers 1984: 374.   [11] Crummy 1992: 31.

The poultry appear to be a raw fragment count. It cannot be stressed too much that such quantification is not ideal. This, though, is the sort of data that is often available. Despite this caveat, the pattern is the same in both cases. The proportion of poultry bone rises with the higher-status occupation. There is a hint here that the consumption of poultry is not just an indicator of the adoption of Roman ways. A high level of consumption may well be an indication of an elite lifestyle. More rigorous quantification of the bone could well be used to explore this.

The consumption of poultry took place not just in a normal domestic context, but also within the setting of a religious experience. Chicken bones, probably indicative of meals consumed during religious ceremonies, have been found at temple sites relating to a variety of religions and these will be examined in more detail later in the book.[12]

It is within the ritual area that poultry may have been consumed, even by those who did not normally favour it. It is noticeable that domestic fowl are often included as grave goods. These may not always have been present as a food item. The cockerel was one of Mercury's attributes, and he was a chthonic deity who accompanied the soul after death.[13] Some of the remains may be sacrifices to the god, in the hope that he would be helpful to the deceased. In others the bird had clearly been eaten before being deposited.

A particularly interesting example of this was found in a rural inhumation cemetery at Foxton.[14] Chicken bones were recovered from a high proportion of the grave fills. They were disarticulated, but those from each individual were found in a compact heap in close contact with the deceased. In the best preserved, most of bones were present, including head and feet. It was suggested that the birds had been cooked, and the flesh stripped from the bones which were then placed either in a small bowl or as a heap. An integral part of the funeral ritual would thus have consisted of eating chicken. As we have seen generally chicken doesn't feature very highly in rural diets. The settlement the dead came from has not been excavated, and so it is not possible to say whether the population of this particular rural settlement did commonly feature chicken in their diet. On some other rural sites it can be shown that chickens feature in the funeral ritual, but were not commonly eaten in the settlement.[15] Eating a

[12] See pp. 211–13 and 215.
[13] Toynbee 1971: 286 footnote 94; MacDonald in Clarke 1979: 410.
[14] Moore in Price *et al.* 1997: 148–9.
[15] Maltby in Davies *et al.* 2002: 168–9; Richardson in Rahtz and Watts 2004: 268, 271–2.

chicken dinner for many of the inhabitants of Roman Britain may thus have been an uncommon, and emotionally charged, event.

Given the pattern established for the exploitation of the birds, it is not surprising that the evidence for the consumption of eggs mirrors it. In urban environments where there has been a systematic environmental sampling programme, eggshell fragments are frequently reported to be common.[16] Conversely, on rural sites with similar programmes, no egg-shell is recorded.[17] Eggs feature lavishly in the recipes of Apicius, often in the form of a *patina*, an egg custard in which various sweet and savoury fillings could be included.[18] The residues identified on a greyware dish at Chelmsford[19] could well be the remains of such a recipe. In Britain, the distribution of the evidence for eggs suggests such dishes could have been consumed in the larger towns, but would have been unknown across much of the country. Evidence from a writing tablet at Vindolanda dated to AD 85–92, suggests egg cookery on a lavish scale, as one shopping list calls for 'a hundred or two hundred eggs if they are for sale there at a good price'.[20] This was probably for the commanding officer's household, and should not be regarded as typical of all military cooking.

Where it is possible to identify the type of bird that produced the egg, it was normally a hen; though duck and goose egg fragments are occasion-ally found as well. At Leicester there was a little evidence of how some of the eggs may have been cooked. Differential colour changes were consist-ent with baking eggs by piercing the narrow end and placing the blunt end in the embers of a hearth.[21] If this was a common way of cooking eggs, then Martial's epigram about the round-bowled spoon called a *cochleare,* in use during the first and second centuries, may be relevant:

I am convenient for snails, but no less useful for eggs. Do you know why I am rather called a snail spoon?[22]

These spoons have sharply pointed handles which could indeed have been used for piercing the shells. In Britain, the use of these seems to decrease

---

[16] O'Connor 1988: 99; Murphy in Crummy 1992: 280; Boyer in Connor and Buckley 1999: 329–33.
[17] Smith *et al.* 1997; Turner 1999.　　　[18] E.g. Apicius IV.2.
[19] John Evans and Going in Going 1987: 91.　　　[20] Bowman and Thomas 1994: 278 no. 302.
[21] Boyer in Connor and Buckley 1999: 331.　　　[22] Martial XIV.121.

as you go down the settlement hierarchy,[23] a pattern very similar to that of the consumption of poultry and eggs.

As with the consumption and use of poultry in ritual contexts, eggs also appear to have played a role in this aspect of life. It is not uncommon to find eggs in funerary contexts;[24] but whether the contents were consumed prior to deposition, or whether they were placed there as a symbol of a new life, cannot generally be established.

[23] Cool 2004a.
[24] Wenham 1968: 106 no. 27, 107 nos. 40, 41; Clarke 1979: 27; Grave: 22; Turner 1999: 224.

CHAPTER 12

Fish and shellfish

INTRODUCTION

The people of the ancient Mediterranean world, or at least those who wrote books, had a somewhat ambiguous view of seafood. It was at the same time a dubious foodstuff, and one that had connotations of great luxury, especially in the Roman milieu.[1] There are ongoing debates as to what contribution to the diet fish actually made.[2] In Britain we do not have the wealth of literary sources, but we do have an increasing number of fish bone assemblages, and patterns of consumption are starting to emerge. For fish bones, sampling and flotation are essential. They can be recovered by hand excavation, but the result will be governed by the competence and knowledge of the excavator, and the size of the bone. I well recall in the mid-1970s, when working as a finds supervisor for a big urban excavation, the sudden appearance of cod and ling vertebrae on the finds trays amongst all the normal potsherds and mammal bone. This took place the day after everyone working on the site had listened to a lecture by a highly enthusiastic fish bone specialist. As fish bones go, these are large; but they had rarely appeared in the preceding weeks. It was a classic example of the phenomenon that what goes on the finds tray is what the excavator recognises. Not all digging teams can have the opportunity of being similarly enthused and, even if they are, they would still miss the smaller species. The best evidence will always come from systematic sampling.

FISH

An appreciation of the role of fish in the Romano-British diet can be gained by looking at the assemblages from urban sites. In these,

---

[1] Purcell 1995; Holland 2003: 183–6. [2] Summarised in Purcell 1995: 133.

comparisons can be made between the Roman and medieval periods.[3] The regular pattern is for the medieval contexts to produce considerably more bones than the Roman ones. Fish formed an important part of the medieval diet, because of the number of fast days imposed by the Church. For almost half the year, Christians were forbidden to eat meat and substituted fish instead.[4] The urban fish bone assemblages suggest that fish is likely to have formed a far smaller part of the diet in the Roman period.

The species regularly identified are freshwater ones, and those which live in estuarine or inshore waters. Freshwater fishes regularly encountered include eel, roach, salmon and trout. The marine fish often include herring, flat fishes like plaice and flounder, sea bream and grey mullet. Cod is only occasionally noted, reflecting the fact that the development of the deep-sea fisheries post-dated the Roman period. The picture appears to be of a rather casual exploitation of what was to hand. At Dorchester, close to the sea, it is noticeable that marine fish dominate;[5] while at Leicester, an inland town in the Midlands, there is a mixture of marine and freshwater species.[6] Some of these fish may have been pre-served rather than fresh. Oily fish spoil quickly, so the presence of herring or mackerel bones at inland sites, such as Leicester, suggests they may have arrived in a preserved form. An amphora found in a Flavian context on the London waterfront had a written label which declared its contents were 'Lucius Tettius Africanus's finest fish sauce from Antinopolis' (modern Antibes).[7] It contained iris and box seeds, and fish-head bones thought to be mackerel. The label specifically says the contents are *liquamen*, so it is possible that some of the oily fish bones arrived as part of fish sauce. The industries that produced fish sauce also produced salted fish;[8] and this might be another way in which these species arrived.

Against this background of low level, sporadic consumption there is a little evidence that fish may have been regarded as a luxury commodity. There are not yet enough adequately sampled sites to say whether con-sumption patterns differed in town and country; though there are occa-sional hints that they might have. In the Dorchester area fish bones are recovered from the urban samples, but appear rare or absent from

[3] O'Connor 1988: Table 32; Jones in Hinton 1988: 433; Locker in Crummy 1992: 278; Nicholson in Connor and Buckley 1999: Table 74.

[4] Kurlansky 1998: 24.

[5] Hamilton-Dyer in Woodward *et al.* 1993: Table 67; Hamilton-Dyer in Smith 1993: 80.

[6] Nicholson in Connor and Buckley 1999: Table 74.

[7] RIB II.6 no. 2492.24.   [8] Curtis 1991: 10.

the rural ones.[9] It is noticeable that fish were consumed at rural sites where there are other signs of prestige development, such as the villa at Gorhambury.[10] An intriguing insight is also gained from looking at the associations of certain unusual fish. Though cod is rare, one of the places where it has been recovered is in the pit at Bishopsgate, London, which has been noted several times as containing evidence for luxury foodstuffs. At Colchester, cod bones were found in association with a substantial town house.[11] In another second-century London pit, bones from a sturgeon were found associated with many chicken bones.[12] If the suggestion that a high level of chicken consumption indicates an elite lifestyle is correct, the sturgeon could well have been consumed by someone in the upper echelons of society. As well as being rare, both cod and sturgeon are large, striking in appearance, and very good to eat. Sturgeon in particular has long been thought of as fit for royalty. In 1529 it was an enormous sturgeon, ceremonially accompanied by a fanfare, that formed the first course of a grand banquet given in honour of the marriage of the Duke of Ferrara to the daughter of the King of France.[13] Literary sources make it clear that rare catches were suitable gifts for patrons in the Mediterranean world.[14] There are hints in the associations of these bones that something similar may have been going on in Britain.

There is also one other piece of evidence pointing to fish, or at least seafood, as being something that featured disproportionately in the diets of the elite. At Poundbury, a sample of the bodies from the fourth-century cemetery were studied using stable-isotope analysis. It was shown that those in what might be considered graves belonging to the richer segment of society, i.e. buried in the mausoleums or in lead coffins, had stable-isotope values that could be associated with a marine diet. Their contemporaries buried in wooden coffins showed no detectable marine element in their diet.[15]

SHELLFISH

We move now from an area where, until recently, there has been all too little evidence to one where there is almost too much. On some sites,

---

[9] Hamilton-Dyer in Woodward *et al.* 1993: Table 67; Hamilton-Dyer in Smith 1993: 80; compare Maltby in Davies *et al.* 2002: Table 20; Smith *et al.* 1997.
[10] Locker in Neal *et al.* 1990: 212.　　　[11] Locker in Crummy 1992: 278.
[12] Drummond-Murray *et al.* 2002: 121.　　　[13] Hollingsworth 2004: 22.
[14] Purcell 1995: 143.　　　[15] Richards *et al.* 1998.

oyster shells are so common that they are discarded and little useful information extracted. In the early 1950s the excavator of the fort at Caister-on-Sea noted 'at first the shells were counted until, at an early stage in the digging, the number passed 10,000, when counting was discontinued'.[16] Until recently they were a category of find that was not thought worthy of specialist attention; and even now, many reports are published where they are treated in only a cursory manner, if at all.[17] This is unfortunate, because the pioneering work of Jessica Winder[18] has shown that a wealth of information can be extracted from them.

The oyster beds in England lie along the south coast, and in the Essex – north Kent area. One of Winder's most valuable observations was that it was possible to identify the source of the shells by studying the infestations they show. The worm *Polydura hoplura* is confined to the southern coast. It leaves blisters on the inner edge of the shell, and shells with this sort of infestation must have come from the south coast. The worm *Polydura ciliate,* which leaves bore holes in the shells, prefers the conditions found in the Essex – north Kent beds, though can occur as well on parts of the south coast. Properly studied, the shells will show where the oysters were coming from. Those eaten in Silchester came, unsurprisingly, from the south coast. Those eaten in Leicester had made the much longer journey from the Thames estuary.[19] Whether other beds were exploited to serve the northern market is unknown, but presumably likely. By the early twentieth century, surveys were noting a distinct paucity of oyster beds in the north-east and north-west coasts;[20] but oysters were common in the Forth until the nineteenth century.[21] It is possible that other beds may have existed in the Roman period. It is unfortunate that, though there is a writing tablet from Vindolanda recording the gift of fifty oysters, the place of origin given is otherwise unknown.[22] Oysters can survive in good condition for up to three weeks out of water, providing they are from inter-tidal beds, where they are exposed to the air for part of each day.[23] What they were transported in is unknown, though wooden barrels or pottery jars would be an obvious solution. Clearly, given their widespread distribution, the trade in oysters was well organised.

---

[16] Ellis in Darling and Gurney 1993: 238–9. [17] References suppressed to protect the guilty.
[18] Winder 1992.
[19] Somerville in Fulford *et al.* 1997: 135–9; Monkton in Connor and Buckley 1999: 340.
[20] Winder 1992: 269. [21] Heppell in Holmes 2003: 136.
[22] Bowman and Thomas 1994: 272 no. 299. [23] Winder 1992: 275.

In Italy oysters were deliberately cultivated,[24] but there is no evidence that there was any need to do that in Britain. The oyster beds appear to have been an under- or non-exploited resource prior to the Roman period, and the shells found give every appearance of coming from a natural, unmanaged population.[25] Where the age of oysters from Roman sites has been considered, it can range widely. At Alington Avenue outside Dorchester, they varied from two to eleven years, with the commonest age being five. In the centre of the town the age ranged from one to sixteen.[26] This contrasts with modern managed populations where oysters are harvested at about four years.

After the conquest, many people seem to have developed a taste for them. This does not appear to be a new foodstuff that the native population rejected, as they can be found on rural and roadside sites of no great pretensions, at some distance from the oyster beds.[27] We generally eat them raw today as they are a delicacy; in the historic past when they were abundant, they were frequently cooked.[28] This can be done by simply placing them on the embers of a hearth. If they were cooked in this way, it might account for the fact that, when the shells have been studied in detail, obvious opening marks on the shells, left by knives and other implements, occur on only a minority.[29] Baking them would lead to the shells opening without any force being required.

British oysters were obviously well regarded in the Roman world as there are several mentions of them in the ancient literature; but whether they actually travelled as far as Rome, as one of Juvenal's satires implies, is open to question.[30]

Although oysters were the shellfish of choice, other species are also recovered. In some cases, their presence on a site may not have been because they were being eaten, but because they probably came attached to seaweed that was being used to improve the soil, possibly having previously acted as packing for the oysters.[31] At Colchester the presence of tiny shells, and shells which had obviously been empty for some time when they were collected, was explained in this way.[32] Mussels were

---

[24] Günther 1897.   [25] Winder 1992: 273.
[26] Winder 1992: 151; Winder in Woodward *et al.* 1993: 348.
[27] Everton in Leech 1982: 144; Alvery in May 1996: 171; Hands 1998: 249; Booth *et al.* 2001: Table 9.22.
[28] Davidson 1999: 564.
[29] Alvery in May 1996: 171; Monkton in Connor and Buckley 1999: 341.
[30] Dalby 2000: 284 footnote 59.
[31] I am grateful to Andrew Jones for this suggestion.
[32] Murphy in Crummy 1992: 277.

probably eaten. With some exceptions,[33] they are always in a noticeable minority compared with oysters. In part, this pattern may be the result of differential survival. Oyster shells are robust; mussel shells less so. It was observed at Leicester that mussel shells were only recovered from the sieved samples, whereas oysters were easily collected by hand.[34] The presence of mussels at inland sites, such as Leicester, again attests to the efficiency of the shellfish trade. As with oysters, mussels occur at inland rural sites, both those of some pretensions such as the villa at Shakenoak, and small villages such as Catsgore.[35]

Other types of shellfish occur in much smaller quantities, and some may have arrived as chance inclusions with the other shells. For others, there is evidence of them being eaten in their own right. A group of cockles found in a ditch by the bath-house of the villa at Halstock,[36] can plausibly be interpreted as a tasty snack enjoyed in the context of taking a bath, which often provided the opportunity of snacking on fast food. It is also noticeable that the carpet shell (*Venerupis* sp.) is noted from time to time in shell reports. At Colchester they were clearly being eaten, as they were found as articulated valves.[37] These are a type of clam that has long fallen from favour as a foodstuff in Britain, but on the continent is still considered a delicacy;[38] as they were by ancient Roman writers.[39] One might assume, too, that the fragments of the shells of edible crabs found at York indicated that these were consumed in the city regularly.[40]

The potential of the evidence for the consumption of fish and shellfish is only just starting to reveal itself. As more sites with good sampling programmes are published, a better picture of fish consumption should become available. It is also to be hoped that oyster and other shells will start to attract a little more attention than they currently receive. However, it is worth entering one note of caution. We should not impose our own standards of luxury when exploring Roman consumption patterns, especially in this category of food. It is salutary to realise that oysters, now synonymous with luxury in Britain, were in the Roman period apparently available to a wide range of society. In the Mediterranean world they could be a luxury delicacy[41] but in Roman Britain, with its prolific oyster beds, they may not have had the same resonance. Availability is all. One

[33] Zienkiewicz 1986: 220 Table 1.   [34] Monkton in Connor and Buckley 1999: 341.
[35] Brodribb *et al.* 1971: 127; Everton in Leech 1982: 144.   [36] Winder 1992: 157.
[37] Murphy in Crummy 1992: 277.   [38] Davidson 1999: 139.
[39] Dalby 2000: 53.   [40] O'Connor 1988: 119; Hall and Kenward 1990: 407.
[41] Dalby 2000: 248.

person's luxury may be another's mundane food. It is useful to remember the poet Edwin Muir's observation on growing up in the Orkneys. He observed that white bread brought at the village shop was a luxury, but that he ate so much crab and lobster as a boy that he had never been able to enjoy them since.[42]

[42] Muir 1954: 59.

CHAPTER 13

Game

INTRODUCTION

There are various strands of evidence that suggest hunting might have been a popular pastime in Roman Britain. According to Strabo, writing at the time of the Emperor Augustus, hunting dogs were one of the items exported from late Iron Age Britain.[1] Hunting is mentioned several times in the Vindolanda writing tablets,[2] and hunting imagery is found in a wide range of contexts such as mosaic floors,[3] large pieces of silver plate[4] and pottery hunt cups.[5] This range suggests that scenes from the hunt were attractive to people both at the upper end of the social hierarchy, and those further down it.

This apparent popularity of hunting as a pursuit is puzzling when viewed from the perspective of animal bone assemblages. Unlike modern British practice which has been, in Oscar Wilde's classic definition 'the unspeakable in full pursuit of the uneatable',[6] the species shown being hunted in the Roman scenes – deer, boars and hares – are all edible ones. If these animals were regularly being hunted, it is to be expected that this would be reflected in the animal bone assemblages. Certainly in the medieval period, when hunting was the preserve of the aristocracy and a popular pursuit amongst them, there is a noticeable increase in deer bones on the sites where they lived.[7] On all types of Romano-British sites, by contrast, evidence for game is generally rare and often absent. This chapter will examine the evidence for the consumption of game, and will conclude with a consideration of why there should be this mismatch between the artistic and the real world.

---

[1] Strabo IV.5.2.
[2] Bowman and Thomas 1994: 206; 2003: 47 no. 593, 48 no. 594, 77 no. 615.
[3] Henig 1995: 159, fig. 85.   [4] Johns 1981: pl. VII; Henig 1995: fig. 96.
[5] E.g. Symmonds and Wade 1999: fig. 5.34 no. 129.
[6] *A Woman of No Importance* Act 1.   [7] Grant 1981: 209.

Table 13.1. *A comparison of sheep/pig and deer bones at selected sites*
(* *indicates present but at levels of less than 0.5%*).

Site	Type	Date	Sheep/Pig (%)	Deer (%)	Total	Quantification
Wroxeter	Fort	c. 60–90	96	4	2003	NISP
Castleford	Fort	c. 70–95	99	1	5176	NISP
Colchester	Town	c. 60–150	94	6	1439	NISP
Wroxeter	Town	c. 90–170	99	1	822	NISP
Wilcote	Rural	c. 50–150	100	*	3193	Zones
Leicester	Town	c. 50–250	100	*	2181	Zones
Colchester	Town	c. 150–400+	93	7	1393	NISP
Leicester	Town	c. 250–400+	98	2	1451	Zones
Caister	Fort	c. 200–400+	84	16	1122	NISP
Segontium	Fort	c. 250–400+	89	11	2445	NISP

VENISON, BOAR AND HARE

Inspection of animal bone reports reveals that, when present, the commonest game species is deer, followed by hare and then, very rarely, by wild boar. In order to gain an insight into how much game might have been consumed, Table 13.1 has been prepared, comparing deer bones to those of pigs and sheep. These were selected to represent the domesticated species because so much of the data are expressed as NISP measurements, and there is a need to discount the distorting effect of heavily butchered cattle bone. As ever, using so much NISP data is less than satisfactory, but it does allow the general pattern to emerge. It should be noted that the more reliable zonal method of quantification, used at Leicester and Wilcote, regularly returns very low figures; suggesting the NISP figures are overestimating the proportion of deer. The urban bone assemblages have consistently low levels, with only Colchester showing a proportion above 5%. Even there, it is clear that bones from the game species are proportionately much scarcer than those from poultry (cf. Table 11.2). This low level is often commented on in other urban assemblages as well.[8] It could be argued that such a pattern is to be expected in towns, and that it is sites in rural areas where game would be more common. The only site that falls into this category in Table 13.1 is Wilcote where the number of deer bones is again negligible. As with the urban

---

[8] Dobney *et al.* 1995: 21; Maltby in Woodward *et al.* 1993: 330–1; Maltby in Holbrook 1998: 368.

sites, this pattern regularly repeats itself in other rural assemblages which it has not been possible to include in Table 13.1.[9]

The military sites show a less consistent pattern, possibly because soldiers, or at least senior officers, included hunting amongst their pastimes. In County Durham the commanding officer of a cavalry unit dedicated an altar to Silvanus after killing a 'wild boar of remarkable fineness which many of his predecessors had been unable to bag'.[10] At Vindolanda, the commanding officer Cerialis wrote to his friend Brocchus, asking for some hunting nets to be sent,[11] and in another note referred to his huntsman.[12] Even if hunting was common around forts, there is often very little evidence that the kill formed more than an occasional addition to the diet. This can be seen in the first-century sites in Table 13.1, which are comparable to contemporary urban assemblages. At other forts, a similar scarcity it often reported.[13] Interesting exceptions to this pattern can be seen in the late Roman military assemblages at Caister-on-Sea and Segontium. Why venison should be so much more popular on these sites is not clear. Both lie in relatively marginal positions, and possibly it is reflecting local abundance. Certainly the garrisons at both sites seemed prepared to exploit various unusual foodstuffs, as seal bones were also very occasionally recovered at Segontium; whilst at Caister-on-Sea badgers appear to have been eaten.[14]

In the table all species of deer were grouped together. The larger red deer was the commonest, but roe deer were also present. The fallow deer, a Roman introduction that did not become properly established until the Norman period,[15] was very rare. There are important differences between the three from a culinary point of view. These days, the small roe deer is considered the best to eat.[16] Certainly the cooks in the *praetorium* at Vindolanda made a distinction between the two types of meat, as did the recipes of Apicius.[17] The record of a gourmet dinner given by Julius

[9] Locker in Neal *et al.* 1990: Table 18; Berg in Wrathmell and Nicholson 1990: 187; Harman in May 1996: 161; Stallibrass in Jackson and Potter 1996: Table 40; Noddle in Price 2000: 235.

[10] RIB I no. 1041.

[11] Bowman and Thomas 1994: 206. (In the interests of accuracy it should, perhaps, be noted that the word could also mean counterpanes, but the editors of the texts prefer hunting nets, feeling it unlikely that these two would be discussing soft-furnishings.)

[12] Bowman and Thomas 2003: 77 no. 615.

[13] Izard in Wilmott 1997: table 34; Stallibrass in Wilson 2002a: 399–400.

[14] Noddle in Casey *et al.* 1993: Table 6.1; Harman in Darling and Gurney 1993: 226.

[15] Grant 1981: 206.   [16] Drysdale 1983: 119; Davidson 1999: 825.

[17] Bowman and Thomas 1994: 157 no. 191; Apicius VIII. 2 and 3.

Caesar also implies that it was roe deer rather than red deer that was the venison of choice for discerning eaters.[18]

What is clear is that venison, and the other larger game species, were an unusual item in most people's diets. So eating game could well have only taken place in special circumstances. When exploring what these were, it is useful to look at both the associations with other animal bones, and which types of deer were being eaten. Given the epigraphic evidence of a link between senior military officers and hunting, the closed group of kitchen refuse from a senior officer's kitchen within the fortress at Caerleon is a good place to start.[19] It has deer, hare and wild boar bones as well as evidence of pork and poultry consumption. Roe deer bones are more numerous than red deer. These associations suggest very strongly that here game is part of an elite dining regime, favouring the rare and the tasty. A similar set of associations can be seen in the Bishopsgate pit in London,[20] where only roe deer is found. A comparison of two wells infilled with domestic rubbish in the second century in Southwark is also informative. The one with the roe deer bones had proportionately more pork and chicken bones in it than the one that did not have the deer.[21] Again the implication would be that roe deer was a delicacy.

At both Caister-on-Sea and Segontium where venison appeared relatively abundant, it was red deer that was the commonest species; possibly suggesting that at those sites it was consumed because it was available rather than because a large amount of elite dining was going on. This would fit the pattern of opportunistic exploitation of other wild animals at these sites already noted.

WILD BIRDS

One of the difficulties of looking at patterns of game-bird consumption is deciding what was present because it had been caught and eaten; and what was there as a chance death within a human settlement. The choice of which birds to eat is very much culturally conditioned, as a brief reflection on modern attitudes to some of the less commonly identified species will show. Golden plovers and snipe[22] are both now generally considered acceptable and tasty. We would have no problem about considering that

[18] Dalby 2000: 248.   [19] Hamilton-Dyer in Zienkiewicz 1993: Table 2 well 2.
[20] Tyers 1984.   [21] Drummond-Murray *et al.* 2002: Table 24.
[22] Parker 1988: Table 1; Gidney in Connor and Buckley 1999: 318 table 66; Maltby in Woodward *et al.* 1993: 333 Table 62; Hamilton-Dyer in Fulford *et al.* 1997: 133.

these were present as items of food. Small passerines are also found.[23] Whether such birds are eaten today, depends on which side of the English Channel you live on. On the continental side, they are considered a delicacy: on the British side, it is culturally unacceptable to eat song birds. On neither side of the Channel is it now considered appropriate to eat buzzards, but a bone from one found at Piercebridge with knife marks, shows that they were being eaten, at least occasionally, in Roman Britain. A list of snares left by one of the garrisons at Vindolanda notes nets for ducks and thrushes and snares for swans as well as a dragnet for fishing, so presumably all of these species were considered edible.[24]

Even if the optimistic view is taken, i.e. that many of the bird bones found in archaeological assemblages are there because the birds had been eaten, it still only reveals a pattern of casual, opportunistic consumption. As with other types of game, many people would never have eaten it. In chapter 11, it was noted that the geese and ducks present on Romano-British sites are often a mixture of wild and domesticated species. It might be questioned though, to what extent the presence of the wild ones indicates wild-fowling, as opposed to the birds themselves appropriating man-made ponds, as may often be seen in public parks today. Setting the ducks and geese to one side, the most commonly encountered wild bird is the raven. These are often found as complete skeletons, sometimes in obviously ritual contexts.[25] The most likely explanation seems to be that these intelligent birds were being kept as pets. Following the raven, the woodcock is the next most commonly encountered species.[26] This is a wader which would have been most likely to have been caught during the winter. It is a bird which today inspires strongly polarised views as to whether it is good eating or not;[27] presumably similar differences of opinion existed in Roman Britain. The bird that is the commonest game bird today, the pheasant, is encountered only rarely,[28] reflecting the fact that then it was a wild bird, whereas today it is commercially bred to provide sport in organised 'shoots'.

One particularly interesting discovery was the remains of at least four cranes in the kitchen waste of the senior officer's household at Caerleon. Crane bones are very occasionally found;[29] but, given the association with

[23] Parker 1988: Table 1; Hamilton-Dyer in Fulford *et al.* 1997: 133.
[24] Bowman and Thomas 2003: 47 no. 593. [25] Parker 1988: 208–9, Table 1.
[26] Parker 1988: Table 1; Cowles in Woodward and Leach 1993: 263; Hamilton-Dyer in Fulford *et al.* 1997: 133; Gidney in Connor and Buckley 1999: Table 66.
[27] Drysdale 1983: 85. [28] Parker 1988: 202.
[29] Parker 1988: Table 1; Maltby in Woodward *et al.* 1993: 333 Table 62; Dobney *et al.* 1995: 51; Harman in May 1996: 163.

other table delicacies, this is the best evidence we have that they were being eaten. The cook clearly did not know the trick given in Apicius, of cooking the bird with its head on, but clear of the sauce. When cooked the head could be grasped in a hot linen cloth and pulled off, bringing the tough tendons out with it. This would not have been possible at Caerleon as the back of the head had been chopped off.[30]

ART, REALITY AND HUNTING

The picture of game consumption outlined in the previous pages is that it was generally at a low, or non-existent, level but was occasionally associated with high-class dining. If hunting was a popular pastime amongst the elite, it has left little trace in the food remains. Why then the pervasive hunting themes in art? One reason may well be that the mosaic floors and vessels with hunting scenes are not depicting a popular pastime but are allegorical, depicting the quest for understanding. In the floor mosaics hunting scenes are frequent in ones with overtly religious symbolism associated with some of the mystery religions where the worshipper passed from initiation to understanding.[31]

Hunting scenes also occur within religious settings in other media. A scene engraved on a mid-fourth-century glass bowl depicting a rider and hounds driving a hare into a net, is often used to illustrate the popularity of hunting in Roman Britain.[32] It belongs to a group of bowls all engraved in the same way with scenes of the hunt depicting stags and boars, as well as hares.[33] Other bowls from the same workshop depict mythological scenes, and ones from both the Old and New Testaments of the Christians. The bowls, including the hunting ones, often have inscriptions around their rims which include exhortations such as 'life to you and yours' and 'live in God'. These are surely better seen as overtly religious items rather than sporting souvenirs. The boar hunt on the Risley Park silver lanx is accompanied not only by Bacchic scenes around the rim, but also by an inscription on the underside recording its donation to a Christian church.[34] The implications would be that the elite of the fourth century, to which many of these items originally belonged, had a greater interest in their immortal souls, than in the chase.

---

[30] Apicius VI.2,ii; Hamilton-Dyer in Zienkiewicz 1993: 136.
[31] Perring 2003: 105.   [32] E.g. Salway 1993: 415.
[33] Harden 1960.   [34] Johns 1981.

Once the link between depictions of hunting and the sport itself is broken, it becomes less surprising that even at a palace such as Fishbourne, evidence for venison consumption is very slight.[35] Hunting may not have been a popular pastime for the elite. Possibly this may have been because, over much of the country, deer and wild boar were not very numerous because the habitat was not available. In the medieval period, hunting was an aristocratic pastime that needed the deliberate creation, and maintenance, of hunting parks. There is nothing in the landscape that suggests a similar policy was being pursued in Roman Britain. Where game was available, as appears to have been the case in the vicinity of Caister-on-Sea and Segontium, it was being hunted and eaten but within a late military milieu. Within this, what may have been of interest was not so much the meat as the trophies. At various military sites, including Segontium, boars' tusks, either mounted in copper alloy or pierced for suspension, have been found;[36] whilst at a site associated with the *Classis Britannica* in Kent, where hunting was clearly being carried out, one of the finds was an impressive antler from a mature stag.[37] In none of these cases can it be proven that the objects were the result of hunting; the boars' tusks may have been from domestic animals and the antler may have been shed. They do, however, hint at an interest in trophies, and provide a context for hunting.

Finally, one reason for the low levels of game consumption could be cultural, as with the current British aversion to eating song birds. Caesar notes the fact that in the Britain of his day, hares were raised but not eaten.[38] Unfortunately, he does not elaborate on the reason for this, though a religious taboo, or the fact that they were regarded as pets, are possibilities. Both stags and boars feature in Celtic mythology,[39] and this too may have set them aside from the food chain.

If hunting for food wasn't much practised in Britain during the Roman period we are left with Strabo's report that hunting dogs were an export prior to the invasion. There does not seem to have been any major change in consumption patterns between the late Iron Age and the Romano-British period, as evidence for game is as conspicuous by its rarity in the earlier animal bone assemblages[40] as it is in the later ones. There is the

[35] Grant in Cunliffe 1971: 378.
[36] Henderson in Bushe-Fox 1949: 141, nos. 173–4; Allason-Jones and McKay 1988: 198, 36 nos. 118–22; Allason-Jones in Casey *et al.* 1993: 202 no. 451.
[37] Harman in Brodribb and Cleere 1988: 273. [38] Caesar V.12. [39] Henig 1984: 18–9.
[40] E.g. Wilson in Parrington 1978: 111 Table X; Grant in Cunliffe 1984: 525; Rackham in Heslop 1987: 107; Grant in Cunliffe and Poole 1991: 478.

question of whether Strabo's evidence can be accepted at face value. He also states that the Britons liked to import glass vessels.[41] Evidence for the presence of pre-conquest imports of these is extremely rare, and certainly does not support any major trade in them.[42] Giving him the benefit of the doubt, however, and assuming British hunting dogs were famous enough to be in demand on the continent, what were they being trained to hunt? Perhaps 'the unspeakable in full pursuit of the uneatable' has a longer history in Britain than has hitherto been suspected.

[41] Strabo IV.5.3.
[42] Price 1996; Cool 2003: 139.

CHAPTER 14

Greengrocery

INTRODUCTION

With fruit and vegetables we revert to a type of foodstuff which will only survive in particular conditions, and which will only be found if a sampling programme has been undertaken. Furthermore, there is a distinct bias between the survival of the two categories. Fruit generally has seeds whilst things classed as vegetables generally don't. Seeds which can become mineralised or charred are more likely to be preserved than the leafy parts of vegetables. The latter may survive in exceptional circumstances, such as the cabbage stalk found in a late fourth-century well at Vindolanda;[1] but in general fruits are more visible in the archaeological record than vegetables. Unlike cereals which were routinely processed by heating, fruit and vegetables are not well represented in the charred-plant-remains assemblages. Most direct evidence thus comes from the waterlogged and mineralised remains. Packaging in the form of amphorae also provides evidence of preserved items, but again this favours fruits.

FRUIT

Good places to start the exploration of the fruit consumed are cesspits. Seeds and pips will often pass through the digestive track, and the conditions in cesspits are ideal for mineralisation to take place. Naturally such environments favour fruits with small seeds. Table 14.1 shows what has been identified in a variety of cesspits, together with material from the outfall of a latrine at Bearsden and from the Church Street sewer within the fortress at York.

As can be seen, fig seeds are ubiquitous. Figs were imported as, though fig trees can survive in Britain, the tiny wasp that is needed to fertilise the

[1] Birley 1977: 89.

Table 14.1. *The incidence of fruit remains in selected cesspits (NB – Bearsden also had evidence for bilberry).*

	Date	Type	Fig	Grape	Cherry	Blackberry	Apple/pear	Sloe	Raspberry	Elderberry	Strawberry
Colchester [1]	44–49	Fort	+	.	+	.	.	.	.	+	.
Colchester [2]	44–49	Fort	+	+	.	.	.	.	+	+	.
Gorhambury	43–61	Villa	+	+	.	+	.	+	.	.	.
Southwark	60/1	Town	.	.	.	.	+	.	.	.	.
Carlisle	Late C1	Vicus	+	+	+	+	+	+	.	.	.
Leicester	Mid C1–mid C2	Town	+	.	.	+	+	+	.	.	.
Dorchester [1]	Late C1	Town	+	.	.	+	+	.	.	.	.
Dorchester [2]	By mid C2	Town	+	.	.	+	.	.	.	.	.
Bearsden	142–58	Fort	+	.	.	+	.	+	+	.	+
Stonea	C3	Rural	.	.	.	.	.	.	.	.	.
York	C2–C4	Fort	.	+	.	+	.	.	+	+	+

flowers cannot.[2] Figs dry well, and we can assume that it was in this form that they were known in Britain. The presence of figs in a cesspit at Gorhambury is of particular interest. The building it was associated with was possibly pre-conquest. At the latest it was burnt during the Boudican rising, but may have been destroyed earlier. It provides evidence that this exotic fruit was being consumed on a native site very early in the Roman period, and possibly pre-conquest.

Fig seeds are often found elsewhere in waterlogged deposits. Even in the early days of the analysis of such deposits, it was pointed out that they were found regularly in London and elsewhere;[3] and the pattern has continued. There are some grounds for thinking they may have been a regular part of the military diet. In their dried form they would store well and would certainly be useful to a quartermaster in case of shortages. They were common at a large campaigning base at Castleford used during the expansion into the north;[4] and they are regularly recovered from waterlogged contexts associated with other military sites.[5] Their presence at both urban and rural sites would suggest they were also a widespread food for the civilian population.

In the Mediterranean world, depending on the variety, figs were both a poor person's staple food and a delicacy for the elite. Cato notes that the bread ration for the chain gang, the lowest type of slave, could be reduced when figs were in season;[6] whilst Roman gourmets delighted in named varieties imported from various islands.[7] Whether such differences were appreciated within Roman Britain is beyond the scope of environmental archaeology to tell us. Fig seeds do sometimes occur in contexts where there is other evidence that the deposits derive from high-class dining activities, such as the kitchen waste associated with a senior officer's house at Caerleon.[8] It is tempting to wonder if these may have been special in some way, as opposed to a more standard issue that might have been consumed by the campaigning army at Castleford.

The other main exotic fruit in Table 14.1 is the grape. Again the presence of them in the Gorhambury pit is important evidence for their consumption by native Britons at an early stage. Though there is now pollen evidence to show that grapes were grown in Britain in at least one

---

[2] Davidson 1999: 297–8; Tyers in Hinton 1988: 448.　　[3] Willcox 1977: 278–9.
[4] Bastow in Abramson *et al.* 1999: Tables 8–10.
[5] Goodwin and Huntley in McCarthy 1991: Fascicule 1 59, fig. 50B; Huntley and Hillam in Buxton and Howard-Davis 2000: 356 Table 32; Kenward *et al.* 1986: 255 Table 255.
[6] Cato 56.　　[7] Dalby 2000: 111, 151.
[8] Caseldine and Busby in Zienkiewicz 1993: 137.

vineyard,[9] most will have arrived preserved. The ancient agricultural manuals provide directions for preserving fresh grapes by sealing the cut stalk with boiling pitch and then sealing the bunches in pottery jars.[10] This would have left behind the 'packaging' as an alien component in the pottery assemblage. Given it is absent, it may be assumed grapes arrived as dried raisins. It would appear these were not uncommon in urban and military environments.[11] At York, as well as occurring within the fortress sewer system, they are regularly present in the later second- to third-century contexts at the General Accident site in the *colonia* and in an early to mid-third-century well fill at Bedern in the fort.[12] It may be noted, though, that in this extensively sampled city, it is the seeds of figs that are more regularly encountered. Though they were not reported from the Church Street sewer, they were present at the General Accident site and the Bedern well, as well as in a layer associated with a late first-century warehouse, and in a well at Skeldergate in use during the second to fourth century.[13] Something similar may be noted at Carlisle[14] and possibly also at Southwark[15] where fig seeds tend to be more regularly present in samples than grape seeds are. Admittedly a fig has many more seeds than a grape, but the presence – absence data does hint that grapes may have been rarer than figs.

The other exotic species in Table 14.1 is possibly the cherry, though it is not always possible to distinguish between the fruit produced by the native gean cherry (*Prunus avium*) and the imported sour cherry (*P. cerasus*); and it is clear that both were eaten.[16] The sour cherries may have arrived as preserved fruits, but one exotic fruit which must indicate that the trees themselves were introduced to Britain is the mulberry. The fruits of these must be fully ripe before being eaten and are very easily damaged. They would not have been transported long distances, so the presence of mulberry seeds in Romano-British contexts indicates the deliberate introduction of the trees. The introduction must have taken place in the first century as the seeds have been found in late-first-century contexts in London. Willcox recorded that they were common in

[9] Meadows 1996.   [10] Columella XII: 44–5.

[11] Willcox 1977: 279; Goodwin and Huntley in McCarthy 1991: 60; Caseldine and Busby in Zienkiewicz 1993: 137; Bastow in Abramson *et al.* 1999: Table 15, 22; Huntley and Hillam in Buxton and Howard-Davis 2000: 356 Table 32.

[12] Hall and Kenward 1990: 407 Table no. 129a; Kenward *et al.* 1986: 247 Table 76.

[13] Kenward and Williams 1979: Table 12; Hall *et al.* 1980: Table 50.

[14] Goodwin and Huntley in McCarthy 1991: 60.

[15] Tyers in Hinton 1988: 48; Gray in Drummond-Murray *et al.* 2002: tables 116–24.

[16] Willcox 1977: 278; Huntley in McCarthy 2000: 77.

London, and they have been noted at Silchester and Colchester,[17] but they have not often been recorded elsewhere. It is possible they were regarded more as an exotic garden plant than as a regularly planted fruit tree.

The other fruits in Table 14.1 are all native species which regularly occur in other waterlogged deposits, though it is only in the cesspits and sewage deposits that we have certain evidence that they were being eaten. The relative scarcity of apple/pear seeds in the cesspits probably hints that the core wasn't eaten as their seeds often occur in deposits that appear to include kitchen waste.[18] The level of their consumption is hinted at by a shopping list probably relating to the provisioning of the commanding officer's house at Vindolanda during the period AD 85–92. It calls for one hundred apples 'if you can find nice ones'.[19]

Fruits with larger stones are naturally not represented in the cesspit deposits, but the exotic ones which would not grow in Britain were clearly being imported as food. Olives are known from both the stones and the amphorae they were imported in,[20] the latter being primarily a first-century phenomenon in Britain. They are also attested in the Vindolanda tablets. The person doing the shopping for apples was also instructed to buy olives, and presumably they would have been preserved in this way. The list calls for a *modius* (8.6 litres) of olives which would have represented about two thirds of an olive amphora.[21] It is believed that the production of amphorae ceased in the mid-second century, but olive stones continue to be found in later contexts indicating they must have been imported in other forms of packaging. At the General Accident site in York, olives were found throughout the mid-second- to mid-third-century sequence.[22] Olives were clearly being eaten at some point between *c.* AD 160 and 240 in the fortress baths at Caerleon,[23] in the late second and third century in London,[24] in the early to mid-third century at Colchester,[25] and in the third century or possibly the early fourth at the villa at Great Holts Farm, Boreham.[26] The distribution of both the amphorae and the olive stones seems in the main limited to major urban and military sites, and currently there is no secure evidence that importation continued in the fourth century.

---

[17] Willcox 1977: 279 Table 1; Murphy in Crummy 1992: 281.   [18] Willcox 1977: 278.
[19] Bowman and Thomas 1994: 278 no. 302.   [20] See p. 68 and fig. 3.1.6.
[21] Sealey and Tyers 1989: 60.   [22] Hall and Kenward 1990: Table 129a.
[23] Zienkiewicz 1986: 224.   [24] Willcox 1977: 278 Table 1.
[25] Murphy in Crummy 1992: 281. Period 4b infill – p. 76.
[26] Murphy in Germany 2003: 209.

Another exotic fruit with a large stone is the date. Date stones have occasionally been recovered,[27] but most evidence for their importation comes from the packaging. Date amphorae are often called carrot amphorae because of their shape.[28] These disappear about the middle of the second century,[29] and unlike the case of the olives, there are no stones from later contexts to suggest the continued import. There is epigraphic evidence that carrot amphorae also transported other palm fruits. An example from a ditch fill dated to AD 84–5 at Carlisle had the inscription KOYK which indicates the fruit was that of the doum palm (*Hyphaene thebaica*). These are large fruits the size of tennis balls with fibrous tough pulp which is edible if soaked, and tastes like gingerbread or caramel.[30]

The commonest carrot amphora has a small capacity: *c.* 3 litres[31] compared to *c.* 13 litres and 30 litres for olive amphora types (see Fig. 3.1 no. 7). Though the amphorae were small, which might indicate that dates and other palm fruit were delicacies, there is good evidence that they were common in the military diet in the first century. The amphorae from Carlisle come from a military context at a time when the fort there was a major northern base. At the Neronian forts at Exeter and Kingsholm they represent 6% and 7% (by weight) of the amphora assemblage.[32] Date amphorae were well represented in the assemblages belonging to the late first-century forts at Castleford;[33] and present, though in relatively small amounts, in the fortress at Wroxeter.[34]

In urban amphora assemblages they appear much rarer. Occasional sherds are found in London but in quantities too small to warrant tabulating in a study that explored the type of amphora-borne commodities present.[35] Similar patterns appear in other major cities such as Canterbury, Dorchester and Leicester.[36] In the smaller urban centres sherds from these amphorae often appear to be absent, even at places

[27] Murphy in Crummy 1984: 40; Caseldine and Busby in Zienkiewicz 1993: 137; Mackinder 2000: 12.
[28] Peacock and Williams 1986: Types 12 and 66.
[29] Sealey 1985: 89.
[30] Caruana 1992: 60 no. 12, 61–2; Tomlin 1992.
[31] Sealey 1985: Table 2.
[32] Holbrook and Bidwell 1991: Table 14; Timby in Hurst 1985: Table 4.
[33] Rush *et al.* 2000: 150 Tables 12–13, 15.
[34] Darling in Webster 2002: Tables 5.15–16.
[35] Symonds in Drummond-Murray *et al.* 2002: Table 102.
[36] Arthur 1986: 253; Williams in Woodward *et al.* 1993: Table 28; Williams in Connor and Buckley 1999: Table 5.

such as Alcester that has seen extensive excavation.[37] Dates appear to have been much rarer in the civilian diet than in the military one. They may have been viewed as a rare delicacy, or alternately an unsuitable food. It is probably no coincidence that the only record of a date stone in a civilian context comes from a most unusual *bustum* burial in London, where it was found as part of a variety of uncommon food items placed on the pyre.[38]

Members of the plum family are not uncommon in waterlogged deposits. Stones of the small native plum, the sloe (*Prunus spinosa*), appear to be the most frequently consumed variety.[39] Their presence in cesspits indicates they were eaten whole, which is an interesting contrast to modern practice. Currently they are considered too astringent to eat in that way, and are used to flavour drinks or to make jam, presumably not an option in Roman Britain in the absence of sugar. The fruits of bullace (*P. insititia*) are larger and less astringent but still not currently thought suitable for eating as fruit. It is not a native species, but is found in contexts as early as the 70s.[40] Plums (*P. domestica*), another non-native species, were clearly being imported at a very early stage of the Roman occupation as one was found in former barracks at Colchester which had been burnt during the Boudican rising of AD 60/1.[41] These could have been imported dried as prunes, or possibly preserved in syrup. A graffito on a globular amphora from Brough on Noe has been read as 'PRVN[A]' (plums) but the reading is disputed.[42]

A most unusual exotic find from London was a peach stone from a first- to second-century context.[43] Peaches would have been an exotic find everywhere in the western empire at that time as the trees only started to be grown in Italy in the first century AD.[44]

Pine nuts from the stone pine are another exotic ingredient that would have been available in Britain; but to what extent they were exploited as a culinary ingredient is hard to judge. They were clearly being used ceremonially as fuel in temples,[45] and many of the records may relate to this type of use. One example where they were regarded as an ingredient, given the associations with other foodstuff, was at the villa at Great Holts Farm, Boreham.[46]

---

[37] Cracknell and Mahany 1994; Cracknell 1996; Booth and Evans 2001.
[38] Mackinder 2000: 12.   [39] Huntley in McCarthy 2000: 77.
[40] Bastow in Abramson *et al.* 1999: Tables 11 and 13.   [41] Murphy in Crummy 1984: 40.
[42] RIB II.6 no. 2493.46.   [43] Willcox 1977: 279 Table 1.
[44] Vaughan and Geissler 1997: 78.   [45] Shepherd 1998: 161.
[46] Murphy in Germany 2003: 212.

NUTS

Nut shells from the native hazel are a common find but not all come from the human food chain. At Carlisle some had clearly been nibbled by small mammals.[47] Hazel nuts have been identified in cesspits and similar deposits;[48] and one of the individuals found at Lindow had clearly been eating raw hazelnuts shortly before his death.[49] The quantities hazel nuts are sometimes found in also indicate they may have been collected and deliberately stored, and this seems to be what was happening in a mid-second-century grain store at Castleford when it burned down.[50]

The other nut most often encountered is the walnut, though it cannot be said to be common.[51] This is not a native species and it is unclear whether the trees themselves were grown in Britain during the Roman period, or whether it was just the nuts that were an occasional import. Almonds have very occasionally been recovered. They were another of the foodstuffs placed on the pyre of the woman buried in the London *bustum* burial which had a variety of unusual offerings.[52] Both their rarity and this unusual context mark almonds out as an exceptional foodstuff.

VEGETABLES

We have one particularly vivid piece of information about vegetable consumption in Roman Britain. It relates to a slave at Vindolanda who considered radishes such a vital part of the Saturnalia festival that he was prepared to spend half a *denarius* on them.[53] Other than that, our knowledge is very sporadic and patchy. Of the different types of vegetables it is the legumes such as beans, peas and lentils that are easiest to recognise archaeologically. In part this is because they are occasionally found as part of charred grain assemblages, where it can be assumed they are accidental contaminants, self-seeding from a neighbouring field or an earlier crop. They are also occasionally recovered in a mineralised form from cesspits.

The Celtic bean had certainly been grown in the south of England during later prehistory, though its introduction into other areas may have

---

[47] Huntley in McCarthy 2000: 77.   [48] Knights *et al.* 1983: 143.
[49] Holden 1995: 80.
[50] Bastow in Abramson *et al.* 1999: 172.
[51] E.g. Willcox 1977: 279 Table 1.
[52] Giorgi in Mackinder 2000: 66.   [53] Bowman and Thomas 1994: 276 no. 301.

come later.[54] Peas, by contrast, tend to be more commonly found on Roman period sites than ones of the late Iron Age.[55] Other types of pea-like seeds also seem to have been consumed. The contents of a jar preserved by charring, caused by the fire that destroyed the north wing of the palace at Fishbourne, seemed to belong to the *Lathyrus* species which includes the vetchlings.[56]

Lentils are not native to Britain and, though they can be grown here, they are not hardy. When they first started to be identified within Romano-British contexts there was some debate as to whether they were chance contaminants of imported grain.[57] The discovery of quantities in kitchen waste that did not contain grain indicated that they were being eaten as a food in their own right, a conclusion that has since been confirmed by the discovery of an account from Vindolanda dated to the period AD 97–102/3 which mentions them.[58] It is possible that they may have started to be imported prior to the conquest as they have been found in the early cesspit at Gorhambury.[59]

Although legumes of any type are only occasionally recorded, it seems likely they played an important part in the diet. At Vindolanda there are records of them being acquired in large quantities for the *praetorium*. A shopping list of AD 85–92 calls for 2 *modii* (17 litres) of bruised beans, and an account of AD 97–102 records the purchase of at least 5 *modii* (a minimum of 47 litres).[60] Elsewhere in the empire too, beans are recorded as being supplied to the army in large quantities.[61]

The consumption of leafy and root vegetables is the most difficult aspect of the diet to explore. It is also one where equating the names in the literary sources to modern varieties can be most misleading, due to the amount of selective breeding that has taken place since the Roman era. A classic example here is the carrot. Modern museum displays will not infrequently include reconstructions of kitchens with produce, including carrots which are invariably orange.[62] Unfortunately orange carrots are a product of seventeenth-century Dutch horticulturalists.[63] The Roman carrot was white, not unlike an early parsnip, and there are some grounds for thinking that the ancient writers sometimes confused the two.[64] For the record, seeds from parsnips are occasionally

[54] Green 1981: 141; van der Veen 1985: 213.
[55] Green 1981: 141. [56] Greig in Cunliffe 1971: 376. [57] Halbaek 1964: 162.
[58] Willcox 1977: 279 Table 1; Bowman and Thomas 1994: 175 no. 204.
[59] Neal *et al.* 1990: 28. [60] Bowman and Thomas 1994: 159 no. 192, 278 no. 302.
[61] Davies 1971: 133. [62] For example Alcock 2001: colour plates 8 and 25.
[63] Vaughan and Geissler 1997: 184. [64] Grant 1996: 107 footnote 53.

found in waterlogged deposits, but those from carrots seem much rarer.[65]

   Brassica seeds are not uncommon, indicating that leafy vegetables such as cabbage and rape were probably eaten. A particularly useful deposit that indicates such seeds do represent food crops, and are not just casual wild inclusions, comes from the garden of the Bancroft villa where they are found alongside the deliberately cultivated seeds of coriander and summer savory.[66] It is also probable that the leaves of vegetables that would normally today be eaten as root vegetables, such as beet and turnip, were eaten.[67] Traditionally in British cuisine young nettles have been seen as a useful vegetable, given they are available earlier in the spring than many others.[68] It is interesting to note that seeds from both the stinging nettle (*Urtica dioica*) and the small nettle (*U. urens*) were present in some quantity in the cesspit at Stonea suggesting they may have been a food item there as well.[69] The range of the green vegetables exploited may have been wider than it is today.

[65] E.g. Bastow in Abramson *et al.* 1999: Tables 8, 10 and 14.
[66] Peterson and Robinson in Williams and Zepvat 1994: 581.
[67] Monkton in Connor and Buckley 1999: 353.
[68] Hartley 1954: 387.
[69] van der Veen in Jackson and Potter 1996: Table 65.

CHAPTER 15

Drink

INTRODUCTION

Prior to the advent of tea and coffee, much of what was drunk in Britain was alcoholic, and this is likely to have been the case during the Roman period as well. One of the advantages of alcoholic drinks was that they were frequently safer to drink than water. Though Roman engineering associated with water supply is often admired, it does not necessarily follow that a pure and healthy product was being delivered. Ancient writers were well aware of the problems that impure waters could bring. Pliny noted that everyone agreed water was better when boiled.[1] It can also be doubted whether liquid milk formed a regular part of the diet of many in Roman Britain. The cattle herds do not appear to have been managed as dairy animals, and most milk would have been turned into cheese. Prior to modern refrigeration, milk would rapidly sour. There was also the problem that it could be disease-ridden. The modern levels of liquid milk consumption owe more to deliberate state-sponsored advertising campaigns to cope with over-production than to long-established drinking habits.[2]

Of the various different types of beverages consumed, it is wine that leaves most evidence archaeologically, both in the packaging and in the utensils used in its consumption. There is also a certain amount of evidence for the brewing of beer. Other drinks may be suspected, but archaeological evidence for them is very scarce. Writers such as Dioscurides and Pliny list a wide range of wines made from fruit and vegetables other than the grape;[3] but unless the pit at Doncaster with the pips of hundreds of apples is evidence of an apple wine or cider-making episode,[4] evidence for these is missing. It might also be suspected that mead would

---

[1] Pliny XXXI.23. [2] Vernon 2000: 699.
[3] Dioscorides V, 28–98; Pliny XIV.18–20.
[4] Buckland and Magilton 1986: 198 and 200.

have been consumed, but the evidence for this is even rarer than evidence for honey. Here we will first look at the evidence for the drinks themselves, before considering what drinking vessels are telling us.

The Roman world already had a well-developed wine culture by the time Britain came within its orbit during the later Iron Age. Italy appears to have undergone an expansion in the production and consumption of wine in the second century BC.[5] By the middle of the first century, wines were ranked in order of merit and knowledgeably discussed in a manner that would do credit to modern wine writers. Pliny even appreciated the importance of what in modern parlance would be called the *terroir*, i.e. the interaction of soil, topography and climate.[6]

From the ancient literature it is obvious that there was a wide range of styles available. Some places such as Cos and Rhodes were famous for making a very sweet wine from grapes that had been allowed to dry to concentrate their sweetness.[7] Falernian, one of the *grands crus*, included a style that was very dry.[8] If wines survived the heat of their first summer, they could be regarded as vintage; and there are good grounds for thinking that some wines aged in sealed amphorae may have eventually resembled something like a dry sherry.[9] One of the problems was producing a wine that would not turn to vinegar. The agricultural manuals of antiquity provide detailed instructions about growing vines and making wine, and some of the instructions such as including seawater are very alien to modern vinification practices. It would appear that boiled seawater and other additives were being used as preservatives, and would not necessarily have resulted in an unpleasant salty taste. Experimental work using Columella's instructions found that generally no salt was detected in the tasting.[10]

Although we know that this sophisticated wine making and drinking culture existed in the ancient world, it is difficult to evaluate the extent to which people in Britain partook of it. Though it is possible to establish where the wine might have come from, that does not necessarily imply it was good wine even if it came from an area of a known *grand cru*. Wines from Campania were put into amphorae with a distinctive black sand

---

[5] Tchernia 1986: 58.
[6] Pliny XIV.viii–ix, see especially viii.70; Tchernia 1986: 350 appendix V.
[7] Tchernia 1986: 105.   [8] Dalby 2000: 48–9.
[9] Tchernia and Brun 1999: 142–5.   [10] Tchernia and Brun 1999: 120–1.

fabric. These would have included not only the Falernian wines, ranked second only to Setinum in esteem, but also those of Pompeii, dismissed by Pliny because they gave him a headache that lasted till noon of the following day.[11] We know that something that purported to be Falernian was present at Colchester and London because there are amphora sherds with painted inscriptions stating this;[12] what we cannot know is whether drinking the contents of other black-sand amphorae would have been a pleasurable experience or one more likely to have given you a hangover.

The Colchester and London fragments suggest there was a market for good wine in Britain. At Vindolanda one account records the acquisition of both a named wine, Massic (a type of Falernian), and quantities of unnamed wine.[13] This would suggest that, at least in the commanding officer's household, different wines were being drunk from choice. Other named wines include Aminean wine, mentioned on a sherd from Caerleon.[14] This is an Italian wine, but it is known the vines were exported, and this particular one would appear to have been Spanish.[15] Sweet wines of unknown provenance are recorded at Mumrills and Exeter,[16] and there is a reference to *mulsum* (a mixture of wine and honey) at Vindolanda.[17]

The earliest wine amphora fragments in Britain are from an Italian type in use during the later second century BC to about the middle of the first century BC.[18] The distribution is limited, being concentrated in Wessex and in the Essex – Hertfordshire area.[19] From the mid-first century BC a wider range of amphora types are noted and it is clear that wine from Catalonia in the north-east part of the Iberian peninsula was also being consumed. Judged by the number of amphora fragments recovered this diversification of supply was not matched by an increase in consumption. If anything the amount of wine imported may have declined.[20] The area of the country which wine reached remained limited to the south. Dragonby in Lincolnshire is one of the most northerly sites with imported pottery prior to AD 43, but there is no evidence of amphora-borne commodities of any type associated with the Iron Age occupation.[21]

In the ancient literature, the Celtic populations outside of the Roman world were notorious for their voracious appetite for wine. It was a trait

[11] Pliny XIV.viii. 62 and 70.   [12] Sealey and Davies 1984; RIB II.6 no. 2492.40.
[13] Bowman and Thomas 1994: 153 no. 190.   [14] RIB II.6 no. 2493.12.
[15] Sealey 1985: 83.   [16] RIB II.6 nos. 2493.14 and 2493.16.
[17] Bowman and Thomas 1994: 278 no. 302.
[18] Peacock and Williams 1986: Class 3 (Dressel 1A).
[19] Fitzpatrick 2003: fig. 2.   [20] Fitzpatrick 2003: 13–4.
[21] Willis 1996: 188; Williams in May 1996: 598.

that set them apart as barbarians, for they drank it neat and not mixed with water as civilised persons were supposed to. The amphora evidence paints a much more complex picture. Whilst the quantities imported into southern Gaul from the second century BC do appear very large, the north appears far more abstemious.[22] The amphorae in late Iron Age Britain also suggests wine was not part of most people's lives even in the south. As a rare and uncommon import it may have conferred distinction on the individuals able to obtain and disperse it. The distribution patterns tend to suggest that how this was done varied in different areas. In the south-central area amphora fragments are found overwhelmingly on settlement sites, whereas in the Essex – Hertfordshire area they form an important part of burial rituals.[23] In some elite graves complete amphorae are found, suggesting the consumption of considerable amounts of wine during the funeral ceremonies. The five found in the Welwyn Garden City burial,[24] and the minimum of seventeen at the Lexden tumulus,[25] would have represented approximately 135 and 460 litres of wine respectively. Such funerary feasts are unlikely to have taken place very often. So, though wine consumption may be more archaeologically visible in the Essex – Hertfordshire area because of the burials, opportunities for wine drinking may have been more frequent in the Wessex area.

Wine does not appear to have been imported in quantity until after the conquest. Much of this will have been for the army. From the literary sources it is clear that the rations of a soldier included *posca* and wine; and that strict disciplinarians insisted the troops drank only the former.[26] In the Anglophone literature *posca* is normally translated as sour wine, whereas the Francophone studies see it as vinegar which was diluted with water at a rate of 1:10.[27] The latter interpretation would explain strict generals' preference for it. That the soldiers had access to wine, even when on campaign, can be seen from the amphora fragments from the early forts. Table 7.1 shows the proportion of wine amphorae in a number of dated assemblages. The first three rows were all early forts, and wine amphorae are present in appreciable quantities. The case of the earliest fort at Castleford is particularly useful here. It was a campaigning base for the early expansion into the north during the 70s. The quantification is by minimum numbers, but if translated into quantities of content, 28% of amphora-borne commodities were wine.[28]

---

[22] Tchernia 1986: 90; Woolf 1998: 179.   [23] Millett 1990: fig. 9.
[24] Stead 1967: 7.   [25] Williams in Niblett 1999: 193.
[26] Roth 1999: 24–5, 38.   [27] Tchernia 1986: 11–13.
[28] Rush *et al.* 2000: Table 18.

Table 15.1. *Wine sources at first-century forts based on amphora weights.*

Site	Date	Gaul (%)	Rhodes (%)	PW10 (%)	Total (kg)
Kingsholm	Mid-60s	4	90	6	22.49
Exeter	c. 55–80	19	24	57	10.13
Wroxeter	c. 57–79	65	25	10	12.42
Inchtuthil	c. 78–84	52	—	48	2.28

Various sources, change up time [handwritten annotation]

One thing that most writers on the Roman army are united about is that the mechanisms of army supply are not understood.[29] There does not appear to have been a central bureaucracy, and it may have been that quartermasters working at a divisional, or even unit, level negotiated the supplies with individual merchants. The supply to first-century forts is certainly varied as can be seen in Table 15.1. Unfortunately the standard wine amphora (PW10) was made in Italy, Gaul and Spain, and attempts are not regularly made to differentiate the fabrics. At Wroxeter, when this was done, it was found the sources included Italy (including Campania), Catalonia, southern Spain and the east Mediterranean.

In addition to the weight data presented in Table 15.1, hints as to the pattern of supply can be gained from other military amphora assemblages less usefully quantified. In the first fort at Castleford occupied between *c.* AD 71–4 and 86 the wine amphorae are either Gallic or PW10, with the former appearing to provide the bulk of the supply (86% of the estimated total capacity).[30] At Blake Street within the fortress at York, Gallic amphora fragments were again in the majority compared to PW10 amphorae in the first two phases of occupation dated to *c.* AD 71–100.[31] At the *scamnum tribunorum* site within the fortress at Caerleon equal quantities of Gallic amphorae and PW10 were estimated for the earliest phase of c. AD 75 to 90 – 100.[32] At none of these sites is there any indication that wine from Rhodes was being drunk. The strong presence of wine from Rhodes in the earlier forts may have been because of state action. The island was incorporated into the empire in AD 44 as a punishment for the deaths of some Roman citizens, and confiscation of wine to supply the army is a possibility.[33] Certainly its disappearance from the Flavian forts and the

[29] Alston 1995: 112; Roth 1999: 264.   [30] Rush *et al.* 2000: Table 19.
[31] Monaghan 1993: Table 117.   [32] Zienkiewicz 1992: Table 3.
[33] Sealey 1985: 134.

Table 15.2. *Wine sources in London during the first century.*

Date	Gaul (%)	Rhodes (%)	PW10 (%)	Total (kg)
50–60/61	44	21	35	4.68
75–100	62	13	27	22.77

growing dominance of the Gallic sources seems to suggest a reorganisation of supply to the military.

To a certain extent the pattern of supply to those parts of the civilian population that wished to consume wine was similar to the military pattern. Wine was certainly reaching what appears to be the native focus of settlement at Colchester in the Gosbecks and Sheepen area in the period AD 43 to 60–1. The amphora fragments have been calculated to represent a minimum of 21 Rhodian amphorae, 5 Gallic and 44 PW10; the last mentioned coming from Italy and Spain.[34] The pre-Boudican figures for London also show a strong Rhodian presence, but the pattern thereafter seems to deviate from the military pattern as Rhodian wines are still present, though in lower quantities (Table 15.2).

The presence of Rhodian wine amphorae in other urban assemblages of the later-first- and/or earlier second-century assemblages can be also be noted.[35] In general though, by the end of the first century, the majority of the wine that was drunk in Britain came from Gaul. Certainly, where wine amphorae can be identified on rural sites, they tend to be the typical Gallic shape.[36] It is also noticeable that most amphorae made in Britain were of this shape;[37] presumably because, to most people in the country, this was the 'proper' shape for a wine amphora.

A curious feature of wine supply to Britain in the second and third centuries is that while the rest of the country is drinking Gallic wine, the soldiers on the northern frontier were not. Gallic amphorae are seriously under-represented in the assemblages from Hadrian's Wall; and it has been suggested, on the assumption that wine of some form would have been drunk, that it came from the Rhineland and was shipped in barrels.[38]

[34] Sealey 1985: Table 1, 7.
[35] Clark in Connor and Buckley 1999: 116; Williams in Woodward *et al.* 1993: Table 28.
[36] Wallace and Turner-Walker in Clarke 1998: Table 11; Williams in Hands 1998: 226; Neal 1974: 231 no. 217.
[37] Symonds 2003.
[38] Bidwell 1985: 182; Croom and Bidwell in Casey and Hoffmann 1998: 178.

Soldiers in contemporary forts in Yorkshire, by contrast, did have access to Gallic wine. As Evans has noted,[39] this implies the Yorkshire forts and the Wall forts were being supplied by different quartermasters. Given this is a regional pattern, this might imply wine supply was coordinated at that time at a divisional level. It opens up the possibility that, by tracing the boundary between those forts with Gallic amphorae and those where they are under-represented, it might be possible to explore the command structure in the north.

The wine supply to the northern forts continues to show differences from that of the rest of the country in the later Roman period. A distinctive form of black-sand amphora from Campania with an almond-shaped rim forms a substantial part of the mid-third to mid-fourth-century amphora assemblages of forts such as South Shields, Newcastle upon Tyne and Wallsend;[40] and in both military and civilian assemblages at York.[41] These amphorae are occasionally found in purely civilian contexts in the north,[42] but are rare elsewhere. In the south, wine from Gaul continues to dominate in the third century, both on military sites such as the Saxon shore fort at Caister-on-Sea and in civilian assemblages such as those from London.[43]

Gallic amphorae cease production in the third century, and with their disappearance we cease to be able to map wine consumption over much of the country. The degree to which wine was shipped to Britain in barrels throughout the period is the great unknowable feature of the wine trade. The manufacture of Romano-British amphorae for transhipment seems to be a first-century phenomenon, but barrels made of silver fir were being reused in third- and fourth-century contexts, and these presumably indicate the continuing import of Gallic wine in large quantities. It is salutary to reflect that at Droitwich five large barrels were found reused in mid-third to mid-fourth-century contexts.[44] They were comparable in size to the Silchester barrels for which capacities of approximately 900 litres have been calculated.[45] Nothing in the pottery report for this site hints at the presence of any amphora-borne commodity; but, unless these barrels were being brought empty over long distances for reuse, considerable amounts of wine were being drunk somewhere in the area.

[39] Evans in Wilson 2002b: 482.
[40] Bidwell and Speak 1994: Table 8.9; Williams in Snape and Bidwell 2002: 150–1.
[41] Williams in Perrin 1990: 345, Tables 23, 27, 30, 31, 32.
[42] Evans in Neal 1996: 71.
[43] Darling and Gurney 1993: Table 29; Miller *et al.* 1986: fig. 76 Phases 4 and 5; Lakin *et al.* 2002: Tables 7 and 9.
[44] Crone in Woodiwiss 1992: 111, Table 7.   [45] RIB II.4, page 1.

The evidence for wine production in Britain is sparse, but the discovery of a vineyard at Wollaston in the Nene valley in the mid-1990s finally established beyond doubt that wine was made in the province. Excavations there uncovered shallow ditches spaced at 5 m intervals, each ditch being lined on either side by post-holes with traces of root balls of plants at 1.5 m intervals. Pollen recovered from the ditches established that the plants had been vines trained onto the wooden supports along the edges of the trench. Over 6 km of these ditches were found, and it is estimated that there would have been at least 4,000 separate vines which could have produced over 10,000 litres of wine.[46] Taking into consideration similar trenches in the area, it is estimated that a figure of 30,000 litres might be more realistic.[47] Though this might seem a great deal, in reality it would have been a very modest amount compared to the volumes produced and shipped in the Mediterranean where a single cargo could amount to more than three times that amount.[48] In addition to the vineyard evidence, it is also clear that amphorae were being manufactured by Romano-British potters, primarily in the first century.[49] Whether these represent the packaging for small-scale production such as that at Woolaston, or are for the distribution of wine originally shipped in large barrels, is unclear. How the Woolaston wine was shipped is unknown. The Nene Valley had a large pottery industry, but none of its products have been identified as being likely amphorae.

On rural native sites it is much more common to find fragments of olive oil amphorae than ones from wine amphorae, but the wine-barrel problem means that it is difficult to be certain that this means no wine was being consumed. It could be of course that wine was coming onto the sites transported in different containers. Another way of tracing wine consumption is to look not at the packaging but at the utensils that were used when drinking it. Within a Romano-British milieu, these show a rather surprising pattern.

Drinking wine in a Roman manner involved mixing it with water, which could be either hot or cold. There were a range of utensils involved in this including jugs for holding the wine and water, large bucket-shaped vessels for mixing, and ladles for decanting the mixture. A unique sarcophagus from Simpelfeld in the Netherlands provides a snapshot of what such a set might have looked like in the later second to third century. The interior of it had been carved to represent an elegant lady reclining on a

[46] Meadows 1996.   [47] Brown and Meadows 2000: 492.
[48] Sealey 1985: 126.   [49] Symonds 2003.

Figure 15.1. Detail of the Simpelfeld sarcophagus showing the wine service. Top row glass cups, mixing buckets centrally, water and wine jugs bottom. (Photo: M. J. Baxter.)

couch along one side, and along all the others her household goods were set out. On the wall facing her, a shelving unit is depicted. On the lowest level there are two jugs, above these are two handled buckets, and above those are three cups, probably made of glass given their shapes (Fig. 15.1). The jugs include a distinctive type with a beaked spout and a narrow-necked funnel-rimmed one. The beaked jug belongs to a family of jugs made from sheet bronze and iron that have hinged lids. Limescale deposits inside them make it clear they were regularly used for heating water.[50] The Simpelfeld sarcophagus makes it clear they were part of wine-drinking sets.

One of the problems with studying metal vessels is that, because they were large, they would generally have been recycled at the end of their

[50] Koster 1997: 30.

useful lives. Fragments from them are much less common in ordinary site assemblages than fragments of pottery and glass vessels, because of different rubbish-disposal practices. Fortunately various of the metal vessels used in serving wine were made from multiple component parts and individual pieces do occur with some regularity. A picture of where they were being used can be built up from these.

For the water jugs, the hinged lids must often have broken and been discarded from the numbers found. The lids themselves commonly had separately made and distinctive knobs inserted into them to aid opening. These too are found in site assemblages, as are the handles. The mixing buckets can be identified from the escutcheons and mounts which were soldered onto the body to hold the handles. The large basins used for hand washing in polite dining regimes also had separately made handles.[51] (See fig. 15.2).

A survey of the finds assemblages of nearly 400 separate excavations is presented in Table 15.3. The types of sites have been divided into broad categories. The military category includes not just forts but the *vici* and *canabae* in their vicinity. The small-town category includes both walled small towns and more straggling roadside settlements. An attempt has been made to distinguish between those rural sites which seemed to have some pretensions to a 'Roman' lifestyle (villas) and those which seem better described as basic farmsteads or villages (rural). As can be seen, less than half of the excavations produced fragments of metal vessels of any type. The number of sites producing fragments of saucepan-shaped *trullea*, water-jug and bucket fittings associated with serving wine, and fittings from the basins and handled dishes used for hand washing are shown in columns 3 to 7.

Saucepans, as probably befits a multi-purpose vessel,[52] were the most frequently encountered type, but water jugs were common finds as well. Both they and the bucket fittings occur all the way down the settlement hierarchy, which is not the pattern seen for the hand-washing equipment. Admittedly they are not common on the rural sites with only 2% of that category of site producing any evidence of them, compared with 8% of the military sites, 18% of the towns, 3% of the villas and 9% of the small towns; but the mere fact that they can be recognised on rural sites does suggest wine was being consumed on at least some of them and in a 'Roman' manner.

It is always possible that the water jugs were being used to heat water for other purposes, but it is difficult to see what else the buckets would

[51] Tassinari 1993: 232.   [52] See p. 47.

Figure 15.2. Metal vessels used for hand washing (no. 1) and the wine service (nos. 2–4) (scale 1 : 6). Nos. 5 and 7 are typical bucket fittings (scale 1 : 2). No. 6 is a water-jug handle and no. 8 a basin handle (scale 1 : 4). Scale bar correct for 1 : 4. (After McCarthy 1991: fig. 78 (5); P. Crummy 1992: fig. 15.5 (6); Frere 1972: fig. 40 (7); N. Crummy 1983: fig. 76 (8). Nos. 1–4 based on originals in Tassinari 1993 and den Boesterd 1956.)

Table 15.3. *Incidence of metal vessels on different types of site.*

Site type	Site total	With vessels	Saucepan	Water jug	Bucket fittings	Basin fittings	Handled dish
Military	126	59	26	10	9	5	3
Town	74	34	5	13	5	6	1
Small town	46	14	1	4	1	2	2
Villa	34	14	1	1	1	2	—
Rural	81	13	2	2	3	—	—
Religious	17	5	1	—	1	—	—
Total	384	148	36	30	20	15	6

have been used for. The escutcheons and handle attachments are generally soldered to the body of the vessel with a lead alloy that would melt at relatively low temperatures, so it would have been impractical to use them for any cooking purpose. There is also some other evidence that might support of the use of the water jugs as part of the wine service in the countryside. At Whitton in south Glamorgan there was not only the lid from a jug, but the terminal from a wine ladle.[53] Though there was no evidence in the form of amphorae that wine was being drunk there, these vessel fragments strongly suggest it was. Sheepen appears to have been the focus of native settlement at Colchester in the pre-Boudican period. Not only were large quantities of wine being drunk, but it was being consumed in a 'Roman' way, as fragments from a minimum of three water jugs were recovered.[54] In fact the whole dining experience may occasionally have been in the Roman fashion as two basin handles were also recovered.[55]

BEER

My fellow soldiers have no beer. Please order some to be sent. (Masclus to Cerialis at Vindolanda[56])

The ancient sources often mention beer as something brewed by the Celtic tribes, and there is also a reference to it in Diocletian's price edict where Celtic beer is priced at twice the cost of Egyptian beer, and half the

[53] Webster in Jarrett and Wrathmell 1981: 182 no. 50 and 51.
[54] Hawkes and Hull 1947: 332 nos. 12–14 and 17.
[55] Hawkes and Hull 1947: 332 nos. 15–16.
[56] Bowman and Thomas 2003: 84 no. 628.

cost of ordinary wine.[57] The basic ingredient was malted grain, i.e. grain that has been allowed to sprout to a point where the starch has been converted to a soluble sugar. The germination is then halted by the application of gentle heat, and the resulting malt ground. When it is mixed with water, the sugars are dissolved out into the liquid, which can then be fermented into an alcoholic drink by yeast. In many beer-making cultures, special yeasts have been developed over the years, but wild yeast in the atmosphere will also produce this effect. The modern Belgian lambic beers, for example, are fermented by wild yeasts.

What would the beer that Masclus's fellow soldiers wanted have tasted like? It would certainly have differed in one way from that of modern Britain, and very possibly in a second. It would have been unhopped as hops only started to be used in European beer-making in the twelfth century. Some writers still regarded them as an alien adulterant to British beer in the seventeenth century.[58] Hops add a certain bitterness to the beer, but more importantly they act as a preservative. The beer of Roman Britain could more accurately be described as ale, and would not have had a very long shelf life. Secondly, it seems very likely that, at least in the south of the country, it was not barley that formed the base of the beer, but wheat. Spelt wheat is the principal grain in all the charred-grain assemblages that can plausibly be interpreted as the result of a malting process.[59] This is unfortunate for those scholars who like to reconstruct the political history of Britain between the invasions of Caesar and Claudius from the coins and the scant historical references. The head of barley on the reverse of some coins cannot have been symbolising beer. This rather spoils the story that different tribes, by choosing barley or vine leaves on their coins, were showing pro- and anti-Roman sympathies.[60]

An eminent modern beer writer has described wheat as producing 'a distinctive, fruity tartness', and resulting in a pale, hazy yellow beer.[61] Modern brewers prefer barley because it has a higher proportion of fermentable sugars, the husk on the grain acts as a natural filter, and the taste of wheat and hops do not combine well. That at least some early brewers realised the advantage of barley in beer is suggested by a deposit of malt found at Colchester in a Boudican context. This had a combination

[57] Pliny XIV.29; Graser 1940: 322.
[58] P. Clarke 1983: 3; Drummond and Wilbraham 1957: 114.
[59] E.g. van der Veen 1991: 312; Letts in Smith *et al.* 1997: 268; Robinson in Houlston 1999: 149; Murphy in Bedwin and Bedwin 1999: 21; Alvey and Smith in Sparey-Green 2002: 300–7; Fryer in Bales 2004: 49–54.
[60] Frere 1987: 31.   [61] Protz 1995: 8.

of spelt and barley in the ratio of 10:1.[62] Other Boudican grain deposits consisted of virtually pure spelt with only the occasional grain of barley, suggesting that the malt was being deliberately manipulated to give a special taste. In the north, given that barley was the staple grain, it might be suspected that beer was brewed from barley. The taste and colour of the beer may have been another way in which the north and the south varied, though at present we lack the debris from malting in the north that would allow us to explore this.

Until relatively modern times, two sorts of beer were produced. Strong ale was produced by the initial fermentation; then small beer, which was only weakly alcoholic, could be produced by pouring more water over the wort. Both types would have made a valuable contribution to the diet, as it has been calculated that even small beer would had the equivalent of 150–200 calories a pint. It is probable that beer was drunk by all sectors of Romano-British society, and that it was looked on as healthy for all ages as home-brewed beer was until moderately recently.[63] Certainly at Vindolanda, it is not just the common soldiers who request beer. Quite large amounts are recorded as coming into, or being dispersed from, the commanding officer's house. In one account which relates to a seven day period in June, Celtic beer is noted on four of the days. For one of the days where there is no reference, there are missing entries; and the final day has only one entry and the note that the 'lords' were away. The quantities of beer are noted in three cases as 2 *modii*, 3 *modii* and between 3 and 4 *modii*. Substituting 2 *modii* for the missing quantity, this account suggests a household consumption of at least 90 litres for the week.[64] Another account that may have been associated with the occupation of centurions' quarters records the acquisition of beer in containers that held 100 pints.[65] Given the whole garrison with servants and dependents would have been well over 500 individuals, a considerable amount of time and energy must have been invested in brewing. It is not surprising that at Vindolanda there were individuals who could be described as both maltsters (*braciarius*) and brewers (*ceruesarius*) as both would have been full-time jobs.[66]

Given the short shelf life of unhopped beer, brewing is likely to have taken place on all sorts of sites, but it is the sort of process that does not

[62] Murphy in Crummy 1992: 282.　　　[63] Drummond and Wilbraham 1957: 114.
[64] Bowman and Thomas 1994: 153 no. 190; conversion following RIB II.2, 58.
[65] Bowman and Thomas 1994: 145 no. 186.
[66] Bowman and Thomas 1994: 131 no. 182; 2003: no. 102.

leave archaeological traces. Brewing tubs are likely to have been of wood, and when made it could have been stored in wooden barrels as was done until recently. The malting process itself can be identified on a small number of sites, of which features excavated at Fordington Bottom, to the west of Dorchester are a good example. There a working area in a late Roman settlement consisted of a yard surface, an H-shaped corn dryer and a pit that had been provided with mortared flint walls faced with *opus signinum* to produce a watertight cistern. Samples from the final use of the cistern and dryer showed that malting had been taking place using primarily spelt wheat with an admixture of 5–6% barley.[67] The whole ensemble can plausibly be interpreted as a maltings with the initial steeping taking place in the cistern, the stone yard surface possibly providing a sprouting area, and the corn drier turning the sprouted grain to malt. The malt may have been for consumption on the farm itself, but its location less than 2 km from the centre of the Roman town would have made it possible to transport either malt or beer to the town for sale.

Though corn driers are occasionally found in the earlier Roman period, they are predominantly a third- and fourth-century phenomenon concentrated in southern and eastern England. The charred grain assemblages show that they were used for a variety of purposes including malting.[68] The development of corn driers may have had an impact on beer production as they probably allowed malt to be produced more effectively. Whether this resulted in more beer being brewed is an open question.

SPICED AND INFUSED DRINKS

The taste for spiced wine in the Roman period is well documented. Not only were spices and aromatics added during the vinification process, but recipes for strongly spiced aperitifs also exist.[69] Though it is sometimes asserted that strainers would form part of the utensils used to serve wine, evidence of this is curiously sparse in the heartlands of the Empire by the first century AD. There are no strainers in the elegant silver drinking service depicted in the tomb of Gaius Vestorius Priscus who died in AD 70 at Pompeii, though all the other vessel types that might be expected are present.[70] The author of the standard work on gold and silver plate felt it was remarkable that 'very few silver strainers have been found at Pompeii

---

[67] Barnes in Smith *et al.* 1997: 217; Letts in Smith *et al.* 1997: 267–70.
[68] van der Veen 1991.   [69] Pliny XIV.xxiv 124–8; Dalby 2000: 245–6.
[70] Stefani 2005: 48 top.

and Herculaneum' and went on to conclude that perhaps by then wine was strained in the kitchen using bronze vessels.[71] Such a conclusion became harder to uphold after the publication of a monumental work cataloguing the extant bronze vessels from Pompeii which showed that strainers formed a very small part of the overall bronze-vessel assemblage.[72] So if the wine was being infused with spices, any straining that was needed would perhaps have been most commonly done using an item such as a sieve made from cloth, like the linen strainer referred to by Pliny as a device for reducing the strength of wine.[73] It is also probable that the host or drinker would not have been called upon to strain the drink at the point of consumption. The recipes Apicius gives for spiced and perfumed wine are for large quantities, made over a number of days and presumably 'bottled' for later consumption.[74]

Long-handled metal strainers and their matching bowls (fig. 15.3 no. 3) seem much more a feature of the areas beyond the frontiers of the empire by the first century.[75] A similar pattern is noticeable in their distribution within Britain. They have been found far beyond the frontiers of the province, at Glenshee and Helmsdale,[76] but are rare within it. The distinctive handles used on both the strainers and bowls were uncommon in the assemblages used as the data set for Table 15.3. They were only recorded at five sites compared to the thirty seven that have produced saucepan handles. Symmetrical flanged strainers are even rarer and again have a predominantly Highland distribution.[77]

The evidence both from Britain and elsewhere does not support the idea that these strainers were a major part of the wine service, and in at least some places they may have been used for the preparation of some other type of infused drink. Helmsdale is far to the north in the Highlands, a long way from any regular supplies of wine; while a grave excavated early in the twentieth century in Denmark, contained a long-handled strainer and bowl, with residues from a drink made with rye and flavoured with cranberry, bilberry, whortleberry and box-myrtle leaves.[78] So it seems more likely that the strainers are reflecting a taste for an infused beer.

Various other types of vessels also indicate a liking for infused beverages. Spouted strainer bowls have been found in late Iron Age and early Roman contexts in south-eastern England (Fig. 15.3 nos. 1–2). Copper-alloy

[71] Strong 1966: 144–5.   [72] Tassinari 1993: 69 type K3000.
[73] Pliny XIV.xxviii.138; see Sealey in Brown 1999: 122–3 for further discussion of this point.
[74] Apicius I. 1 and 4.   [75] Koster 1997: 46.
[76] Curle 1932: 386 no. 64, 392 no. 79.   [77] Tomalin 1989.
[78] Cited by Curle 1932: 307.

Figure 15.3. Strainers used for infused drinks. (After Niblet 1985: Mf fig. 33 (no. 1); Stead 1967: fig. 12 (no. 2); den Boesterd 1956: pl. III (no. 3); Grimes 1930: figs. 72–3 (nos. 4–5).) scale 1 : 8.

examples have come from a rich burial at Welwyn of the later first century BC, one of the conquest period graves at Stanway, a late-first-century AD burial at Wheathamstead and various domestic sites in Bedfordshire, Suffolk and Norfolk.[79] Pottery versions are quite common in pre-Boudican contexts at Sheepen outside Colchester and are also known in London.[80] In general the distribution is in eastern England, north of the Thames and

[79] Stead 1967: 24; Crummy 1997: 67; Anon 2004: 33; Sealey in Brown 1999: 121; Sealey in Bales 2004: 30–1.
[80] Hawkes and Hull 1947: 273–5 figs. 50 no. 8 and 57 no. 12; Niblett 1985: fig. 33. Marsh 1978: 181 Type 46.

south of the Wash.[81] The Stanway bowl contained the remains of worm-wood which would have produced a very bitter drink. There is a recipe in Apicius that uses wine and wormwood to produce a Roman absinth;[82] but, as Paul Sealey has pointed out, fragments of these bowls are found on sites with no evidence of wine consumption, and so there is the distinct possi-bility that they were used to make an infused beer.[83] Whether it was always infused with wormwood is open to question. The Stanway grave also contained surgical instruments and an amphora of fish sauce, so the contents of the bowl may have been medicinal rather than enjoyable.

There are various other pottery vessels that could have been used as strainers for infused drinks, though they always very rare. In the case of the open bowls with perforations in their lower sides and bases, it is possible that they were multi-functional utensils as they could have functioned like a modern colander (fig. 15.3 no. 5). In the case of the utensil long-termed 'wine-coolers', the association with the preparation of an infused drink seems secure. These are bowls with an integral lid that rises from the interior of the wall to a central narrow aperture (fig. 15.3 no. 4). The narrowness of the aperture means that it could only have been used with liquids, and the lid has many small perforations so that it could have functioned as a strainer. These vessels have been the subject of a detailed study by Scott Martin.[84] He has shown that they occur primarily on urban and military sites and were produced in the later first- to early second-century period. They are widely spread through the province, but often give the impression of being special commissions, and were clearly not in the regular repertoire of any of the larger pottery industries. It is suggested that they functioned by having the liquid and infusing ingredi-ents introduced through the central aperture which was then stoppered with a bung. The ingredients would be left to infuse and then the liquid drained off by tipping the bowl to allow it to flow through the perfor-ations. The resulting drink seems very likely to have been alcoholic because the perforations on an example from Germany spell out a drinking slogan in a suitably incoherent form,[85] but whether what was being spiced was wine, beer or mead is unknown.

Both the strainer bowls and the wine coolers have a fairly limited period when they were in use, and were not common. The strainer bowls appear most popular amongst the native population in East Anglia during

---

[81] Sealey in Brown 1999: 121.   [82] Apicius I.3.
[83] Sealey in Bales 2004: 30. See also Sealey in Brown 1999: 122–4 for an extended consideration of this.
[84] Unpublished.   [85] Marsh 1978: 181.

the late first century BC and first century AD. The wine-coolers were favoured by some elements of the military and urban communities during the later first to early second centuries. and may reflect a passing taste for a style of drink that originated in the Rhineland. The rarity in Britain of both these styles of vessels and the metal strainers, suggests that the taste for infused and/or spiced drinks was never widespread within the province. Had it been, it seems very likely that the prolific Romano-British pottery industries would regularly have featured utensils to cater for it, but they never did.

PINTS AND HALF PINTS

The type of glasses people drink out of can tell you much about the drinking habits of the community they live in. The British have long consumed beer in pint (c. 0.6 l) or half-pint quantities. With the rise of wine drinking, the standard glass offered in a public house is now 175 ml or 250 ml. Across the Channel in much of western Europe, the standard beer glass comes in 0.2 l and 0.4 l sizes, and you are more likely to receive a glass of wine in a 125 ml size.[86] The difference in glass sizes provides an immediate insight into the different drinking cultures. Differences that in Britain lead our political and medical establishment to berate us for overindulgence, and on the continent mean that in some areas there is an equation between being British and being a drunken yob. Archaeology struggles to recreate the intricacies of drinking practice and rituals in all their nuances, but some insights can be gained by looking at the vessels it was consumed from.

Tall pottery vessels, often made in finer fabrics, have long been known as beakers. Some of the beakers can have a very large capacity raising the question of whether they were all drinking vessels. Fortunately this can be examined via a group made in the Moselle valley in the third century which very conveniently have drinking mottos written on them (fig. 15.4). These say such things as 'Drink', 'Serve unmixed wine', 'Mix for me', 'Wine gives strength' and 'Spare the water'; as well as more general good wishes such as 'Good luck to the user' and 'Be happy'.[87] Even when the mottos don't explicitly refer to wine or drink, they are frequently decorated with vine

---

[86] Observations by the author over many enjoyable years. The continental figures do not apply in resorts frequented by many British tourists where litre glasses can often be observed.

[87] RIB II.6 89–97; Tyers 1996: 138–40; Steures 2002.

Figure 15.4. Pottery beakers with drinking mottos from Verulamium (no. 1) and York (no. 2). (After Frere 1972: fig. 133; RCHME York: pl. 35.) Scale approximately 1 : 4.

leaves or bunches of grapes. Their association with wine drinking thus seems well established. Fig. 15.5 plots the rim diameter against the height of a number of these beakers from British sites together with broadly

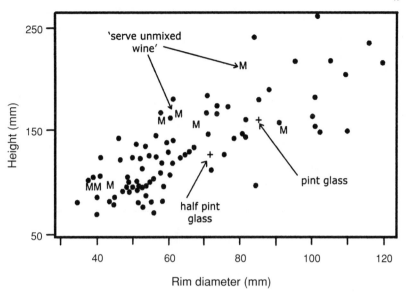

Figure 15.5. Plot of the size of late second- to third-century pottery beakers. Beakers with mottos relating to drinking indicated by 'M', standard 'straight' pint and half-pint glasses given for comparison.

contemporary beakers of late second- and third-century date, and a standard modern pint and half-pint glass for comparison. As can be seen, the motto beakers are found throughout the size range seen for the other beakers, suggesting it is safe to consider that beakers are drinking vessels, or at least vessels associated with drinking.

Pottery cups and glass drinking vessels are at the lower end of the capacity of the beakers. Pottery cups are a regular feature in first- and second-century assemblages, but become scarcer in the third century as samian pottery ceases to be imported. The native fineware industries, whose products replaced the samian products, made beakers not cups. Interestingly from the late second century onwards there is a noticeable increase in the number of glass cups found. A cylindrical colourless form starts to be found on many sites of that date, often in quite large numbers.[88] By the fourth century, vessel glass assemblages are dominated by drinking-vessel fragments,[89] again indicating high levels of use on many sites. Small capacity vessels would thus appear to continue to be

[88] Cool and Price 1995: 82–5.   [89] Cool and Baxter 1999: 88–9.

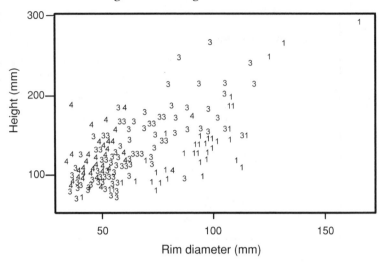

Figure 15.6. Comparison of the sizes of first (1), third (3) and fourth (4) century pottery beakers.

available throughout the Romano-British period, though increasingly made of glass from the late second century.

Fig. 15.6 compares the beakers plotted in fig. 15.5 with those from first- and fourth-century contexts. Whilst the early group includes some that are as large as the late second- and third-century ones, the fourth-century group generally lacks the medium to large ones. This suggests that the way in which drink was consumed may have changed by the fourth century. There are various options to explain this. It could be that the larger beakers were used for a particular type of drink that went out of fashion. The motto beakers though show that both large and small beakers were associated with wine drinking. It could be that some of the larger ones were used as mixing bowls for wine and water, and other vessels were used for this in the fourth century. This type of use seems at odds with the mottos, where even large examples admonish their users to fill them with unmixed wine or to spare the water; though admittedly these could just be a joke intended to entertain a drinking party. One from Verulamium with the motto 'Serve unmixed wine' (fig. 15.4 no. 1) would have held well over 800 ml (*c.* 1.5 pints).[90] The two other possibilities are that the larger

[90] RIB II.6 no. 2498.4; capacity based on Steures 2002: fig. 3.

beakers were communal vessels which were shared amongst several drinkers, or that some individuals drank truly prodigious amounts. The different sizes and materials of the vessels associated with drinking, together with the hints that there may have been changes with time, suggests that it could be profitable to look in more detail at the types associated with particular well-dated episodes to see if any additional light can be shed on drinking rituals. An attempt will be made to do this in Chapters 16 to 19.

CHAPTER 16

The end of independence

INTRODUCTION

Up to now we have been exploring the different foods and drinks one by one. The next four chapters examine patterns of eating and drinking chronologically. They look at what particular communities' preferences were, and how these change with both time and place.

We start with the late Iron Age. It is not possible to draw a boundary between prehistoric and Roman Britain at a particular date. In the south-east of England some communities were adopting what looks like a 'Romanised' lifestyle a century or more preceding the formal invasion. So much so that it has been argued that the south-east could be regarded as occupied by a series of client kingdoms between Caesar's raids and the Claudian invasion.[1] Elsewhere much of the population carried on their lives after AD 43 happily oblivious to the fact that they were now part of the Roman empire. In many sites in Gloucestershire, for example, noticeable changes in the way people dressed and the things they used are not detectable until the second century.[2]

This chapter explores some of the variety in eating practice that can be detected in the century or so prior to the conventional date of the conquest. As a convenient shorthand, areas will be referred to by the *civitas* names they were to become known as during the Roman period, even though these were probably administration entities that emerged in the Roman period, and do not necessarily reflect the tribal names or boundaries of the later Iron Age.

When looking at late Iron Age communities, we are faced with a major problem concerning chronology. Pottery in large parts of the country is not a helpful chronological indicator.[3] The advent of intensive radiocarbon

---

[1] Creighton 2000.   [2] Cool in Miles *et al.* forthcoming.
[3] See Willis 2002 for discussion.

dating programmes has often shown that sites were occupied for much longer than would have been suspected from their sparse finds assemblages.[4] So, though an attempt will be made to concentrate on the last century BC and the earlier first century AD, in some areas this is impossible and a broader period of up to half a millennium has to be considered.

POTS AND PANS IN THE LATE IRON AGE KITCHEN

Pottery was central to the preparation and serving of food in many parts of Roman Britain. This does not appear to have been the case in many parts of the country during the Iron Age, a state of affairs that has interesting implications for cooking practice. Simplified greatly, in the later Iron Age the area to the south and east of the Severn – Humber line used pottery whilst to the north and west it is much rarer and in some areas absent. It is always possible that in these aceramic areas more pottery might have been used but has just not survived. Some northern Iron Age vessels are very crudely made and poorly fired; so much so that in some cases they can easily fragment after only gentle handling or even, it sometimes feels to anyone unfortunate enough to have to deal with them, simply by being looked at.[5] The prognosis for such pottery surviving in large quantities is small. Equally its use as a cooking pot is also unlikely as fabrics such as those would be unlikely to survive the thermal shock associated with heating for very long. It seems reasonable to conclude that whatever cooking method was favoured in these areas did not rely on the use of pottery.

During the later centuries of the first millennium BC, well-defined regional styles of vessels developed in the pottery-using areas but the range of forms in use was limited, consisting mainly of jars and deep bowls.[6] Both were used as cooking vessels judged by the sooting and carbonised deposits recorded on them, though there may have been regional preferences. At a settlement at Abingdon occupied throughout the later Iron Age, virtually all of the sooted vessels which could be assigned to a form were jars, despite the overall jar – bowl assemblage having a ratio of 60 : 40.[7] At the broadly contemporary northern site at Thorpe Thewles over a

[4] E.g. Roberts *et al.* 2001: 249.
[5] For example Cool 1982: 93 Type I; Type II puts up a little more resistance.
[6] Cunliffe 2005: figs. A:15–30.   [7] De Roche in Parrington 1978: 42–65 Table IV.

quarter of the predominantly jar assemblage had cooking residues.[8] At Danebury, by contrast, both jars and bowls were sooted, including finely decorated examples.[9] Despite this, it can be questioned to what extent the use of any type of pottery vessel was central to the cooking process even on pottery-using sites. On those with relatively large late Iron Age pottery assemblages, the actual amount of pottery found is often small in comparison to what will be found later on Roman period ones. As a very crude measure, the c. 8,000 Iron Age sherds from Abingdon can be compared to the 11,400 from the Roman road-side settlement at Asthall in the same area (c. 26 km apart).[10] Both were settlement sites of no great pretensions probably occupied for broadly similar lengths of time. The disparity does not appear too great until the area excavated is considered. In the case of the Iron Age site this was 5,100 m², whereas for the Roman site it was only c. 900 m². At Asthall 90% of the assemblage, judged by the most reliable measure the EVE, consisted of jars, reflecting the large number that will be used and thrown away if they form a regular part of the cooking regime. No Iron Age site appears to match the rate of jar use seen on many Roman period sites, even if allowances are made for the fact that some may have been so poorly made that they have not survived.

An analysis of over 250 Iron Age sherds from southern England has shown that a high proportion with detectable lipids were associated with the processing of dairy products (ranging from 39% to 71% of those with lipids).[11] The authors conclude that this shows that dairy products were 'an extremely important commodity during the period'.[12] This conclusion is questionable because pottery is not that common. What the analysis does suggest is that, within the later Iron Age communities that used them, pottery vessels might have had quite a specific culinary role rather than being used for a wide range of ones as they were to be later.

How then was food cooked? The popular image is of a cauldron suspended over a central hearth, but the evidence points to cauldron use being restricted to a small part of society, probably for special magical or religious purposes.[13] So, if lots of people were not using either pottery vessels or metal cauldrons to cook with, what were they using? The honest answer is that we don't know. In earlier prehistory there was a tradition of cooking food in troughs of boiling water that had been heated by hot stones (pot-boilers). Experimentally this has been shown to be

---

[8] Swain in Heslop 1987: 63.
[9] Brown in Cunliffe and Poole 1991: 286 Table 67.
[10] Parrington 1978; Booth 1997.
[11] Copley *et al.* 2005: 489.
[12] Copley *et al.* 2005: 493.
[13] See p. 49.

quite an efficient way of cooking,[14] but if it was a widespread cooking method it might be expected that large numbers of heat-affected pebbles would be present on later prehistoric sites. Though this is indeed the case on some such as at Dinorben where they were described as 'abundant' and 'numerous',[15] many other site reports make no specific mention of them.

TABLEWARES IN LATE IRON AGE SOCIETY

Most later Iron Age pottery assemblages lack tablewares such as shallow bowls, dishes, bottles and jugs. If these were required, it has to be assumed that they were made in other materials such as wood and leather though there is little evidence of this, even in sites where there is good organic preservation. From the late second century BC some potters in southern Britain started using the wheel to make vessels, giving them the ability to produce different shapes. The implications of why the wheel was introduced into Britain so late compared with areas across the Channel has rarely been commented on,[16] but clearly it has important implications for eating and drinking as a whole range of new shapes such as closed flagon or bottle forms became much more simple to produce. Previously there does not appear to have been the need for a differentiated suite of cooking and eating vessels. Where sooting and limescale have been studied, fineware and finely decorated vessels that might be assumed to have been tablewares are just as likely to show evidence of being cooking vessels as more superficially utilitarian ones.

In many places the introduction of the wheel does not appear to have radically changed the range of shapes being made. In others, new shapes did start to be made. Some parts of those societies were clearly developing a need for them, suggesting dining practices were changing. Towards the end of the first century BC these new vessels include shallow platters and dishes, cups, pedestal beakers, large capacity beakers and flagons (see fig. 16.1). Some of these vessels were imports from Gaul and the Rhineland, primarily from the *terra nigra* and *terra rubra* industries of north Gaul,[17] but others are local imitations.[18] Shape cannot automatically be used to identify function, but in the case of the beakers, cups and platters it does seem very likely that they were tablewares. The imported

---

[14] Alcock 2001: 102. [15] Gardner and Savoury 1964: 179; Savoury 1971: 55.
[16] Hill 2002: 151. [17] Tyres 1996: 161–6.
[18] Pollard 1988: 31; Symmonds and Wade 1999: 212.

Figure 16.1. Pottery tablewares found in the King Harry Lane cemetery showing the range of sizes of tazze (1), platters (2), cups (3), flagons (4) and beakers (5). (After Stead and Rigby 1989). Scale 1 : 8.

examples are carefully made, frequently thin-walled vessels with carefully fired slips and burnished surfaces producing glossy vessels in a range of red to orange and black to grey colours. Some independent evidence of their use comes from graves where the platters have been recorded as containing animal bone, suggesting their role was to serve food.[19]

The core area where such vessels were popular prior to the Roman conquest is the Kent – Essex – Hertfordshire area where both platters and beakers were being produced by local industries. Further north and west

[19] E.g. Stead and Rigby 1989: 302 no. III.

the take up of the new suite of vessels was variable, and often did not take place until well after the conquest. Although it is well-established that Caesar's conquest of Gaul resulted in an increase in cross-Channel contacts and trade between Britain and the continent, this alone cannot explain this inrush of new forms and their imitations; nor why some areas adopted them and some did not.

What we are seeing in the core south-eastern area is a major change in eating and drinking habits. This has occasionally been doubted. It has been pointed out that the metal vessels found in elite graves are those associated with sacrifice and not wine drinking, and so should be seen as a 'do it yourself Roman ritual kit'.[20] In part this is true, but the jug and handled bowl set were used in both sacrifice and polite dining. The notion that these sets are being acquired simply for sacrifice overlooks the scale of the change in the pottery assemblage. That is reminiscent of the boom in tea drinking in the eighteenth century, the rituals of which required not only the tea services for serving and drinking the beverage, but also pots in different materials for brewing it, canisters for keeping it in and teaspoons for stirring it. Different tea services were kept for green and bohea tea.[21] It was not until after the Commutation Act of 1784 that the price fell. Even before this, though initially the preserve of the rich, people of quite modest social standing aspired to it. The case of Nicholas Peacock, a farmer and land agent in County Limerick, and his wife Catherine who came from gentleman-farmer stock, is instructive.[22] His accounts relate to the 1740s and 1750s both before and after the marriage. This couple was positioned quite a distance down the social scale; indeed before his marriage the vessels in the house were made of wood and the cutlery of base metal. After the marriage the consumption of tea becomes necessary, and the accounts tell of the purchase of the tea itself, the teacups and even silver spoons.

In the late Iron Age context the range of new vessels is presumably associated with the rituals surrounding both new items of food and drink, for which there is contemporary evidence from the amphora assemblages, and new ways of consuming established items. The well-documented growth in tea drinking provides a useful model against which to explore this change in late Iron Age society. When first introduced it was the preserve of the rich, and the 'correct' vessels to drink it from were imported Chinese porcelain tea bowls. Local ceramic industries such as

[20] Creighton 2000: 201.   [21] Barnard 2004: 128–9.
[22] Barnard 2004: 107–8, 131, 135–6.

that of Josiah Wedgewood soon began to make the tea-wares necessary for its polite consumption, even when it was still an expensive, highly taxed commodity. As their manufacture spread, they evolved into new forms that took them away from the Chinese originals, for example, larger handled cups rather than small bowls. Early in the nineteenth century a new meal, teatime, evolved. This could either be the elegant and dainty afternoon tea favoured by the upper classes or the high tea with more substantial food offerings enjoyed by those who had to work for their living.[23] By the nineteenth century tea was the national British drink but, as is often the way of commodities that go from being the preserve of the elite to being available to all, attitudes to it have changed. So much so that when today a senior politician states that it is his beverage of choice, suspicions arise that he is trying to manipulate his image to appear an ordinary man of the people, for tea-drinking would not be expected for a person of his class.[24]

Alas, archaeology does not enable us to reconstruct such a richly textured account; but the evidence we do have allows us to see if something similar was happening in the late Iron Age. We could expect that sites where a high proportion of the new vessel forms were actually imported would be the elite sites. The extent to which the new food and drink items were adopted by the rest of society should be reflected in both the number of the new forms that are found further down the settlement hierarchy, and the ratio of imported to native versions. With time, elite sites might be expected to move on to a different type of assemblage as some other commodity took on the role of being a mark of elite distinction. The next section explores whether this is indeed what happens.

NEW FASHIONS IN HERTFORDSHIRE

We are fortunate that a group of sites of varying status belonging to the final half century or so before the Roman conquest have been excavated in the Hertfordshire region. They provide data against which the model proposed above can be tested. The first is the settlement in the Braughing – Puckeridge area. This lay at the boundary of the Catuvellaunian and Trinovantian *civitas* areas. Its precise status, whether it was a royal centre or not, has been the subject of much discussion.[25] What is clear is that people of the

---

[23] Davidson 1999: 6 and 380–1.   [24] Burkeman 2005.
[25] Summarised in Potter and Trow 1988: 156–8; see also Creighton 2000: 205.

highest social status lived there. It is, for example, one of only two sites of this date in the entire country where imported glass vessels have regularly been found.[26] Two sites excavated within the complex are particularly useful: the Skeleton Green excavations[27] and those alongside the later Ermine Street.[28] In both cases the main focus of activity was in the last decades of the first century BC and the first quarter of the first century AD. At Skeleton Green, buildings, pits and wells were recovered, while at the Ermine Street site pits but no buildings were found.

The second site is at Gorhambury which lies to the north of Verulamium which at this point was a tribal centre for the grouping that was to become known as the Trinovantes.[29] Here a set of enclosures and buildings were recovered. Occupation appears contemporary with that at the Braughing sites but continued into the Roman period when the site eventually developed into a masonry villa. During the late Iron Age the objects found provide no hints that this was the residence of part of the tribal elite, and its inhabitants were probably someway down the social hierarchy compared to those at Braughing.

The Braughing sites were excavated in 1971–2, that at Gorhambury in the 1970s and early 1980s, and this has some influence on the nature of the data that can be extracted from the published sources. On the whole the pottery was not quantified in any of the ways that would allow direct comparison between sites. The only measure in common is the minimum number which is far from ideal. By using it we can acquire a broad picture, but a more accurate one would come from the use of EVEs. The date of the excavations also make it unlikely that the phenomenon of structured deposition[30] would have been recognised, either during the digs themselves or later during analysis of the results. In at least one case at Gorhambury, the description of the pottery from a lower ditch fill as consisting of 'semi-complete vessels'[31] strongly suggests that it was taking place. Given that much of the pottery used here derives primarily from the pit fills, there is the distinct possibility that it may have been biased by special choices. This cannot be explored further here, but in future a comparison of the vessel types chosen to be part of structured deposits with those in contemporary use might provide further insights into how they were perceived and used.

---

[26] Charlesworth in Partridge 1981: 72 no. 18, 119 nos. 1–3; Price and Cool in Potter and Trow 1988: 81 nos. 1–5.

[27] Partridge 1981. [28] Potter and Trow 1988. [29] Neal *et al.* 1990.

[30] See discussion p. 13. [31] Parminter in Neal *et al.* 1990: 178 context 105.

In addition to the settlement sites, various burial sites provide data. The most important for our purposes are two at Verulamium – the King Harry Lane cemetery[32] and the Folly Lane burial[33] – and one at Welwyn Garden City.[34] King Harry Lane is a cremation cemetery where a wide cross section of the community were buried, judged by the age and sex profiles of the deceased. Ignoring the intermittent use of the area as a cemetery later in the Roman period, the excavators favoured a date range of *c.* AD 1 to 60 for its period of use based on the ceramic evidence. The dating of the numerous brooches found has caused Mackreth to challenge this.[35] He would place its use slightly earlier, starting *c.* 15 BC and running on to *c.* AD 40. What is certain is that this was the burial place of a predominantly pre-conquest population, though possibly not of those of highest rank. The Folly Lane burial and that at Welwyn Garden City were clearly those of high-ranking members of the tribe. At Folly Lane a complex series of ceremonies surrounded the cremation and burial of an adult in about AD 55. The date of the Welwyn Garden City burial is uncertain. It contains a pair of imported platters dated to *c.* 30 BC[36] but lacks the wider range of Gallo-Belgic wares seen at the end of the century.

The pottery from the Braughing sites, excluding mortarias and amphorae, has been quantified in Table 16.1 according to shape and whether the vessels were imported or made locally. Whether an item was imported or not would have been visually very obvious to its users. The continental potters achieved much greater control of the firing conditions than the native potters did, so the colour of the imports was much more uniform than that of the native vessels which had more variegated surfaces. The top five categories (platters, cups, beakers, flagons and tazze) can be regarded as new tableware forms. At Skeleton Green they make up make up over half the assemblage and of that nearly 80% are imported. At the Ermine Street site, the tablewares make up 44% of the assemblage. It is not possible to assign all the flagons to either the local or imported category from the published information, but if they are ignored, then 72% of the tablewares were imported. These figures can be compared to those from Gorhambury (Table 16.2). There tablewares form less than a quarter of the assemblage and less than a third of those are imported. Despite the inadequacies of the quantification method, the evidence would suggest that the new patterns of consumption were not limited to the elite, but

---

[32] Stead and Rigby 1989.   [33] Niblett 1999.
[34] Stead 1967.   [35] Mackreth in Jackson and Potter 1996: 318.
[36] Fitzpatrick and Timby 2002: 163.

Table 16.1. *Pottery vessels from the Braughing excavations by source (minimum numbers).*

Form	Skeleton Green				Ermine Street			
	Italian	Gallic	Local	Total	Italian	Gallic	Local	Total
Platters	10	55	20	85	4	37	17	58
Cups	7	16	—	23	3	22	—	25
Beakers	—	43	16	59	—	41	25	66
Flagons	—	7	2	9	—	?	?	15
Tazze	—	2	—	2	—	2	—	2
Jars	—	28	41	69	—	3	65	68
Storage jars	—	—	18	18	—	—	34	34
Bowls	—	—	40	40	—	—	40	40
Lids	—	—	15	15	—	—	39	39
Total	17	151	152	320	7	105	220	347

Table 16.2. *Pottery vessels from Gorhambury by source (minimum numbers).*

Form	Italian	Gallic	Local	Total
Platters	—	2	3	5
Cups	1	—	1	2
Beakers	—	1	4	5
Flagons	—	—	1	1
Tazze	—	—	—	0
Jars	—	—	27	27
Storage jars	—	—	3	3
Bowls	—	—	12	12
Lids	—	—	1	1
Total	1	3	52	56

were adopted lower down the social scale just as in the case of tea-drinking.

An interesting feature of the tablewares at the sites is the presence or absence of tazze (bowls on high feet – fig. 16.1 no. 1). They are a rare but consistent presence at Braughing but absent at Gorhambury. In the slightly earlier elite burial at Welwyn Garden City, three of the thirty-six pottery vessels are tazze. Two other elite burials in the same tradition

Table 16.3. *Tableware forms in formal burials at the King Harry Lane cemetery.*

Phase	Date	Platter	Beaker	Cup	Pedestal cup	Tazza	Flagon	Total
1	1–40	27	55	9	4	5	15	115
2	35–55	34	41	7	3	—	17	102
3	40–60	32	81	9	—	—	14	136
?	—	—	14	—	—	—	—	14
Total		93	191	25	7	5	46	367
Urn		—	121	—	—	1	17	140
Accessory		93	70	25	7	4	29	227

found at Welwyn also contained pottery tazze.[37] There may be hints here that different strata of society adopted different aspects of the new table services and these can be explored at the King Harry Lane cemetery.

In the King Harry Lane report, 472 burial features are recorded for the Iron Age cemetery. A small number are inhumations but most reflect cremation burial activity. The descriptions of the features make it clear that not all of them are formal burials; there are also deposits of pyre debris and other types of deposits of the type that is normal in a cremation cemetery.[38] In what follows, only the deposits that are clearly urned cremation burials or formal cremation deposits with grave goods are considered. In the tables, the dating given for the phases follows that presented by the excavators.

Table 16.3 shows that of all the new open tableware forms, tazze are the least popular in the cemetery and restricted to the first phase. Their rarity is even more pronounced than the figures show as one example had been reworked in antiquity to turn it into a low platter. Of the four deposited as tazze, two came from burials with three vessels, one was part of an assemblage of seven vessels and the fourth came from the grave with the most vessels found (ten). In phase 1 more than two thirds of the formal burials only had one or two vessels so, if status can be equated with the number of vessels in a grave, tazze are associated with the higher-status graves. This is also suggested in the case of the burials with seven and ten vessels as each had a high proportion of imports in it. Tazze were thus an

[37] Smith 1912: 3.   [38] McKinley 2000.

Table 16.4. *Incidence of cups in the graves at King Harry Lane.*

	Number of pottery vessels in grave									
	1	2	3	4	5	6	7	8	9	10
Total	214	80	32	18	6	3	3	—	2	1
With cups	1	1	3	4	1	3	2	—	2	1
Percentage	<1	1	9	22	17	100	67	—	100	100

early part of the service, possibly confined to the highest society. Their role in the new patterns of consumption was obviously not found to be vital as these patterns spread to other parts of the community.

The King Harry Lane evidence suggests that the role of the cup (fig. 16.1 no. 3) was also changing. Overall the ratio of platter : beaker : cup amongst the accessory vessels in the cemetery was very similar to that seen at Braughing, but when the distribution and types of cups are considered, again there are suggestions that they were restricted to the more wealthy members of the community. Over 80% of the cups in the formal burials are imports and, as can be seen in Table 16.4, they are overwhelmingly concentrated in graves with large numbers of vessels in which there was often more than one cup. The evidence would be consistent with a divergence in what was considered an appropriate part of the service in different parts of society; with an increasing number of people considering that beakers were central to drinking rituals, but with the elite considering cups were essential too.

The Folly Lane complex provides further insight into the ways in which the different vessels were used and possibly regarded. There were obviously very elaborate ceremonials surrounding the funeral held there in c. AD 55. A funerary chamber was constructed possibly for the display of the body before it was cremated. Some of the pyre debris was placed in the funerary chamber which was then deliberately dismantled and buried. Amongst this debris were fragments of pottery vessels that had presumably been used in the ceremonies surrounding the display and burning of the body. Some showed clear signs of having been on the pyre. Overwhelmingly, this pottery consists of tablewares and the remains of a minimum of thirty-five platters and ten cups, but only one beaker, were recovered.[39] If this can be regarded as a representative sample of the vessels used during

[39] Niblett 1999: 182–93.

the funerary feasts, then again it is suggesting that cups were preferred, or seen as appropriate, for those of the highest rank.

The patterns of use for the different vessels suggest that not only were new habits of dining emerging in large parts of the community, but that there may well have been subtle differences between those practised by the leaders and those down the social scale. The next section explores what these habits might have been.

NEW PLATES, NEW CUISINE?

Given the amphora evidence of wine imports during the first century BC, there is a temptation to associate the tableware services with wine consumption. Some of the tribal chiefs of the middle first century BC were certainly buried with grave goods that suggest a knowledge of polite drinking rituals in the Roman world. One of the Welwyn burials not only had a wine amphora but also a large bronze bowl of the type used for hand washing during dining,[40] and it is likely that the large cylindrical bronze bowl from the Welwyn Garden City burial served a similar purpose.[41] As we have seen, however, the new table service extends down the social hierarchy, and it does not appear to be the preserve merely of the elite. Were it to be associated regularly with wine drinking, it could be expected that far more evidence for wine amphorae would be recovered, but it is not until after the Roman conquest that wine appears to have been imported into the country in any quantity.

The capacity of the beakers would also suggest that they were not habitually used for wine (see fig. 16.1 no. 5 for range). Fig. 16.2 shows the beakers used as accessory vessels from the King Harry Lane cemetery together with the third-century motto beakers from fig. 15.5. As can be seen, the beakers from the King Harry Lane site tend to have a much larger capacity than the motto beakers which themselves included some of the larger beakers plotted in fig. 15.5. Considerable amounts of wine, even if diluted, would have been needed to fill a King Harry Lane beaker. Given their size, beer would be a much more appropriate drink to put in them; and even then, given the size of many larger ones, they were possibly vessels for communal rather than individual use.

As Tables 16.1–16.3 make clear, the serving of food had as important a role, possibly a more important one, than the drinking vessels. Platters are

---

[40] Smith 1912: 3 first vault no. 3, fig. 11; see also p. 138.
[41] Stead 1967: 26, fig. 14.

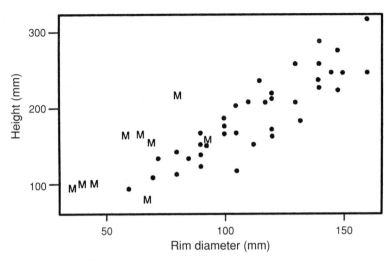

Figure 16.2. Sizes of beakers used as accessory vessels at the King Harry Lane cemetery compared to the size of motto beakers (M).

the commonest vessel type at each settlement site and equally are the most numerous type of accessory vessel at King Harry Lane. At that site, the platters range in size from 130 mm to 320 mm diameter with half of the examples lying between 170 mm to 215 mm (see fig. 16.1 no. 2). This is about the size of a small modern dinner plate and it would be reasonable to assume that it was used for serving individual portions. In one of the very few discussions of what the significance of this pottery might have been, as opposed to the minutiae of its typology, Hill has pointed out that platters like this allow food to be presented in a very different way than is possible in a bowl.[42] Bowls are ideal for gravy-rich stews where all the ingredients are mixed in the cooking process. Plates allow different foodstuffs to be presented individually, with the possibly of saucing the individual elements differently. This sort of cooking means more work for the cook; a stew normally needs less time and attention than several different dishes that only come together as a whole at the point of serving. Plates also allow more attention to be paid to the visual presentation of the food, and the possibility of individuals picking and choosing which elements of the meal they will eat.

---

[42] Hill 2002: 149.

Plates are very useful if a society develops a differentiated cuisine of the type discussed in Chapter 5. One of the requirements for that is access to a range of different ingredients, and the late Iron Age certainly saw an increase in the range of foodstuffs available. As well as the amphora-borne commodities such as olive oil and salted fish products, the domestic fowl first appears in Britain at this point. Other exotic ingredients are suggested by finds such as the distinctive mica-dusted jars which were being imported from the central Loire area of Gaul.[43] There would have been little point in importing this fundamentally utilitarian form for itself, and a role as packaging seems much more likely.

Some of these new ingredients definitely imply new and more careful ways of cooking. A chicken can be stewed in much the same way as the types of meat available before, but the use of fish sauce in an unpractised way can lead to quite disastrous results. It could be argued that the presence of fish sauce amphorae in elite Welwyn-style burials such as Mount Bures and Snailwell, each of which had three examples,[44] was just a matter of elite display and it does not imply that the contents were necessarily regarded as cooking ingredients. Such an argument becomes doubtful when only fragments are found in a probable pyre debris deposit at King Harry Lane;[45] and it certainly does not hold in the case of the broken fragments on settlement sites. These can be found not only at sites such as Braughing,[46] but also at the Sheepen site outside Colchester in pre-conquest contexts.[47] Such finds imply the contents were being used, presumably as a culinary ingredient. Other changes in cooking practice are suggested by the presence of early mortaria at the elite sites at Braughing and Sheepen in pre-conquest deposits.[48] As discussed in Chapter 6, there are strong reasons to suspect that in some places in Britain the popularity of the mortaria *cannot* be taken as an indication of the adoption of a Romanised cuisine.[49] In this case, given that the mortaria are present as part of what might be thought of as a package of ingredients and tablewares, it does seem reasonable to view them as indicative of new cooking practices.

---

[43] Tyers in Partridge, 1981: 102; Tyers 1996: 142–3.
[44] Stead 1967: 53; Tyers 1996: 52; Lethbridge 1953: 25, pl IV.
[45] Stead and Rigby 1989: 326 no. 206.1.
[46] Williams in Partridge 1981: 202; Williams in Potter and Trow 1988: Table 13.
[47] Hawkes and Hull 1947: 252 Form 185.
[48] Hartley in Partridge 1981: 198 nos. 16 and 17; Hawkes and Hull 1947: 254 Forms 191A and B.
[49] See pp. 45–6.

Table 16.5. *Associations of the principal types of tablewares at the King Harry Lane Cemetery. (infants are aged 0 to 5, immature are 5–18).*

	Infant	Immature	Male	Female	Adult
Platter	3	8	21	4	35
Beaker	1	6	13	3	20
Cup	1	3	2	2	10
Flagon	—	12	11	5	14
Total identified	10	20	59	21	156

An intriguing question arises as to what part of society developed these skills. Hill has suggested that the additional time needed in preparation might have led to a greater separation between the cooks and the consumers; and has wondered, rather provocatively, whether this might have been a women/children versus men division.[50] Whilst it might traditionally be felt that woman's place is in the kitchen, the associations of the different vessel types in the King Harry Lane cemetery provides no support for the theory that men were the primary beneficiaries of the new meals.

Table 16.5 shows the associations of the four principal types of tablewares in those graves where it is possible to age and sex the individuals buried in them. The cases where more than one individual is present in a grave are omitted, and the bottom line shows the total number of aged and/or sexed individuals in each category. As can be seen, all the forms are fairly evenly spread amongst all the different types of individuals when the total number in each category are considered. By comparing the number of male and female graves with platters with the numbers without, it can be shown that there is no statistically significant difference between them.[51] Whoever was doing the cooking in the community that buried its dead at King Harry Lane, all ages and sexes appear to have been considered equally in need of the vessels that would ensure a good meal in the next world.

Taken as a whole, the evidence points to quite fundamental changes in cooking and dining practices in the south-east during the century preceding the Roman conquest amongst the Trinovantes, the Catuvellauni and probably part of the Cantii of Kent. There is every sign that a differentiated cuisine was developing. The mere availability of foreign imports was not sufficient to trigger such a change elsewhere; so the interesting question is,

---

[50] Hill 2002: 150. [51] For methodology see Cool and Baxter 2005.

why here? The answer must surely lie within the internal dynamics of these communities. At the time as the eating changes are taking place, the same people develop the need to bury their elite dead with spectacular funerals consuming large amounts of resources. Dining and drinking parties may well have been another arena in which the standing of the household was displayed; and there are distinct hints in the record that it may have been judged by presentation and taste as much as by quantity.

MEANWHILE ELSEWHERE

The area of England that has been considered in detail in the previous two sections always tends to dominate any consideration of late Iron Age Britain because it is so visible archaeologically. Not only are large ceramic assemblages not uncommon; but spectacular burials are found from time to time and a form of historical narrative can be pieced together from the ancient sources and the native coinage. Then as now the south-east does not give a representative picture of what was going on in Britain as a whole. It is interesting to look as a comparison at the lands of the Durotriges in the Dorset area, where there is evidence for the importation of exotic foodstuffs in the late Iron Age, but no evidence for the widespread development of a differentiated cuisine.

Hengistbury Head, probably at the border of the territories of the Durotriges and their neighbours the Atrebates, has produced important evidence for the import of amphora-borne commodities in the first half of the first century BC.[52] The commonest appears to have been wine, but olive oil and fish sauce are also present. The site is believed to have been an import point rather than a settled community and the distribution of early wine amphorae in an arc of sites around it in Dorset and Hampshire would seem to confirm this.[53] Alongside the amphorae at Hengistbury Head there are also other pottery imports from the continent in the form of jars and bowls from Armorica, but these are not found much beyond the immediate hinterland of the site.[54] With the turmoil brought about in Gaul by Caesar's campaigns, the trade route leading into Hengistbury Head was obviously disrupted, but later wine amphora finds continue to be found in the region, suggesting that not all links had been severed.[55]

[52] Tyers 1996: 50 Table 12.   [53] Fitzpatrick 2003: Fig. 2.
[54] Fitzpatrick and Timby 2002: 162–3.   [55] Fitzpatrick and Timby 2002: 162.

The Durotrigian potters did start to use the wheel, and there is evidence that by the end of the Iron Age in this area, pottery production was a centralised rather than a domestic industry. The forms produced continued to be based on traditions stemming from the middle Iron Age and were primarily bowls and jars.[56] Some new forms such as tazze and handled tankards did appear, but the platter and beaker forms are missing from the range. The Durotrigians obviously also felt no need to acquire these from the Gallo-Belgic industries when these products started to pour into the country further to the east. It is clearly not the case that the potters would have been unable to produce shallow forms allowing food to be displayed had there been a demand. When the army provided one after the conquest, a range of shallow dishes and bowls were produced by this industry.[57]

Everything suggests that despite the early exposure to exotic ingredients, this had no impact on cooking practice or patterns of dining. The only changes that might perhaps be detected are in drinking vessels. The appearance of the pottery tankards is broadly contemporary with the first appearance of those made of wood with copper-alloy fittings, whose earliest examples occur in one of the Welwyn graves discussed above, and in a broadly contemporary one at Aylesford in Kent.[58] The use of the wood and copper-alloy tankards runs well into the Roman period and they have a scattered distribution, but there are two distinct concentrations; one in the Hertfordshire – Essex – Suffolk area and one in the Dorset – Somerset one.[59] The latter can be seen as part of marked regional interest in this vessel form as it was to become a very common product of the later Severn Valley pottery industry.[60]

That the Durotrigian potters were making the tankard form in the late Iron Age shows that their customers had a use for it, and that the vessels they needed were starting to diversify; but compared with the changes seen in the south-east, this diversification seems minimal. Durotrigian society was very different to that of the Trinovantes and Catuvellauni. There was a continued preference for using hillforts. Equally, though there was a well-developed tradition for inhuming the dead, the community obviously did not feel the need for spectacular elite burials. The lack of interest in diversifying their cuisine may well have been part of this attitude to life.

---

[56] Brown in Sharples 1991: 198–203.   [57] Sharples 1991: 108 Type 33.
[58] Corcoran 1952; Smith 1912: 21 fig. 21; Evans 1892: 357.
[59] MacGregor, M. 1976: Map 19; more are now known but the pattern is not broadly changed.
[60] Tyers 1996: 197.

A similar picture emerges further north. The east Midlands was a pottery-using area throughout the first millennium BC with what has been described as a ceramic industry of 'daunting diversity' during the final century before the conquest.[61] This diversity continued to be played out within the traditional jar and bowl assemblage. In this area imports of other forms are very rare,[62] and there is very little diversification of the form repertoire. At Dragonby in north Lincolnshire it is possible to study quite an extensive sequence of pottery use running from the later Iron Age to the later Roman period. Such diversification that takes place centres on the drinking-vessel element with local imitations of the beaker forms appearing to replace smaller capacity cups in the early to mid-first century AD.[63] Platters and dishes do not become visible until after the conquest.

Moving north into the territory of the Brigantes, we enter a society that seems to have had little use for pottery. In the West Yorkshire area Dalton Parlours has a sequence of enclosures and roundhouses and a long occupation dated by radiocarbon to the second half of the first millennium BC. It also has one of the larger pottery assemblages for the area but this amounts to only some forty vessels in total, primarily jars.[64] Other sites in the area occupied over a similarly long period have often produced no pottery whatsoever,[65] or only a single vessel that has all the hallmarks of being placed as a special structured deposit.[66] On such sites the only evidence for eating practices is often the quern and charred grain assemblage, as soil conditions frequently mean that not even animal bone survives. What they were eating and how they cooked it, is a matter of guesswork.

CONCLUSIONS

What are these patterns telling us? The reason why the continental commodities themselves and the pottery tablewares that aided their consumption are *not* found in many areas of Britain in the later Iron Age is sometimes discussed in terms of those areas being actively prevented from acquiring them, perhaps by tribes further south controlling the trade networks.[67] This is presumably based on the assumption that

---

[61] Knight 2002: 136.   [62] Willis 1996: 185–91, figs 2–3.
[63] Elsdon in May 1996: 415 Type 11.
[64] Sumpter in Wrathmell and Nicholson 1990: 130.
[65] Burgess in Roberts *et al.* (eds.) 2001: 72–83.
[66] Evans in Roberts *et al.* (eds.) 2001: 158 no. 22.
[67] Willis 1996: 191.

naturally everyone will have wanted these things. Perhaps a better way of looking at this is that there wasn't the demand for them. It would be wrong to think that these communities could not acquire exotic imports. They are found occasionally in even quite small settlements. The excavation of roundhouses and enclosures in the vicinity of the Ferrybridge henge in West Yorkshire, dated to the early to mid-first century AD, produced not only a Gallo-Belgic eggshell beaker and an imported Alésia brooch, but also a grape pip.[68] Further north at Stanwick which was clearly a major tribal centre, the imports include a black obsidian cup.[69] Even within Italy this would have been a sign of great luxury, and it was probably one of the most expensive imported items in the whole country.

The reason why imports from the Roman world are not more visible in large parts of the country probably lies more in the social than the political realm. In many communities there appears to have been neither the desire to experiment with a new cuisine, nor internal pressures that could have led to its adoption. It would probably be unwise to cast this within the models of active or passive resistance to 'Romanisation' that have become popular,[70] though of course it would be possible to do so. More likely we come back to the fish sauce problem. Exotic ingredients are only desirable if you know how to cook with them properly. Today when supermarkets bring us delicacies from all around the world, and bookshops and television screens provide instant instruction on how to prepare them, it is easy to forget this. Yet, less than forty years ago when my father was a greengrocer in a small rural town, attempts to introduce new items failed because people did not know what to do with them. The avocado pear was a case in point. One elderly couple was perfectly happy to try them, but reported back later that they didn't think much of the experience. Questioning established that they had eaten them as you would a dessert pear, and had naturally found them wanting. In the face of innate conservatism in matters of food, what is truly interesting is probably not why most of the country saw no reason to change well-established eating and drinking habits in the late Iron Age; but why parts of the south-east did.

---

[68] Roberts 2005: 135 no. 17, 155 no. 6, 184.
[69] Cool and Price 1995: 14.
[70] For example Mattingly (ed.) 1997.

CHAPTER 17

A brand-new province

INTRODUCTION

There can be no doubt that whatever influence the Roman state had in southern Britain before the Claudian conquest, it was only after it that the major impact of being formally part of the Roman world started to be seen. People and goods poured into the new province. Soldiers, administrators, traders and craftsmen arrived as did items that virtually no Briton would have seen before, such as glass vessels. New patterns of eating and drinking were introduced, but it would be wrong to see a simple Roman – native dichotomy developing. There was no more a single Roman way of doing things, any more than there was a single native way. In this chapter, five case studies relating to the first to second centuries are presented to show some of the patterns. They do not represent all of the ways of life being practised at this time, but they do give a taste of the diversity that emerges from the archaeological record.

SOLDIERS AND SETTLERS AT COLCHESTER

Colchester (fig. 17.1) provides a good place to start exploring practices introduced by the Roman forces. In the late Iron Age an important tribal centre existed there in the Sheepen – Gosbecks area, and it was the place where Claudius came to take official possession of the new province. A fortress was built to the east of the native centre by the Twentieth Legion and following its redeployments to the west of Britain in AD 49, the site became the first colony to be established in the province. The colonists were, no doubt, drawn from the soldiers of the invasion army due to be discharged. It was clearly intended to be the capital of the new province but it was burnt to the ground in AD 60/1 during the Boudican rising.[1]

---

[1] For general account see Crummy 1997: 9–84; see also Tacitus *Annales* XII.32; XIV. 29–39.

Figure 17.1. Colchester: location of different areas (A) and location of the excavated sites within the fortress (B). (After P. Crummy 1997.)

The fortress and *colonia* lie beneath the modern town. Excavations in advance of the redevelopment of large parts of the centre in the 1970s and 1980s provided a wealth of evidence. Being built on a previously un-occupied site and then destroyed sixteen years later means that Colchester provides an almost unparalleled opportunity to see how the soldiers and colonists lived. All the material from the excavations has been published, though not always in strictly comparable ways. Within the sites it was variously possible to assign some phases to the fortress occupation before the legion departed in AD 49, and others to that and an initial phase of the *Colonia* thought to end about AD 55. Elsewhere the stratigraphy does not make it possible to separate the occupation within the AD 44 to AD 60/1 period, but the pre-Boudican deposits are always distinct from the occupation that came afterwards when *colonia Victricensis* was refounded.

The production of the *Colchester Archaeological Reports* was a remark-able achievement by what has always been one of the smaller professional units.[2] There are minor problems with assessing the evidence because of when the excavations took place. For those conducted in the 1970s there is less environmental evidence than would be normal now; but sieving did take place on many sites and has produced some useful results. A more fundamental problem concerns the pottery. From the published

---

[2] Sites and environmental evidence – Crummy 1984; 1992 and Crummy *et al.* 1993. Small finds – Crummy 1983 and Crummy 1992. Animal bone – Luff 1993. Glass vessels – Cool and Price 1995. Pottery – Symonds and Wade 1999.

Table 17.1. *Proportions of the principal domesticates at Colchester in contexts dated to AD 49–60/1.*

	End date	Cattle (%)	Sheep (%)	Pig (%)	Total weight (kg)
Culver Street A	60/1	64	10	23	4.058
Culver Street E	49	72	10	13	7.291
Culver Street E (2)	60/1	72	8	14	50.902
Gilberd School A (1)	49	69	14	13	12.310
Gilberd School A (2)	60/1	61	14	16	21.029
Gilberd School A (3)	60/1	62	12	15	25.153

material it is impossible to reconstruct pottery assemblages that would have been associated with particular areas of the fort and city. This is particularly unfortunate, as the site reports occasionally indicate very distinctive suites of vessels were present in particular areas. Here a general picture can be presented with occasional detailed snapshots relating to particular groups of people at particular times. There can be no doubt that a much more richly textured understanding would result if the pottery was subject to reanalysis.

As is clear from Table 17.1, beef was the principal meat consumed by both the soldiers and colonists. Taking into consideration the differential waste associated with sheep and pig carcasses (see Table 9.2), it is likely that pork and ham products were consumed in greater quantities than lamb and mutton. The bones of domestic fowl occur regularly in contexts of this date, and it is clear that eggs were also being eaten.[3] Most of the meat consumed came from domesticated species, suggesting hunting and snaring played a negligible role in this community. Evidence for venison is so rare as to be almost non-existent on most sites; and it is also noticeable that geese and duck bones were much rarer than those of domestic fowl.

The Boudican conflagration provided ideal conditions for the preservation of cleaned grain in stores awaiting consumption. It is clear, both from grain stores and debris close to cooking hearths, that the preferred grain for bread-making was spelt wheat. Emmer is found less commonly

[3] Luff 1993: Table 5.1; Murphy in Crummy 1992: 280.

Table 17.2. *Amphora-borne commodities in Colchester AD 44–60/1 by weight kg (* = amphorae made in Britain).*

Contents	Source	To AD 55	To AD 60/1	Total
Wine	Italy/Spain	7.159	35.492	42.651
Wine	France	2.689	7.505	10.194
Wine	Rhodes	4.809	5.938	10.747
Wine	Crete	0.050	0.469	0.519
Wine	Unknown	0.235	2.826	3.061
Wine	Britain*	—	7.474	7.474
Subtotal (wine)		14.942	59.704	74.646
Defrutum	Spain	1.595	6.167	7.762
Olives	France	1.131	8.592	9.723
Fruits	Italy	—	3.045	3.045
Dates	Unknown	—	0.029	0.029
Fish products	Spain	12.158	18.184	30.342
Olive Oil	Spain	42.903	215.823	258.726
Unknown		0.100	2.270	2.370
Total		72.829	313.814	383.616

but fully cleaned samples were found on two sites indicating that a range of flours would have been available for different types of baking.[4]

The presence of exotic fruits is indicated by both the evidence of amphorae (see Table 17.2) and by mineralised and carbonised remains. Carbonised dates were found in a Boudican destruction context at Lion Walk. Judged by the quantities of the relevant amphora fragments found, they are likely to have been a rare delicacy.[5] Dried fruit may have been imported in greater quantities. Mineralised grape and fig seeds were present in two latrines belonging to the military phase, alongside seeds of locally available fruits such as elderberry, raspberry and cherry.

These latrines also produced bones indicating the consumption of fish. The species included mackerel and herring though naturally much was not identifiable to species. Generally fish remains were not very common even on the sites where quite extensive sieving was carried out,[6] and it seems that fresh fish was not often consumed. Fish sauce and salted fish products were popular ingredients judged by the amphora evidence (Table 17.2), and it might be suspected the remains in the latrines came

---

[4] Murphy in Crummy 1984: 105, 108, 110; Murphy in Crummy 1992: 281–2, 330.
[5] Murphy in Crummy 1984: 40.   [6] Locker in Crummy 1992: 278.

Table 17.3. *Pottery-vessel forms from Colchester AD 44–60/1 (quantified by EVEs).*

Form	To AD 55	To AD 60/1	Total
Flagon	17.14	42.60	59.74
Cooking jar	14.63	35.49	50.12
Beaker	7.90	27.89	35.79
Bowl	8.37	21.45	29.82
Storage jar	3.44	20.64	24.08
Lid	4.29	19.14	23.43
Dish	3.31	10.97	14.28
Jar	2.90	9.76	12.66
Cup	5.30	3.94	9.24
Mortarium	2.06	5.84	7.90
Constricted-neck jar	1.13	5.33	6.46
Cooking dish	1.06	4.98	6.04
Handled jar	3.14	1.32	4.46
Cheese press	—	0.11	0.11
Total	74.67	209.46	284.13

from eating these, rather than fresh fish. Certainly the species identified are oily ones of the type used to make salted fish products. An interesting feature of the amphora assemblage is that while the proportion of wine amphorae stays approximately level at 16–17% in both the military contexts and those of the later *colonia*, that of the fish products plummets from 14% to 5%. Either tastes were changing or perhaps the colonists found them too expensive when they no longer had their salaries as soldiers. Certainly the figures would suggest that it was a much less common part of the diet in the years immediately prior to the Boudican rising than it had been earlier.

It is clear from the wine amphorae present that both the soldiers and the colonists had access to a range of different wines. The brewing of wheat beer is attested by a deposit of malt carbonised in AD 60/1.[7] If we can equate large-capacity drinking vessels with beer and smaller capacity ones with the consumption of wine, then there are hints of an intriguing difference in consumption patterns. Table 17.3 shows the different forms of pottery vessels present. In it bowls, dishes and cups are under-represented

[7] Murphy in Crummy 1992: 282.

as samian vessels were not quantified in the report. This is a particular problem for estimating how many small-capacity cups were used, as those in samian pottery were likely to have been very common. In the 1970 excavations at Sheepen, for example, approximately 350 fragments of samian vessels were recovered from precisely contemporary contexts, and of these half came from cups.[8] All that can be said from Table 17.3 is that beakers were one of the commonest forms, and cups are present but in unknown quantities. Twice as many samian cups as those in all other fabrics would have to be present to bring them up to comparable levels with the beakers.

An exceptional number of cups were found in one of the military latrines. A minimum of twelve Italian eggshell examples and at least two similar cups in other wares were present, whilst a third is associated with the house.[9] The only other pottery catalogued as coming from the deposit were fragments of a large decorated samian bowl,[10] though this of course does not rule out the possibility that other uncatalogued items were also found. It can be stated categorically that no glass vessels were found in the latrine.

The latrine was part of a large courtyard house facing onto the *principia* across the *via principalis* and would have been the home of one of the senior officers in the legion. One can only speculate on why so many cups were found in this deposit. Was it the result of one particularly riotous party, or did particular individuals make a habit of retiring to this multi-seater facility with cups of wine for quiet contemplation? What the evidence does point to is that wine was probably the drink of choice of the officers who lived there. Within the sites at Colchester, Culver Street where this latrine was found can be regarded as a high-status area during the fortress period. Not only were parts of tribunes' houses excavated, but there were also the centurial quarters of the First Cohort of the legion. On two other sites, Lion Walk and the Gilberd School, parts of barrack blocks were recovered, and these areas may be thought of as lower-status ones. The possibility exists that it might be possible to map differences in the drinking preferences of the officers and the men by looking at the assemblages from these fortress-period contexts. The way the pottery has been published means that it is impossible to establish the beaker and cup proportions at particular sites, but some progress can be made with the glass vessels.

---

[8] Dannell in Niblett 1985: MF2 D3–D11.
[9] Symmonds and Wade 1999: 227 no. 43, 242 nos. 1–3 and 4, 259 no. 85, 444 no. 37.
[10] Dannell in Symmonds and Wade 1999: 30 no. 459.

Table 17.4. *Glass-vessel forms from Colchester AD 44–60/1 (quantified by EVEs).*

Type	To AD 49	To AD 55	To AD 60/1	Total
Large bowl	2.40	3.20	8.00	13.60
Cup	—	1.00	4.60	5.60
Jug	0.42	0.98	2.80	4.20
Jug/flask	0.80	0.20	2.60	3.60
Beaker	—	0.40	2.80	3.20
Bowl (other)	—	1.20	2.00	3.20
Bottle	0.28	0.42	1.54	2.24
Cantharus	—	—	0.60	0.60
Jar	—	0.17	0.38	0.55
Amphorisk	—	—	0.28	0.28
Total	3.90	7.57	25.60	37.07

As can be seen from Table 17.4, the glass from the pre-Boudican contexts is dominated by large bowls. These are primarily of the pillar moulded form and all have the sort of rim which would allow them to be large drinking vessels, as opposed to other forms of bowls where the rim formation would make this impossible. Smaller-capacity cups and beakers also occur, but do not appear to become very common until the later part of the period. When the distribution of these forms is looked at across the military contexts, the large bowls dominate the assemblages from the men's barracks at Lion Walk and the Gilberd School but are surprisingly rare on the high-status site at Culver Street. If the pillar moulded bowls were used as drinking vessels then, taken with the evidence of the cups from the tribune's latrines, it hints at a difference between the drinking habits of the officers and men. This might be a wine – beer difference or an individual cup – communal bowl one. It would be a fruitful area to explore within pottery assemblages in the future.

Another difference in drinking habits is suggested by the absence of spouted strainer bowls from the city-centre sites. These large bowls are found in a variety of primarily native contexts both before and after the conquest in this area.[11] Whatever the precise drink was that they were used to make, the soldiers and colonists don't appear to have developed the taste for it.

[11] See pp. 144–6, fig. 15.3 nos. 1–2.

The pottery vessels cast useful light on cooking practices. As can be seen in Table 17.3, cooking jars are very numerous. It is likely that they were the commonest form present, as the flagon total may be inflated by the fact that flagon rims tend to break as complete or substantially complete circuits. The shallow dishes and lids with non-stick surfaces (Pompeian-Red ware and the like), occur in some numbers and as far as can be judged from the catalogued examples, across all the sites. Given that mortaria are always regarded as the Roman kitchen utensil *par excellence*, the relatively small amount recovered is interesting. It could be argued that this is because mortaria were used communally and might not often be broken, unlike individual drinking vessels which would be needed in large quantities and be subject to high levels of breakage. The same considerations would apply equally to storage jars, yet they are far more numerous. The figures appear to be telling us that mortaria were not regarded as essential in all kitchens. This again throws into stark relief the popularity that the mortaria was gaining amongst some sections of the British population. If this most Roman of communities did not see the form as truly essential, why was it found to be so useful elsewhere?

It is worth asking, though, whether or not this is a 'Roman' community. The legionary soldiers and the colonists would indeed have been Roman citizens but it would be a mistake to think that should be automatically equated with an Italian ethnicity. It is known that the first six governors of the new province were Italian as were the known legionary commanders.[12] Given the army command structure at the time, there are likely to have been Italians amongst the lower-ranking legionary officers and the commanders of the auxiliary units. It has been estimated that twenty years or so before the conquest in 43 approximately half the men being recruited came from outside of Italy, especially from Spain and Gallia Narbensis, and it would have been these individuals who would have supplied the pool of retiring soldiers.[13] Three of the legions, including the Twentieth that was to be stationed at Colchester, came from bases in the Rhineland while the fourth came from the Danubian garrison in Pannonia and men from these areas are to be expected too. Amongst the auxiliary units there were Batavians from the mouth of the Rhine and units from Thrace.[14] Thus the bulk of the population of pre-Boudican Colchester is likely to have had a much wider range of ethnic affiliations than simply an Italian one. They may have thought of themselves as

---

[12] Birley 1979: 39; Webster 1980: 90–2.
[13] Millett 1999: 195.   [14] Webster 1980: 85–7.

'Roman', but their tastes in food and drink may have been very different from those of a contemporary Italian.

This seems to be borne out by several features of the early Colchester data. It was beef not pork that was the preferred meat. This is a German preference, not an Italian one.[15] If the men did indeed prefer beer, then this too might reflect ethnic preferences. After all, fifty years later at Vindolanda, Batavian troops were complaining that they had run out of beer, not wine.[16] As far as drinking goes, it may be that the lower ranks of the legion had more in common with the native population than they did with their officers. This can only be speculation at present, but could be tested by further work on the pottery from the excavations.

LONDON LIFE

It is hard for a modern British audience to conceive of a time when London did not dominate national life, but that was the situation when the first colony at Colchester was thriving. London had not been a centre of native occupation prior to the conquest as Colchester had been. At the time of its destruction during the Boudican rising in AD 60/1, Tacitus described it as not being a Roman colony but rather a centre for traders and merchandise.[17] Its precise status, both then and later, is unclear; but after the Roman authorities had defeated Boudicca's forces and regained control of the province, it was clearly a boom town and probably the seat of provincial government.

The excavations at Leadenhall Court in London provide a most useful snapshot of life in London as this new city became established. Not only can deposits relating to relatively short-lived periods of occupation be identified; but the site has been published in an exemplary manner, so properly quantified data can be extracted to build up a detailed picture.[18]

The site lies in the heart of the developing city. Prior to about AD 70 the area was still rural, occupied first by a small cemetery and then by a farmstead. Recognisable urban land-use started about AD 70. Occupation continued for about fifteen years and then the area became a building site for the erection of the city's forum and basilica. It is with the urban occupation of c. AD 70–85 that we are concerned here (site Period 3). The site was occupied by a large multi-roomed building, strip buildings, outhouses and middens (Fig. 17.2). The outhouses at the back of the

---

[15] King 1999: 189.   [16] Bowman and Thomas 2003: 84 no. 628.
[17] Tacitus *Annales* XIV.33.   [18] Milne and Wardle 1996.

Figure 17.2. Leadenhall Court, London. Location of the site at the north-west of the later *forum and basilica* (A). Main excavation area (within dotted lane) showing structures of site Period 3. Cross-hatched structures relate to latest developments (B). (After Milne and Wardle 1996: figs. 10–11.)

properties seemed to have served a variety of purposes. One was alongside a latrine pit and so may have been a room for ablutions. They may also have acted as storerooms as the highest concentration of amphorae were noted in them. Hearths and ovens were associated with the strip buildings and multi-roomed building rather than the outhouses, so it can be surmised that the kitchens were in the main buildings. Given the relatively small amount of occupation on the site prior to this phase of occupation, residuality is only a minor problem. What was found associated with the Period 3 contexts should, on the whole, reflect what was used and consumed on the site.

The inhabitants consumed a considerable amount of pork as well as beef. The division between the meat of the three main domesticated species is 49% cattle, 35% pork and only 16% lamb.[19] Numerous chickens were also eaten, but the contribution of any other type of meat was negligible. The charred plant remains were too few to be able to judge what the preferred grain was. Both spelt wheat and barley were present. What is clear is that the final cleaning of grain for consumption took place on the site, and it was ground there using imported lava querns. The inhabitants had access to imported foodstuffs such as lentils and figs, but the range of spices and flavourings revealed by the waterlogged remains is meagre. Only poppy seed and an unusually early occurrence of summer savory represent this area of foodstuffs. The inhabitants were heavy users

---

[19] Based on West in Milne and Wardle 1996: Table 6, the meat yields would be beef 8.785 kg, pork 6.357 kg, lamb 2.786 kg. See Table 9.2 and Appendix for calculations.

Table 17.5. *Pottery and glass vessels associated with Phase 3 contexts at Leadenhall Court, London (EVE data).*

Building number	Large building B6	Strip building 10 and 12	Outhouses 14 and 16	Total
Pottery beaker	2.93	3.45	4.00	10.38
Pottery cup	1.22	2.76	5.57	9.55
Glass drinking vessel	—	2.40	2.20	4.60
Pottery flagon	3.90	5.17	9.43	18.5
Glass jug	0.28	0.28	0.84	1.40
Pottery bowl	2.69	5.52	6.55	14.76
Pottery dish	1.71	1.38	5.39	8.48
Glass bowl	0.40	0.80	1.20	2.40
Pottery jar	7.31	10.34	13.27	30.92
Pottery lid	0.73	2.41	2.70	5.84
Mortarium	1.46	1.72	0.89	4.07
Glass bottle	—	0.70	0.14	0.84
Total	22.63	36.93	52.18	111.74

of olive oil as 84% of the amphora assemblage[20] consisted of olive oil amphora sherds. They also had a marked taste for *garum* and other fish products (6% of the sherds). Wine (9% of the sherds) came from a range of sources including Gaul, Rhodes and elsewhere in the Mediterranean. Sherds from the distinctive amphorae that shipped olives and dates indicate that these too were occasional delicacies.

The pottery and glass vessels being used are summarised in Table 17.5. It would appear that smaller-capacity drinking vessels (pottery cups and glass drinking vessels) were marginally preferred overall to the larger-capacity beakers. Bowls were also marginally preferred to the shallower dish and platter forms but sufficient of each are present for a variety of stews and drier dishes to be served. The ratio of glass drinking vessels to glass bowls (pillar moulded variety) shows a noticeable difference to the pattern seen in pre-Boudican Colchester. There the bowls dominated the glass assemblage and were especially common in the barrack areas. The inhabitants of Leadenhall Court appear to have had less interest in acquiring them, even though they were still common at this time.

[20] Quantified by weight.

Amongst the kitchen wares jars dominate, and again mortaria have low figures. They are the least common of the pottery forms and make up only 4% of the assemblage. They are even less common than glass drinking vessels. Some cooks may have been using stone mortars instead of pottery ones, as fragments of a Purbeck-marble mortar were found in a context belonging to this phase. Some use was made of non-stick Pompeian-Red ware vessels, but the quantity of fragments made in these fabrics suggests such use would have been the exception rather than the rule. Fragments of glass bottles are rare. This may be due to the date of the site as they do not become common until the end of the first century, though it is noticeable that they are much commoner in contemporary military assemblages (see next section).

Other utensils are rare. No knife blades or handles were associated with contexts of this date, though a single round-bowled spoon was recovered from a Period 3 latrine.

In general the finds from this site do not indicate that the inhabitants were particularly wealthy. Even the more elaborate multi-roomed building had only poor-quality painted wall plaster. Some of the buildings had tiled roofs but most would probably have been thatched. The inhabitants should probably be regarded as of the middling sort: rich enough to acquire the latest fashionable colourless glassware and to have efficient lava querns, but not of such status to have well-built and decorated homes. What the ethnicity of the people living here was is unknown. Their preferred meats fall into the immigrant rather than native consumption pattern and they obviously were happy to consume other imported foodstuffs such as lentils. As already noted, the precise status of London during the period under consideration here is unclear, but it seems likely that it was primarily populated by an immigrant community.[21] The consumption patterns seen at Leadenhall Court could be taken to be those of not particularly wealthy, civilian immigrants.

LIFE ON CAMPAIGN

The period under consideration at Leadenhall Court was the time when northern Britain was absorbed into the province. Up to about AD 70 the border had lain in the Midlands. To the north had lain the lands of the Brigantes. Their queen Cartimandua was probably a client of Rome, but

---

[21] See, for example, Millett 1996.

she fell from power in AD 69. The reasons that Tacitus gives for this are the stuff of historical romance.[22] Indeed it is surprising that the story hasn't been adapted as a best-selling historical saga with associated television series. Whether or not the reason her husband took control of the territory was really as a result of her setting him aside and taking his standard bearer as her consort, or whether there was some other reason, the result was the same. The Roman authorities now appeared to be faced with a hostile power on their northern border. At the same time a new dynasty, the Flavians, came to be in power in Rome. The new emperor Vespasian had seen military service in Britain as one of the legionary commanders in the Claudian invasion force, and possibly this influenced what happened next. The decision was taken to absorb the rest of Britain into the province. During the next fifteen years or so the army advanced to the north, sweeping through northern England, southern Scotland and on into the Scottish Highlands.[23] Tacitus says this was the period when Britain was conquered and then immediately thrown away.[24] His view was undoubtedly coloured by the fact that his father-in-law Agricola had been the final governor of Britain involved in this expansion; and it was his conquests in Scotland that had been abandoned when the frontier was settled on the Tyne – Solway line by the end of the century.

During the period of the Flavian advance, the garrison of Britain consisted of four legions with a nominal strength of 20,000 men and an equivalent number of auxiliary troops. The redeployment of the army resulted in many new forts being established. Some were temporary, some saw intensive occupation for a short period before the army moved on, while the sites of others became towns which are still occupied today, such as Carlisle and York. Castleford in West Yorkshire provides a very good place to look at how a campaigning army provisioned itself. Urban occupation there is relatively recent, and in many places the Roman deposits are relatively undisturbed. A series of excavations took place between 1974 and 1985 and the results appeared in three monographs between 1998 and 2000,[25] though much of the specialist work was completed between five and ten years before the volumes appeared. This leads to some problems when attempting to extract data for a synthetic approach. The quantification of the pottery, for example, is somewhat

[22] Tacitus *The Histories* III.45.
[23] Frere 1987: 81–104 is still a good general account though some details are now clearly incorrect.
[24] Tacitus *Annales* I.2.
[25] Cool and Philo 1998; Abramson *et al.* 1999; Rush *et al.* 2000.

idiosyncratic reflecting the fact that the report was written at a time when different types of quantification were being experimented with. On the whole the data are clearly presented, and some sites had the great advantage of having waterlogged deposits which preserved an important sequence of organic remains. The only noticeable absence appears to be any report on the bird or fish bones.

The army arrived sometime during the governorship of Petilius Cerialis (AD 71–73/4). There was then intense occupation until about AD 95. This occupation is normally described in terms of two separate forts with their associated civilian settlements (*vici*). The first of these is dated to the period up to about AD 86/7. During that period the same area was often occupied by a succession of different buildings and the layout does not conform to the normal internal organisation of a fort. Nor have any defences been identified. This is in contrast to the second fort belonging to the period of the mid-80s to the mid-90s where the line of the defences can be suggested, and the layout of the buildings conforms a little more to what is normally expected of a fort. There are some grounds for thinking that what is described as the first fort and *vicus* was in fact one of a series of different base camps for a large campaigning force, intermittently occupied. In what follows we shall be looking at the evidence derived from this first phase of occupation, before the second fort and *vicus* were established. Precisely which units would have been in the garrison is unknown. Various aspects of the finds recovered suggests the force may have been mixed, with both legionary and auxiliary troops being present.

The mammal bone was the subject of a very detailed study quantified by fragment count, diagnostic zones and minimum numbers. Judged by all measures and in all the separately studied groups the order of frequency of the three main meat animals is cattle, sheep and then pig. Table 17.6 shows the division between these in two groups. One is derived primarily from slaughter waste incorporated into levelling and make-up layers (Tr15IV/15V/18). The other group is derived from a waterlogged midden in Trench 14 and is a mixed group of both slaughter and cooking waste.

By any measure, beef was the main meat consumed. An attempt has been made to quantify the lamb and pork intake using the average weights provided in Table 9.2 and the minimum numbers. These show that pork may have been commoner in the diet than the other measures suggest, but it would not have been as common as it was in the diet of the people in Colchester and London. The reason for that is probably because the units garrisoned at Castleford were living off the land. It is noticeable that the

Table 17.6. *Animal bone from the principal domesticates from selected Fort I contexts at Castleford.*

	Quantities	Trench 15/18	Trench 14
Cattle	Fragment count (NISP)	1,638	1,727
	Zone count	552	1,057
	Minimum number	79	61
	Notional meat (kg)	18,157	11,072
Sheep	Fragment count (NISP)	755	999
	Zone count	(?)	789
	Minimum number	69	55
	Notional meat (kg)	1,328	1,089
Pig	Fragment count (NISP)	301	416
	Zone count	(?)	371
	Minimum number	20	18
	Notional meat (kg)	1,185	1,067

age range of the cattle at this time is much broader than was to be the case for the cattle consumed in Fort II.[26] The soldiers might well have been seizing what they could find with little concern for maintaining the viability of the herd. The butchery patterns seen on even low-meat-yielding parts such as cattle mandibles show that the butchers of Fort I were anxious to maximise the amount of meat acquired from each carcase. The Fort I midden on Site 14 is also the only place in all of Castleford where cattle scapulae have been found with the typical knife marks and punched holes indicative of preserving by salting or drying.[27] Everything points to the meat supply having to be eked out. The soldiers might have preferred to eat pork and ham, but what was more easily available was lamb and mutton. Interestingly, despite the obvious need to maximise the meat supply, hunting does not appear to have been seen as a way of doing this as game was very rare.

The problems with the meat supply could have come about because the supply chain for fresh produce was erratic. A similar pattern of living off the land is revealed in the charred grain assemblages where barley is the dominant grain in the assemblages associated with the early fort whereas wheat is dominant by the second century.[28] Barley would have been what

[26] Abramson *et al.* 1999: 228 Table 39.
[27] For the butchery see Abramson *et al.* 1999: 233; see also p. 89 and fig. 9.1.
[28] Bastow in Abramson *et al.* 1999: Tables 17, 19 and 20.

was locally available in bulk. There does not appear to have been as great a problem with staples that could be stockpiled, though there appears to have been an emphasis on commodities regarded as essential. Amphorae show the presence of olive oil, wine, fish sauce and other fish products.

The fragments have been quantified by minimum numbers which is not ideal, but the minimum amounts they would have carried can be calculated.[29] The Phase I fort contexts and the contemporary contexts in the area that was to become the *vicus* in Period 2, produced fragments of sufficient amphorae to have transported *c.* 9,600 litres of goods. This will be only a small sample of what was imported, but probably broadly reflects the proportions coming into the fort. 77% would have been olive oil, 20% wine, nearly all of which was from Gaul, and 3% would have been preserved fish products. These were obviously regarded as essential. Other amphora-born commodities were not and are only represented by a carrot amphora that would have contained dates. This is in interesting contrast to the amphora from earlier military assemblages such as at Kingsholm and Exeter where amphorae transporting preserved fruit, olives, fruit syrups etc. accounted for 9% and 5% of the assemblages.[30] The rarity of exotic fruits in the diet of the soldiers is well demonstrated by comparing the number of fig seeds from the waterlogged midden in Trench 14 with the number recovered from mid-second-century water-logged pits on Site 10 in the *vicus* area. In the 8.4 kg of the midden that was sampled for environmental analysis, there were only 18 fig seeds in total. This compares to just under 4,000 seeds from a 1kg sample from one of the pits.[31]

Acquiring products from the vicinity also extended to utensils as can be seen in the quern assemblage.[32] Fragments from imported lava quern-stones are present in the Fort I contexts but the local beehive querns are well represented too. All of the flat rotary querns from the early contexts for which a diameter can be calculated are of the size suitable for hand mills. There is no evidence of mechanisation even though the numbers in the garrison would probably have been large.

The pottery and glass vessel assemblages are summarised in Tables 17.7 and 17.8. Amongst the pottery vessels, jars and flagons dominate as they did at Leadenhall Court, but here there are almost twice as many cups as there are beakers. Whether this reflects different drinking habits from the

---

[29] Rush *et al.* 2000: Tables 18 and 19.   [30] See Table 7.1.
[31] Bastow in Abramson *et al.* 1999: Tables 8–12, 15.
[32] Buckley and Major in Cool and Philo 1998: 241–7.

Table 17.7. *Pottery vessels from Fort I contexts at Castleford (minimum numbers).*

Form	Number	Percentage
Cup	143	4.3
Beaker	77	2.3
Dish	262	7.8
Bowl	295	8.8
Lid	53	1.6
Flagon	733	21.8
Jar	1,719	51.2
Mortarium	71	2.1
Cheese press	3	—
Total	3,356	

Table 17.8. *Glass vessels from Fort I and the Phase 1* vicus *area at Castleford (EVE data).*

Form	Fort area	*Vicus* area	Total
Drinking vessel	2.40	0.20	2.60
Pillar moulded bowl	2.00	1.20	3.20
Other bowl	0.40	—	0.40
Jar	0.19	—	0.19
Jug	0.42	0.42	0.84
Bottle	2.24	0.28	2.52
Total	7.65	2.10	9.75

civilian population in London is open to question. Military sites tend to have large quantities of samian pottery supplying what might be considered the personal tablewares (dishes, bowls and cups). The samian industry produced cups rather than beakers so the preference for cups may just be reflecting what was easily available. What is less easy to explain is that again the pillar moulded glass bowl form is dominating the glass-vessel assemblage as it did in the barrack areas at Colchester. Pillar moulded bowls frequently dominate first-century military assemblages, and whatever their purpose, they were obviously ones that had an appeal for the military. Conversely, glass drinking vessels were much less used at Castleford than they had been at Leadenhall Court.

Mortaria were obviously in little demand, and the cooks also appear not to have used the non-slip Pompeian-Red ware platters for cooking.[33] Amongst the utensils, small round-bowled spoons were very popular as no less than five of the twelve examples found were stratified in contexts associated with the earliest occupation.[34] Knives and cleavers, by contrast, were much less common, though this possibly reflects the fact that iron was not well preserved here.

What is interesting about the Castleford data is what was regarded as essential by this 'Roman' community. Adequate supplies of olive oil were essential, probably because of the range of purposes it served. A certain amount of wine was important too, but relishes like fish sauce could, on the whole, be done without. They would eat whatever varieties of meat and grain were locally available, but they would probably cook and serve them by their normal procedures. Certainly the number of bowls and dishes indicate the need for deeper vessels presumably for the more liquid dishes (soups, stews, porridge), as well as shallower ones for drier foods. The number of spoons also suggests a different way of eating than that which would have been practised in the surrounding native sites.

COUNTRY LIFE

Rural sites rarely provide the precision of dating that has been possible for the urban and military sites just considered, and longer timespans have to be considered. To provide examples of consumption patterns amongst the native populations, two rural agricultural sites have been selected. The first is in Gloucestershire at Claydon Pike to the east of Cirencester, excavated between 1979 and 1983. Some post-excavation work was carried out in the 1980s, but the bulk of the analysis was completed in the past few years.[35] The second is Orton Hall Farm on the fen edge in Cambridgeshire. This was dug in the early 1970s with final publication in 1996.[36]

The dates of the excavations means that there were no systematic sampling programmes. Perversely, the delays in publication have been useful as, though the quantification methods used are variable, some useful figures can be extracted. This would probably not have been the case had they been published soon after they were dug. Both sites have the advantage that it is possible to separate out the earlier occupation from

---

[33] Rush *et al.* 2000: 93 type 26, Tables 21–2.
[34] Cool and Philo 1998: 94 nos. 449–53, 455–7, 459–61; also Greep in the same: 277 no. 138.
[35] Miles *et al.* forthcoming. [36] Mackreth 1996.

Table 17.9. *Animal bone from the principal domesticates from Period 2 contexts at Claydon Pike and Period 1 contexts at Orton Hall Farm.*

		Claydon Pike	Orton Hall Farm
Cattle	Fragment count (NISP)	964	712
	Minimum numbers	12	—
	Notional meat (kg)	2,178	—
Sheep	Fragment count (NISP)	722	1,160
	Minimum numbers	22	—
	Notional meat (kg)	424	—
Pig	Fragment count (NISP)	173	48
	Minimum numbers	8	—
	Notional meat (kg)	474	—

that belonging to the late Roman period. In the case of Claydon Pike, occupation started early in the first century prior to the conquest. Phase 2 relates to the occupation from the early first to the early second century, prior to a major reorganisation of the landscape which seems to have been associated with a much more Romanised lifestyle. At Orton Hill Farm, occupation started about the middle of the first century AD and the first period of occupation extended to about AD 175 when again there was a major reorganisation of the site with the establishment of rectilinear buildings where before there had been roundhouses.

The bone from the three main meat animals are shown in Table 17.9. The quantification methods are not ideal, but it will be realised that there are striking differences when compared with the proportions of bones recorded from Colchester, London and Castleford. At Orton Hall Farm, for the first time the numbers of sheep bone fragments are in a clear majority. On rural sites such as these, it could be questioned whether all animal bone represents food waste in the way it must do on an urban site. The other functions of cattle and sheep in providing traction, dairy produce and wool may have been as important. At Claydon Pike it was noted that, during Phase 2, the sheep tended to be slaughtered earlier than they were to be later on the site. At the age of one to two years they would have been prime young meat animals, suggesting they were being produced primarily for meat rather than wool or milk. The butchery marks on the cattle bones also indicate they were being processed for meat. Given this, a notional meat yield for the minimum numbers of beasts at Claydon Pike has been calculated using the average weights provided in Table 9.2. As ever, these should be read with health warnings, but it does make clear that even when fragment-count and minimum-number measures are large for sheep, the amount of meat they are contributing may be low. Even allowing for this, the figures for Orton Hall Farm suggest that sheep meat featured more on the menu there than pork.

One thing that these two rural sites do share with the military and urban sites already discussed is an avoidance of game. In both cases evidence of deer consists merely of antler fragments and thus does not indicate venison was being eaten. There are two fragments of hare bones from Orton Hall Farm, but at Claydon Pike hare bones do not appear until later in the sequence. Whether this avoidance was cultural, or simply means there was not the game in the vicinity to be exploited is unknown; but the absence on a wide range of sites shows that not eating game was the rule rather than the exception. Other sources of animal protein were provided by poultry. At both sites domestic fowl, ducks and geese are present, with domestic fowl being the commonest type represented.[37] At Orton Hall Farm, oysters were also eaten, even though the site was 50 km from the sea.[38]

The presence of the oysters is a useful reminder that rural sites were not necessarily isolated. They could acquire foodstuffs and other items from outside if they were required. At Orton Hall Farm a lava quern was acquired at this time, which must have been a great boon for whoever had to grind the corn.[39] The presence or absence of things is thus partially a matter of choice on the part of the inhabitants as well, of course, as of the vagaries of archaeological discovery. At Orton Hall Farm lava querns and oysters were found useful, but amphora-borne commodities appear to be absent. The converse was true at Claydon Pike where a small number of amphora sherds suggest some olive oil and fish sauce was reaching the site.[40]

As can be seen in Table 17.10, the pottery assemblages from these two sites are strikingly different to those from the urban and military sites. In both cases it is dominated by jars, and the tablewares are much less common than they were in the assemblages discussed earlier in this chapter. Taking beakers, cups, dishes, bowls and flagons as tablewares, at Leadenhall Court they made up 60% of the assemblage (see Table 17.5). At Claydon Pike they contribute only 16%. At Orton Hall Farm they represent 19% of the coarse pottery assemblage. The overall figure is higher but cannot be calculated because, unlike at Claydon Pike, the samian pottery has not been usefully quantified by EVEs. Even if every

[37] Harman in Mackreth 1996: 218–9; Sykes in Miles *et al.* forthcoming.
[38] King, J. in Mackreth 1996: Mf 8; B13 Table 80. [39] Mackreth 1996: Mf 8: B12 sf11321.
[40] Williams in Miles *et al.* forthcoming.

Table 17.10. *Pottery vessels from Period 2 contexts at Claydon Pike and Period 1 contexts at Orton Hall Farm.*

	Claydon Pike	Orton Hall Farm	
	All pottery (EVE)	Coarse pottery (EVE)	Samian (fragment)
Beaker	0.40	1.73	—
Cup	0.75	—	5
Flagon	0.44	6.61	—
Tankard	0.93	—	—
Bowl	4.69	1.34	12
Dish	0.62	1.69	46
Lid	0.09	1.34	—
Jar	36.2	47.06	—
Mortaria	0.09	0.25	—
Total	44.20	60.02	63

one of the samian fragments identified was a rim sherd though, it is highly unlikely that the tableware figure would come anywhere close to the level seen at Leadenhall Court. It is clear that the tableware forms were not so important to the inhabitants of these rural sites as they were to the inhabitants of the urban and military ones. This is reflected in the glass-vessel assemblages from the sites too. These are meagre in the extreme, consisting at both solely of a single fragment of a glass drinking vessel.

An interesting difference does start to emerge if the figures from the two sites are compared. Though the tableware levels are reduced in comparison to those of urban and military sites, the inhabitants of Orton Hall Farm assemblage did seem to show a greater interest in them than the people at Claydon Pike did. The latter primarily wanted bowls, the former appear to have had a greater use for flagons and shallow dishes. This may well be reflecting the different parts of the country the sites are in. Orton Hall Farm lies on the edge of the area where a diversified range of forms was available in the late Iron Age. Claydon Pike lies in an area where diversification did not happen, and from the look of the first- to early second-century pottery assemblage on the site, the inhabitants continued to find little use for a wider range of forms even when they became more widely available. So while these are both comparable rural sites with similar ingredients available, the way they were being prepared was probably different. Bowls continued to suffice for the people of Claydon Pike. The dining regime at Orton Hall Farm obviously required more diversity.

POLITE DINING

A group of late first- and second-century graves in the south-east and south-central part of Britain allows an insight to be gained into dining practices. Their location, often in rural settings or outside towns with little evidence of major immigrant communities, strongly suggests that these are the graves of native Britons. They frequently contain suites of vessels that appear to be place settings and evidence for food in the form of animal bones from joints of meat. Some also contain other suites of equipment relating to activities such as a visit to the baths or writing. Not all elements are present in all the burials, and localised traditions have been identified amongst them.[41] They do give a very good picture, though, of how some elements of the native elite were aspiring to live, and what was thought necessary for a good life. The combinations of vessels found provide some of the best indications we have of what these people were eating and drinking out of, and how some of the vessels may have been used.

Though excavated nearly two hundred years ago, the cemetery at the Bartlow Hills in Essex is a good place to start exploring this phenomenon. These were cremation burials placed below barrows in the second century. Most of the material was long since destroyed in a fire, but the accounts published in *Archaeologia* between 1834 and 1842 allow the groups to be reconstructed and, in some cases, dated.[42] Generally elite burials like these are found only as single examples or as pairs, but at Bartlow there are six examples which can be compared. The groups are summarised in Table 17.11.

The graves clearly demonstrate various different aspects of what it was to be 'Roman'. The first barrow dug (1834/I) provides a good example of a group designed for dining. It consists of two jugs (glass and pottery), four samian cup-and-dish sets, two pottery beakers and a glass bottle. The group dug in 1836 focuses on other aspects of a 'Roman' life. There is equipment for the baths (strigils, an enamelled flask for oil, and a glass unguent bottle), a folding iron stool of the type used by magistrates and senior military officers,[43] a jug and *trulleum* set and a lamp. This combination of jug and *trulleum* is the one associated with washing hands before making a sacrifice.[44] The recorded positions of the four from the Bartlow

---

[41] E.g. Millett 1987.
[42] Gage 1834, 1836, 1840; Gage Rokewode 1842. I am most grateful to Miss Brenda Dickinson for providing the dates of the samian stamps described therein.
[43] Jessup 1954: 22–8.   [44] See p. 47.

Table 17.11. *The grave goods from the Bartlow burials (* = contained chicken bones).*

	1834/I	1842	1840	1834/II	1834/III	1836
Samian date	100–25	160–90	150–80	—	—	—
Coin date	—	—	—	117+	—	—
Samian cup	4	2	1	—	—	—
Samian dish	4	1	1*	—	—	—
Glass drinking vessel	—	1	1	1	—	—
Pottery beaker	2	4	1	—	—	1
Wooden tankard	—	—	—	1	—	—
Pottery flagon	1	—	—	—	—	—
Glass jug	1	—	—	—	—	—
Glass bottle	1	—	2	1	2	1
Water jug	—	—	—	—	—	1
Lamp	1	1	1	—	1	1
Jug and *trulleum* set	—	1	1	—	1	1
Glass flask	—	1	—	—	—	1
Ointment pot	—	—	—	—	—	1
Strigil	—	—	—	—	—	1
Chair	—	—	—	—	—	1

cemetery make it very clear that they were indeed seen as a set. In each case they were found together with the jug placed in or on the *trulleum*, and it is tempting to see them as representing the ability to sacrifice in the 'correct' manner. The goods with the individual in 1836 could be seen as demonstrating authority, proper relationship with the gods and appropriate hygiene. It seems reasonable to conclude that the graves with place settings were also regarded as 'correct' for a 'Roman' life.

A cremation burial from Stansted, dated to the early to mid-second century, makes it even easier to identify these different aspects of the Roman life, given the way in which the grave goods were laid out (see fig. 17.3).[45] Centrally the cremated remains had been placed on a pewter tray. To the left of this was equipment for sacrifice (a jug and *trulleum* set) and bathing (a bath saucer). A large copper-alloy basin with a samian dish placed internally was also on the left side. To the right was equipment for dining (seven small samian bowls and dishes of varying sizes, one samian cup, one copper-alloy pedestal cup, a glass flask and a two-handled

[45] Havis and Brooks 2004: 217–27.

copper-alloy amphorisk). Beyond the bottom edge of the tray there were three groups of items. These were, from left to right: a carrot amphora and a pottery beaker, a pillar moulded glass bowl and a glass drinking vessel, and a joint of pork with a bone-handled knife.

It is tempting to see this last group of material as the remains of food. This is certainly true of the amphora, which would have contained dried dates and other palm fruit, and the joint of pork. There are noticeable gaps in the layout of the grave goods in this area which is curious given the crowding seen in the tablewares on the right of the tray. The pork joint had been placed directly onto the base of the chest, and so other solid foodstuffs that have not survived could have been placed similarly in the gaps. If there was food to the left and right in this area, this would open up interesting questions about the role of the pottery beaker, positioned with the amphora. Perhaps it was acting as a serving vessel of some form.

Generally, within these graves, cup forms far outnumber beakers. Where both are recovered, and the position of the vessels has been carefully recorded, the beakers and the cups are not placed together. This can be seen in the late first-century Burial 2 at Victoria Road, Winchester (see fig. 17.4).[46] The main focus was a shale tray on which had been placed a large dish and cup, both of samian, bones from two joints of pork with each group having its own knife, and a single copper-alloy spoon. To one side were three samian cups and two jugs (one copper-alloy jug and one glass). Extending to the end of the grave from the tray were three samian dishes. One had another dish inverted over it, the other two each had a pair of samian cups placed in them. At the end of the grave there was a large pottery flagon and a pottery beaker placed on either side of the row of dishes. The beaker was thus placed at almost the maximum distance possible from the jug and cup group. It is possible it was for the consumption of whatever was in the large flagon, but the position away from the main focus of the tablewares possibly suggests that, as at Stansted, it could be viewed as a food container.

There is no doubt that the samian dishes can be regarded as vessels for eating out of, as bones from meat are sometimes found in them. The deliberate covering of one at Grange Road also suggests that when it went into the grave it contained something that needed to be protected. Where multiple sets of dishes are recovered, there is often a single larger one suggesting a serving dish from which individual portions were taken. At

---

[46] Biddle 1967: 230–45.

Figure 17.3. Cremation Burial 25 at Stansted. Scale of vessels 1 : 8 apart from nos. 1, 6 and 9 (1 : 16). (Based on Havis and Brooks 2004: figs. 145–52.)

Figure 17.4. Burial 2 at Grange Road, Winchester. (Courtesy of the Winchester Excavation Committee.)

Grange Road the largest dish was placed on the platter alongside the meat joints suggesting that perhaps it also contained food when placed in the grave.

The role of the vessels generally called cups is more equivocal. In some cases the interpretation of them as drinking vessels seems very reasonable. The grouping of the cups and jugs at Grange Road suggests that all were concerned with drinking, but it is noticeable in that grave that whereas there are four individual-sized dishes, there are eight cups. All are the same form though two are noticeably smaller. The separation of the cups into a group with the jugs and another group of four, including the small ones, with the dishes suggest they may have been serving two functions even though they were the same shape. Certainly the goods accompanying a contemporary grave at Verulamium excavated in 1989 suggest this.[47] The interim publications available unfortunately do not describe the internal

---

[47] Frere 1991: 259–60, pl. xxvi; Anon 1990: 413–5.

layout. Amongst the finds, however, there are clearly four identical place settings in samian pottery, each consisting of a shallow dish with one large and one small cup.

Whilst it is always possible that the different sizes were needed for different drinks, it is equally possible that many of the samian 'cups' actually functioned as individual bowls for food. This would certainly have been the case at Stansted. Four of the small samian dishes there are of a type traditionally termed a cup (Dragendorff Form 35), but given they have a wide out-turned rim with relief decoration in the form of barbotine leaves, they are very unlikely to have functioned as drinking vessels. They are much more likely to have been vessels for eating from. This might explain the wear marks seen internally on some cups and thought to have been brought about by stirring.[48] Even if some of the 'cups' in the graves were in fact bowls, what is clear is that the drinking vessels preferred were small-capacity ones.

Some of the graves make it very clear that two containers were considered necessary for whatever liquid was being served, suggesting this may indeed have been wine that needed to be mixed with water. The forms of the containers though are very varied. At Bartlow 1834/I and Grange Road, jugs were used made of pottery and glass, and of glass and copper alloy respectively. At Stansted this part of the service was supplied by a glass flask and a copper-alloy amphorisk. Elsewhere it has to be suspected that glass bottles were being used. At both Bartlow 1840 and the grave excavated at Verulamium in 1989, a pair of glass bottles were present and there were no other candidates for any liquid container.

Two other interesting features emerge from the graves with dining equipment. One is the presence in the graves of joints of pork. Given the scarcity of pork on native sites normally, this too would appear to be yet another way in which the deceased were being marked out as adopting Roman ways. It is clear, however, that the Roman 'package' was not being bought wholesale in its entirety. In these graves utensils such as knives and spoons are rare. Even when they occur in graves where there would appear to be multiple place settings, they occur in numbers that suggest that it was not thought important that everyone should have their own. This is not the pattern that would be suspected from sets of silver plate from the heart of the empire.[49] It is also not the pattern that emerges from the soldiers at Castleford or from the soldiers and settlers at Colchester where

---

[48] Biddulph 2005.   [49] See p. 53.

spoons were found with some regularity on the pre-Boudican sites.[50] The native elite might have been prepared to accept many aspects of 'being Roman', but changing table manners and the actual act of conveying the food to the mouth may have been one step too far.

CONCLUSIONS

This examination of the eating habits in five broadly contemporary communities has shown how varied they were. Major differences can be observed between the immigrants and the natives, but equally there are differences within these communities. The inhabitants of Leadenhall Court and Castleford were eating different things and probably drinking in different ways. If the people living at Claydon Pike had been invited to dinner in the households of the native elite buried at Winchester and Bartlow, they would probably have thought both the food and the way it was served strange and alien. Equally though, they would probably have been just as uncomfortable dining at Orton Hall Farm.

The studies also show that the way in which the results of excavations are analysed and reported can have important consequences when we try to look at the wider, rather than site-specific, picture. How much more nuanced this chapter could have been if assemblages of the same type of thing had been quantified uniformly!

[50] Crummy 1983: 69 no. 2008; Crummy, N. in Crummy, P. 1992: 156 no. 535, 215 no. 124.

CHAPTER 18

Coming of age

INTRODUCTION

The previous chapter showed some of the different patterns of eating and drinking that can be identified during the first to second centuries. This chapter continues the story into the later second and third centuries, by which time much of Britain had been part of the empire for a century or more. It is during this period that the impact of belonging to this wider world can start to be seen more regularly on the rural sites where many of the native British population would have continued to live. Here we will explore first how the habits of the native population were changing, before going on to look at the evidence from particular types of activities being engaged in by both native and immigrant communities.

LEICESTER: A BRITISH TOWN

The lifestyles of the two urban communities described in the previous chapter were those of immigrants. The excavations at Causeway Lane, Leicester, provide an opportunity to look at how the British adapted to town life. Leicester (*Ratae Corieltavorum*) was the *civitas* capital of the Corieltavi. It had been a tribal centre prior to the conquest but did not acquire the formal trappings of a city such as a planned street layout and a forum until the second century.[1] Causeway Lane is situated in the north-west of the town, and the remains recovered included structures facing onto the road and backyards with rubbish pits and wells. It was excavated in 1991 with an extensive sampling and sieving programme which yielded good environmental evidence. The publication is of very high quality with well-quantified find assemblages.[2] Here we will concentrate on the

---

[1] Wacher 1995: 343–5.   [2] Connor and Buckley 1999.

evidence of the Phase 3 contexts, dating from the middle second to early third centuries.

Looking at the type of meat consumed is complicated during this phase because, in addition to food waste, the bone and horn debris from a tannery was deposited as the infill of a ditch. Ignoring this material, the division between the species is 50% cattle, 34% sheep and 16% pigs (based on a zonal count).[3] Allowing for the varying quantities of meat the species can provide, this probably reflects a primarily beef diet with approximately equal amounts of pork and lamb as alternatives. Compared with the quantities recovered from the late-first- to mid-second-century contexts on the site, there is an increase in the number of pig bones compared to those from sheep. Possibly this reflects an increasing acceptance of pig-meat products.

As ever, evidence of game consumption was very slight, and the principal type of poultry represented was the domestic fowl. The number of eggshell fragments recovered suggest that the consumption of hens' eggs was common, occasionally augmented by goose eggs.[4] The remains of fish were rare both at this period and during the rest of the Roman period. This was especially noticeable because occupation continued into the medieval period, and the much higher consumption of fish then is immediately apparent from the figures recorded.[5] It is possible that some of the small amount of fish consumed came in the form of salted fish products as the species list includes herring and mackerel. Unfortunately the amphora report does not differentiate the types recovered by phase, but in general those associated with *salaison* industries are poorly represented. They form only just over 1% by weight of the entire assemblage.[6] The population of Leicester, or at least the part of it living at Causeway Lane, do not appear to have developed a taste for fish, either salted or fresh.

The amphora assemblage in general shows that both olive oil and wine from a range of sources was reaching the site. The quantity of olive oil amphora fragments (*c.* 124 kg) looks impressive until they are put into context. The area of the site excavated was 1,875 m[2] and the figure represents the numbers recovered from at least a century or possibly two, depending on how late olive oil continued to arrive at the site. By contrast, at Leadenhall Court with its immigrant population, 107 kg of

---

[3] Gidney in Connor and Buckley 1999: Table 65 (total zones 2279).
[4] Gidney in Connor and Buckley 1999: Table 66; Boyer in Connor and Buckley 1999: 329–33.
[5] Nicholson in Connor and Buckley 1999: Table 74.
[6] Williams in Connor and Buckley 1999: Table 5.

olive oil amphora fragments were recovered from an excavation of less than half the size (*c.* 890 m²) and representing a time period of slightly under fifty years.[7] This pattern can be seen within other *civitas* capitals as well. The 1988 excavations at County Hall, Dorchester were approximately the same size as the Leadenhall Court ones, but only produced a total of 13.2 kg of olive oil amphora fragments.[8] It is always possible that people were acquiring their oil and wine in smaller quantities and bringing it home in other containers but, judged by the amphora evidence, the Britons who lived in towns appear to have used less olive oil and drunk wine much less commonly than those where the population was primarily of immigrant stock.

A process of change is apparent in the types of vessels being used. Those made of pottery and glass vessels are summarised according to the principal forms in Table 18.1. This shows that the proportion of jars in the assemblage falls after the mid-second century. In part this may be because there was a need for more tablewares, but it may also be because in Phase 3 Black Burnished ware (BB1) vessels started to be available. These were specialised cooking wares made in Dorset which were available not only as jars, but also as shallow dishes. The rise in the proportion of dishes from Phase 2 to Phase 5 reflects the increasing number of these that were in use. This hints that there may have been a diversification of cooking practices taking place, away from a primarily jar-based technique. Another change appears to be the greater need for mortaria in the later period compared to low levels of use in the earlier phases.

Some change might also be underway in the drinking-vessel assemblage. At Causeway Lane, pottery beakers always outnumbered pottery cups, but it is possible that the use of smaller-capacity drinking vessels was actually increasing as time progressed. The glass-vessel assemblage is small, but a marked increase of glass cups is apparent from the late second century onwards.

A broadening of the culinary horizons can certainly be seen in the Causeway Lane assemblage. The inhabitants might not have liked fish, but they were prepared to try lentils, flavour their dishes with coriander,[9] eat more pork and possibly bake as well as stew. It was not a 'Roman' lifestyle that was emerging, but it was certainly different from what was going on in much of the countryside.

---

[7] See p. 182; amphora data from Groves in Milne and Wardle 1996: Tables 7–9.
[8] Williams in Smith 1993: Table 15.
[9] Monckton in Connor and Buckley 1999: 353.

Table 18.1. *Principal pottery and glass-vessel types from contexts of Phases 2, 3 and 5 at Causeway Lane, Leicester (* indicates residual in this phase. PMB = pillar moulded bowl).*

| | | 2 | | 3 | | 5 | |
| | | Late 1st to mid-2nd century | | Mid-2nd to early 3rd century | | Late 2nd to mid-4th century | |
Phase		EVE	%	EVE	%	EVE	%
Pottery	Cup	7.26	6	4.33	8	8.56	5
	Beaker	11.57	10	8.98	16	23.21	13
	Flagon	7.94	7	4.53	8	18.65	10
	Bowl	17.03	14	7.88	14	23.92	13
	Dish	12.16	10	6.99	13	28.80	16
	Lid	2.66	2	2.16	4	2.88	2
	Jar	59.89	49	18.05	33	63.82	35
	Mortarium	2.61	2	1.76	3	10.50	6
	Total	*121.12*		*54.68*		*180.34*	
Glass	Drinking	0.20	—	0.80	—	2.00	—
	PMB	0.60	—	—	—	0.40*	—
	Bowl	0.40	—	—	—	0.20*	—
	Jug	0.42	—	0.14	—	0.84	—
	Jar	0.57	—	—	—	—	—
	Bottle	0.42	—	0.70	—	0.20	—
	Total	*2.61*	—	*1.64*	—	*3.64*	—

THE COUNTRYSIDE REVISITED

In the previous chapter the evidence from Claydon Pike for the first to early second century was examined. At some point during the first half of the second century, the site saw a major reorganisation of the landscape with rectilinear buildings and enclosures replacing everything that had gone before. The main aisled building had a tiled roof and painted walls internally. The change in the landscape was associated with major changes in lifestyle. People started to wear hob-nailed shoes, women started to wear their hair in Roman styles using hairpins. Furnishings were augmented by some luxurious items like a metal oil lamp. This phase of occupation (site Phase 3) lasted until the late third century, and the material associated with it can be used to see whether all these changes were matched by changes in eating and drinking.

The site at Parlington Hollins in West Yorkshire provides a useful comparison to Claydon Pike. Approximately one quarter of a hectare was

Table 18.2. *Principal pottery and glass-vessel types from Claydon Pike (Phase 3) and Parlington Hollins. Figures in brackets for Claydon Pike are the percentages of the forms present in Phase 2 as shown in Table 17.9 (*note the flagon category covers flagons at Claydon Pike and constricted neck jars which served a similar purpose at Parlington Hollins).*

		Claydon Pike		Parlington Hollins	
		EVE	%	EVE	%
Pottery	Beaker	3.6	2 (1)	0.16	2
	Cup	4.6	3 (2)	0.12	2
	Flagon*	3.4	2 (1)	0.74	10
	Tankard	3.9	3 (2)	—	—
	Bowl	17.3	11 (11)	0.40	6
	Dish	7.3	5 (1)	0.55	8
	Lid	2.1	1(<1)	—	—
	Jar	110.3	70 (82)	4.48	62
	Mortarium	4.4	3(<1)	0.77	11
	Total	*156.9*	—	7.22	—
Glass	Cup/Beaker	1.80	—	—	—
	Bowl	0.40	—	—	—
	Jug	1.42	—	—	—
	Flask	0.40	—	—	—
	Jar	0.36	—	—	—
	Bottle	1.12	—	—	—
	Total	*5.50*	—	—	—

dug in the mid-1990s in advance of road construction.[10] Being a recent excavation it had all the benefits of environmental sampling, but this generally only provides information about the grain consumed as bone does not survive well. This site also underwent a major transformation in the second century when rectilinear enclosures were laid out. There was at least one rectilinear building in the vicinity, judged by the roof tiles recovered, and it continued in occupation to the end of the third century.

It is instructive to look at the pottery and glass vessels first as the evidence from these is directly comparable, in a way that the animal bone is not. The assemblage from the Phase 3 contexts at Claydon Pike and the complete assemblage from Parlington Hollins is summarised in Table 18.2. The most notable feature is how small the assemblage from the West Yorkshire site is, despite the large area excavated. This, it has to be

[10] Holbrey and Burgess in Roberts *et al.* 2001: 83–105.

Table 18.3. *Animal bone from the principal domesticates from Period 3 contexts at Claydon Pike and Roman contexts at Parlington Hollins.*

	Claydon Pike		Parlington Hollins	
	NISP	%	NISP	%
Cattle	941	53	70	19
Sheep	682	38	289	77
Pig	168	9	15	4
Total	1,791	—	374	—

realised, is one of the more prolific sites in the area! This part of the country had not habitually used pottery during the later Iron Age. Figures such as these suggest that even people like those who lived here who did change some aspects of their life, continued to find little use for pottery vessels, even in the third century. Judged from the sooting on the vessels, dishes were being used to cook with as well as jars. Quite what the relatively large numbers of mortaria were being used for is unknown, but it seems highly unlikely that here they were being used in the Classical manner envisioned in Apicius's recipes. One is recorded as being burnt around the rim so use in some cooking, as opposed to preparation, process might be suspected. At Claydon Pike, pottery vessels were more central to cooking and eating. The second to third centuries saw a slightly increased demand for pottery tablewares and a variety of glass-vessel types became acceptable. A copper-alloy water jug probably also belongs to this phase of occupation. On the whole, however, the vessel assemblage continued to be dominated by jars, and does not show the type of diversity seen on contemporary urban sites.

Approximately equal quantities of mammal bone were found at Parlington Hollins and in the main domestic area at Claydon Pike (6345 and 6672 fragments respectively), but the poor preservation meant that only 9% could be identified to species at the former site, whereas 29% could be at the latter. This means that the Parlington Hollins data will probably under-represent young beasts and pigs whose bones are known not to survive well in adverse conditions. Even allowing for this, the data presented in Table 18.3 would suggest that sheep meat featured more strongly in the diet at Parlington Hollins than it did at Claydon Pike.

At Claydon Pike the overall distribution between the species remained much the same as it had been in Phase 2, but an interesting pattern arose when the distribution of the species across the site was considered. It was noticed that pig and domestic-fowl bones accounted for 60% of those associated with the main aisled building. In one well fill of this period, fowl and pig bones were also associated with a small amount of bone from roe deer and hare, which was otherwise very rare. It was thought that this might represent the debris from a single high-status meal. These observations open up two interesting possibilities. One is that different elements of the people living on the site were favouring different diets. The other is that, for special occasions, the meats selected were perceived to be of higher status. The combination seen in the well is very reminiscent of the debris from the senior officers' kitchen at Caerleon.[11] They will not have eaten like that all the time, but for a feast a more 'Romanised' cuisine was seen as appropriate. Perhaps it was at such occasions that the lamp and the water jug for the wine service were brought out. The amphorae suggest olive oil and Campanian wine were reaching the site during this phase. The quantities were small, so perhaps these too were special-occasion commodities. Certainly, for the lamp to have functioned, oil would have been needed, reminding us that not all olive oil was used for cooking.

One thing that both sites have in common is that in both cases the principal grain was wheat (emmer and spelt).[12] This is unexceptional at Claydon Pike, but barley would normally be expected in West Yorkshire. The choice of grain might be one additional way in which the inhabitants of Parlington Hollins marked themselves out from their neighbours.

These two sites demonstrate that rural Britain continued to be different from urban Britain, but equally there was no one rural way of life. The inhabitants of both these sites aspired towards things Roman as is demonstrated by the tiled roofs, but this did not result in the same way of doing things. Regional differences of habits continue to play a very important role; and the mere availability of new types of goods and consumables in an area does not mean that all communities will adopt them. The inhabitants of Parlington Hollins may have been regarded as dangerously modern by their neighbours who, because they found no use for much Romanised material culture, will have continued to live in an

---

[11] See p. 83.
[12] Young and Richardson in Roberts *et al.* 2001: 221 Table 44; Straker, Jones and Perry in Miles *et al.* forthcoming.

essentially late Iron Age way. This, of course, makes them relatively invisible to archaeology in this area.[13]

One intriguing feature of the data from both these sites relates to the question raised in Chapter 5 of whether or not a differentiated cuisine, with all the cultural stratification that implies, can be discerned within Roman Britain. Whilst one might expect to observe it in obviously Romanised sites, these two native rural sites also appear to be showing different facets of what might be expected of such a cuisine. The inhabitants of Parlington Hollins were definitely differentiating themselves in many ways, including what they were eating, from their neighbours, whilst at Claydon Pike the choice of what has regularly featured as elite dining ingredients for a special meal, suggests an awareness that different food was appropriate for different occasions.

AN OUTING TO THE BATHS

There is some evidence that certain places were associated with particular eating habits. The next two sections explore two of these cases. A visit to the baths in the Roman period was not just about getting clean. The larger ones provided opportunities to take exercise, get beauty and health treatment and to generally enjoy oneself. Seneca's letter complaining about the noise emanating from a public bath-house describes the type of people involved and, interestingly for our purposes, notes the cries of pastry cooks, sausage sellers, confectioners and other hawkers of refreshments.[14] Drains in bath-houses often provided traps for the detritus of activities carried out in them. Analysis of these assemblages show that the finds are precisely the sort that would be expected from the known activities that went on in the baths. Fragments from glass flasks used to hold the oil needed for cleaning the skin are numerous; whilst amongst the small finds the types of personal ornaments are precisely those most likely to be kept on when people aren't wearing many clothes. Many women lost the pins they were using to fasten their hair, whilst the steam clearly loosened the adhesive that held intaglios in finger-rings and many were washed away.[15] Given the evidence of these finds, it is reasonable to suppose that any evidence for food and drink in the drains will relate directly to what was being consumed during visits to the baths.

---

[13] See p. 170.
[14] *Epistulae Morales* 56 – quoted in Zienkiewicz 1986: 17.
[15] Cool *et al.* 1995: Table 138, 1642; Cool and Baxter 1999: 81, fig. 4.

In Britain the best place to study bath-house activity centres on the baths in the legionary fortress at Caerleon.[16] There a 28 m stretch of the drain from the *frigidarium* was found with its vaulted stone roof intact. The baths had been built in the 70s and silts and rubbish in the drain had built up to the early second century when the drain had been remodelled and enlarged. This had involved laying a new stone floor on those silts and replacing the roof at a higher level. Silt then continued to accumulate until *c.* AD 230 when the baths went out of use. Drain Group 1 material was sealed below the remodelled floor, and securely relates only to activities in the bath-house. Drain Group 4 material is from above the new floor and is dated to *c.* AD 160 – 230. It relates primarily to activities in the bath-house, but there is some evidence that unrelated rubbish was washed in after disuse and when the baths were being decommissioned in the later third century.

The excavations were completed in 1981 and a sieving programme retrieved the bones from small animals. Unfortunately the conditions in the drain had not resulted in any waterlogged or mineralised plant remains. This gap in the evidence can be plugged by reference to what was found in a sewer associated with the Church Street bath-house in the fortress at York. This was excavated in 1972–3, a time when a group of specialists in York were pioneering methods of acquiring environmental evidence, and one of the earliest in-depth environmental reports resulted from the excavations. The sewer is neither as well dated nor as undisturbed as the Caerleon drain deposit, but it does contain a similar range of small finds and glass vessels and will have been reflecting similar activities.[17]

The bone from the Caerleon drain makes it clear that food vendors specialised in finger food.[18] This can best be seen in the remains from Drain Group 1 which is dominated by chicken and sheep bones, the latter consisting in the main of rib and vertebra fragments indicative of the consumption of lamb or mutton chops. These often had knife cuts but they were also well chewed, a good indication of being held whilst eaten. Evidence for pork is much less common but again is indicative of snack food in the form of chops and trotters. Cuts like these continued to be consumed judged by the deposits accumulating during the later second to

[16] Zienkiewicz 1986.
[17] Site – Whitwell 1976; small finds – MacGregor, A. 1976; environmental evidence – Buckland 1976.
[18] O'Connor in Zienkiewicz 1986: 226–30.

third century, but during that time there was an increase in debris from the main meat-bearing bones. In part this might be due to contamination, but it could also indicate a growing taste for meat sliced off the bone.

Other snack foods available included shellfish. Mussels were consumed throughout the use of the baths, but oysters became more popular later on.[19] Mussel and oyster shells were also recovered from the York sewer with the latter being commonest.[20] There is some tantalisingly ambiguous evidence of the consumption of other seafood snacks at York. The remains of a number of immature fish of species typical of a riverine habitat close to tidal influences were recovered.[21] The specialist that studied them suggested these were young fish washed into the sewer when the River Ouse was in flood, and then trapped there; though he considered it interesting that the commonest species, the smelt, had penetrated that far inland. An alternative interpretation might be that these were the Roman equivalent of whitebait – a dish of very young small fish served deep-fried and eaten whole.[22] There is no record of such a dish being eaten in the Roman period, but it would fit the picture of fast food snacks that emerges from the animal bone and seashell deposits.

Drain deposits such as these are not the places where large amphora fragments are likely to accumulate, but the availability of amphora-shipped delicacies is indicated by the recovery of an olive stone at Caerleon and grape pips at York.[23] Seneca's reference to pastry cooks and confectionaries are a timely reminder that many items of food tend to be invisible archaeologically, though perhaps the seeds from strawberries, raspberries and blackberries found at York might hint of their presence. This might be the debris of raw fruit, but all would make good tarts. Equally, though the poppy seeds found there might have had a medicinal purpose as doctors were known to practise in baths, they could also have been the debris from seed-encrusted cakes and buns.[24]

The heat of the baths and the taking of exercise, not to mention the consumption of all the snacks, would undoubtedly have given people a thirst. The number of beaker fragments recovered in the drain deposits at Caerleon certainly underlines the fact that liquid was being consumed there.[25] What was in them, unfortunately, is unknown.

[19] Zienkiewicz 1986: 222 Table 1.   [20] Rackham in Buckland 1976: Table 5.
[21] Wheeler in Buckland 1976: 33–4.   [22] Davidson 1999: 846.
[23] Zienkiewicz 1986: 224; Greig in Buckland 1976: 24.
[24] Greig in Buckland 1976: Table 2.   [25] Greep in Zienkiewicz 1986: fig. 14.

The picture presented of the baths as a place to indulge in fast food snacks has been derived from two military bath-houses because they are the two sites with the best-preserved drain deposits. It is likely that similar practices went on in public bath-houses in the towns, and even sometimes in domestic baths. The taste for a saucer of shell fish to nibble whilst relaxing after a bath was certainly not restricted to the legionaries and their families. It can also be seen at the Halstock villa in Dorset, where a group of forty-seven cockles were found in the ditch outside the bath-house, reminiscent of the debris of a single snack.[26] It is possible that the type of food eaten at bath-houses might have cut across normal consumption patterns, because in the public bath-houses you would have been buying it in. The preference for lamb or mutton chops at the Caerleon bath-house, for example, is not one seen in the contemporary barracks where people cooked for themselves.

WORSHIPPING MERCURY AND MITHRAS

The role of food and drink within religious ceremonies varied according to the deity being worshipped. In some a communal meal was central, in others there is more ambiguity as to what happened to the sacrificed animals. Here the rites surrounding two known gods will be explored; one with a large temple complex at Uley in rural Gloucestershire who probably attracted predominantly native worshippers, the other outside the fort of Carrawburgh on Hadrian's Wall with a military congregation.

Part of the temple complex at Uley was excavated between 1977 and 1979.[27] Religious activity on the hilltop started early in the first century AD, possibly focusing on a sacred grove, and involving the construction of palisades and a timber shrine. In the second century a masonry Romano-Celtic temple was built surrounded by other masonry buildings, presumably for the use of the priesthood and worshippers. This continued in use with various modifications until the early fifth century, by which time all the buildings had been demolished. During the Roman period the god being worshipped was clearly Mercury. The variety of epigraphic evidence makes it clear that though the worshippers expressed themselves using Latin, none had the *tria nomina* of the Roman citizen. Their names were either Celtic or derived from Roman *cognomina*,[28] and it seems likely that this was a British congregation.

---

[26] Winder 1992: 157.   [27] Woodward and Leach 1993.
[28] Tomlin in Woodward and Leach 1993: 117.

One of the most remarkable features of the discoveries at Uley was the animal bone assemblage consisting of nearly a quarter of a million fragments. These overwhelmingly belonged to sheep or goats. Most unusually on a British site, many goats could be identified and, apart from the earliest phase of religious activity, they outnumbered sheep. Similarly the numbers of domestic fowl after the initial phase were very high. Given that the goat and the cock are attributes of Mercury, it seems very reasonable to conclude that the unusual composition of the animal bone assemblage is the direct result of these two animals being sacrificed. The report on this material by Bruce Levitan is exemplary, and the reader is warmly recommended to consult it in its entirety.[29] Here I will concentrate on the evidence associated with the second and third centuries (site Phase 4), as it is possible to map patterns that cast light on how sacrificial beasts were regarded.

In Phase 4 parts of three buildings were excavated in addition to the temple itself (see fig. 18.1), and animal bones were associated with two of them; Structure X to the north and Structure IV to the south. These are summarised in Table 18.4.

As can be seen, there were differences between the two groups. That from Structure IV was overwhelmingly dominated by ovicaprids, and amongst them goats were in the majority. Structure X had a more mixed range of animals and a more equal division between the sheep and goats. When other aspects of the bones were considered, it could be seen that the differences between the two went further. A feature of the ovicaprine bones from Uley, much commented on in the report, was the very low level of butchery marks seen on them. This was much lower than is normally seen in a domestic assemblage. The assemblages from the structures showed markedly different rates. In Structure IV less than 1% of the bones had evidence of butchery. In Structure X, by contrast, 8% showed butchery. Different parts of the carcase dominated in the different structures as well. In Structure IV skulls and lower-limb bones were much more numerous than they were in Structure X.

The evidence of the more mixed species, the butchery marks and the types of bones present suggests that Structure X may represent the debris from animals that were being eaten. The remains in Structure IV in contrast suggest either that the animals were not being eaten or, if they were, they were being cooked in a different way. Spit-roasting whole would be a

---

[29] Levitan in Woodward and Leach 1993: 257–301.

Figure 18.1. The Uley temple complex. (After Woodward and Leach 1993.) Structure X lay below the later Building IX.

Table 18.4. *Animal bones from Phase 4 contexts at Uley (number of identified bones).*

	Building IV		Building X	
	Number	%	Number	%
Sheep/goat	960	72	73	13
Cattle	22	2	103	19
Pig	24	2	103	19
Domestic fowl	322	24	273	49
Total	1,328	100	552	100
Sheep : goat ratio	95 : 204		59 : 54	

possibility. A difference in function between the two buildings is also hinted at in the pottery report. Though the data are not presented in a way that can be properly examined, it is noted in passing that Structure IV has relatively little pottery, whilst Structure X is one of the buildings with an essentially domestic assemblage.[30] This too might suggest that cooking and eating was being carried out in Structure X but not in Structure IV.

Where it could be established, the age and sex of the bones from Structure IV would support the idea that these were sacrificial animals. The ovicaprids were predominantly young and male. The ages of the domestic fowl were more mixed, but again males were in the majority. The evidence from these two structures points to sacrificial animals being regarded in a different light from ones it was permissible to eat. If they were eaten, they would certainly have been cooked differently. The presence of goats in Structure X makes it clear that goat meat and domestic fowl were not excluded from ordinary meal preparation, so it must have been something special about these particular animals that set them apart.

Whilst feasting may well have played a part in the festivals held at Uley in the summer, there is no evidence that it played a central part in the worship of the god in the same way that it did in the worship of Mithras. He was a saviour god whose adherents looked to a life after death and were initiated into various grades of the mysteries. It is known that a meal was an important part of the gatherings because early Christian writers inveighed against it as a devilish imitation of their own ritual meals.[31]

[30] Woodward and Leach 1993: 245, 248.   [31] Clauss 2000: 108–13.

Figure 18.2. The *mithraeum* at Carrawburgh. (After Richmond and Gillam 1951.)

In Britain his worshippers were overwhelmingly drawn from the Roman army.[32]

He was worshipped in *mithraea* and these were of a very distinctive form with benches down either side which would have allowed the worshippers to recline whilst eating. The best-preserved temple in Britain was that found outside the fort of Carrawburgh. It was discovered in 1949 when a dry summer meant that the peat that had engulfed it shrank to reveal the tops of altars still *in situ*. It was dug by the leading Romano-British archaeologist of those days and published with admirable promptness,[33] but of course this was a considerable time before the development of environmental archaeology. The waterlogged conditions of the site would have been an ideal environment for the preservation of plant remains, but this was an opportunity lost. The animal bones do provide an insight into the meals consumed there.[34]

The *mithraeum* was built and used in the third century and underwent various alterations whilst always maintaining the same basic plan (fig. 18.2). It would have attracted senior members of the garrison to worship there as all three altars recovered were dedicated by the commanding officers of the unit.[35] The congregation can never have been very

[32] Henig 1984: 97–109. [33] Richmond and Gillam 1951.
[34] Fraser in Richmond and Gillam 1951: 89–90. [35] RIB nos. 1544–6.

large as the building is small measuring only *c.* 4.9 by 6.7 metres internally in its first phase, though later extended to an internal length of 11 metres. Meals appear to have been cooked in the building. A hearth was present in the anteroom from the enlargement onwards and sooted cooking vessels are associated with the structure from the earliest phase. Animal bones were associated with various phases of the second and third *mithraea*. In the first and third phases of Mithraeum II, the animal bone from the anteroom where the food may have been prepared suggests primarily a liking for pork and some lamb. Beef is much rarer. It is noticeable that all the animals represented were young. A broadly similar pattern was found amongst the bones found incorporated into the floor levels of the nave. In the third phase and in the floor of the final *mithraeum* they came from pigs and sheep. In both cases pig bones were most numerous and again the beasts were generally juvenile. In the second phase, bones of domestic fowl were recovered from the nave floor.

A similar picture of the selection of domestic fowl together with young pigs and sheep as suitable for Mithraic feasts emerges from the study of the copious remains deposited in pits outside the *mithraeum* at Tienen in Belgium, thought to have arisen from a single very large event in the mid-third century.[36] There, only cocks appeared to have been consumed, possibly because of the association of cockerels with the dawn, and of Mithras with the sun. The sex of the domestic fowl on the nave floor at the Carrawburgh *mithraeum* is not commented on, but bones from cocks were present there incorporated into the wattle revetments which fronted the benches.[37]

Just as the choice of meats was different from that which would normally have been consumed within the fortress, so too was the pottery assemblage. It was dominated by pottery beakers to a much greater extent than is normal from military sites in the third century.[38] This evidence of the drinking activities that went on as part of the worship of Mithras is also evident in the pottery assemblage from the contemporary *mithraeum* at the fort at Rudchester where beakers were numerous.[39]

What becomes apparent from looking at the animal bones associated with the worship of two very different gods by two entirely different communities, is that there may have been something in common. Food for the god, or food eaten in the company of the god, appears to be different from that eaten under normal circumstances. The animal for

---

[36] Lentacker *et al.* 2004.
[37] Platt in Richmond and Gillam 1951: 91.
[38] Evans 1993: 114 Appendix 1.
[39] Gillam and MacIvor 1954: 216.

sacrifice and/or consumption varied according to the deity, but the unifying factor was that juvenile or sub-adult animals were preferred. This is true not just at these two sites, but at other temple sites where the animal bones have been examined in detail such as at Harlow and Chelmsford.[40] A variety of reasons could be suggested for this. Perhaps they tasted better and were regarded as delicacies; perhaps if you were offering something to a god it wasn't worth expending the resources to raise the beast to adulthood. Another possibility may be that the animal needed to be unblemished to be a suitable offering, and young beasts provided the best opportunity of this. In the case of the Uley beasts, it was certainly noted that they were fit and healthy.[41]

It would be interesting to pursue the age and state of health of the animals from temple sites, but currently there is relatively little data available.[42] If animals for the gods did have to be unblemished, then it would open up an interesting vista on how the population of Roman Britain regarded their world. It is unlikely that such a belief would have existed in isolation, and not have been part of an outlook that encompassed other aspects of life. Douglas has shown how the rules laid down in Leviticus on how Jews should live their lives, including all the dietary prohibitions, stemmed from the belief that things had to be complete. The injunction that animals for sacrifice had to be unblemished was just one part of this.[43] Plainly the population of Roman Britain was not Jewish, and even if they too thought sacrificial animals had to be unblemished, it need not have meant that they had such strict dietary and other rules. It would, though, suggest that concepts of purity and taboo were active, and might go some way to explaining why certain things like game were so rarely eaten.

FOOD AND DRINK FOR THE DEAD AT BROUGHAM

The cemetery at Brougham provides an opportunity to examine what elements of food and drink were though necessary for different parts of a military community in the third century. The site was excavated in 1966 and 1967 in advance of road building, but the archive was not analysed

---

[40] Legge and Dorrington in France and Gobel 1985: 127; Luff in Turner 1999: Table 142 (Phase IV data).
[41] Levitan in Woodward and Leach 1993: 301.
[42] Subsequent to writing this a very useful survey of just such data has been published – King 2005.
[43] Douglas 1966: 42–58.

and published for nearly forty years.[44] The date of the excavation means that no sampling procedures were in place to acquire the carbonised plant remains that were undoubtedly present. There were also problems in that some elements of the archive had gone missing in the time between excavation and analysis. The data are flawed, but the analysis has revealed that what remains are internally consistent and tell quite a remarkable story.

The cemetery lies outside the fort and was in use during the period *c.* AD 220 to 300. Both this and the military equipment found in the burials and other deposits indicate that it was soldiers and their families that were buried there. The unit in garrison was a *numerus,* a cavalry unit recruited from the tribes on the empire's border. Various strands of evidence from the cemetery itself including epigraphy, the types of objects found and some burial practices strongly suggest that this unit came from territory bordering the Danubian provinces centred on modern-day Hungary. There can be no doubt that this was an immigrant community, but it would probably have been regarded as alien not just by the local British community, but also by the soldiers in the neighbouring forts.

The burial rite was cremation and the deceased were given items at two stages of the funeral. There were pyre goods burnt with the body and vessels placed with the burnt remains in the formal burial. By looking at the associations between the age and sex of the deceased, and the goods that were associated with them, it was found that different items were thought appropriate for different people.

With regard to food items, one of the most interesting observations is who had joints of meat placed on their pyres. The burnt animal bones could be divided into two categories; those where sufficient fragments from a range of the different parts of the skeleton survived to suggest the entire animal had been placed on the pyre, and those where the fragments were limited to a particular part such as a leg, which suggested that they had come from a joint. The whole carcases included three horses, one cow, two sheep and one dog. As neither horses nor dogs are normally regarded as meat sources, it seems likely that the animals burnt entire may have served a purpose other than food provision, such as sacrifice. Attention will focus here on the associations of the meat joints. These are summarised in Table 18.5 for those deposits which contained the remains of a single individual who could be aged.

---

[44] Cool 2004b; animal bone – Bond and Worley in Cool 2004b: 311–31.

Table 18.5. *The pyre good meat-bone associations for burials at Brougham.*

	Sheep	Bird	Cattle	Pig	Total deposits
Adult	9	3	2	—	73
Male	7	3	—	1	24
Female	4	7	2	—	27
Immature	2	—	—	—	23
Infant	—	1	—	—	15
Total	22	14	4	1	162

The first surprising feature of this table is the dominance of sheep. Elsewhere in the area, beef was the main meat in urban and military contexts. This can be seen from the bone assemblages associated with a building occupied in the second to third century in Carlisle, some 35 km to the north, and that associated with third- to mid-fourth-century granaries in the fort at Birdoswald, a further 25 km along Hadrian's Wall. Both were dominated by cattle bone, ovicaprid bones were much scarcer, while pig bones were present at the military site but absent in the small urban assemblage.[45] The Brougham community, however, felt sheep meat was the most appropriate thing to place on the pyre. Pork was surprisingly rare. There is evidence of it on one pyre and in one burial where an unburnt shoulder of pork was placed on a dish in the grave. In both cases the association was with an adult male of high status. The bird bones were mainly from small domestic fowl, though goose was also present. Whether they were placed on the pyre as food, or were there for a ritual purpose,[46] is unclear.

The second striking feature of Table 18.5 is the rarity of any evidence for meat on the pyres of people younger than eighteen. A domestic fowl was present on the pyre of an infant, but this could have been present as a sacrifice. Two immature individuals (five–eighteen years) had joints of sheep meat but otherwise this category of individuals had no meat remains despite being well represented in the cemetery. It can be shown using statistical significance tests that this pattern would not have come about by chance.[47] In this community meat, or at least meat on the bone, was not considered an appropriate pyre good for young people. It is here

---

[45] Rackham in McCarthy 1990: Table 30 Period 9; Izard in Wilmott 1997: Table 33.
[46] See p. 101.   [47] Baxter in Cool 2004b: 469.

that the absence of any environmental remains is particularly to be lamented as it might be that vegetable-based foods such as fruit and grain were thought appropriate for the young people.

Some interesting attitudes to vessels also emerge, of which two have direct relevance to eating and drinking practices. In this community, glass drinking vessels were seen as the preserve of adult males and were placed in their graves. Several adult females had large copper-alloy buckets of the type used to mix wine.[48] Though it seems dreadfully stereotypical to suggest it, the data would support the view that it was woman's work to prepare alcoholic beverages, and man's role to drink them. In the previous chapter the role of samian cups was questioned, and it was suggested that they were probably also used as serving bowls. This seems unequivocal at Brougham where samian cups are only ever found in graves where the individual is younger than eight. Where it was possible to age the children closely, one was two to three years and another three to four. It would seem much more likely in these circumstances that they should be regarded as feeding dishes for toddlers rather than drinking vessels.

The evidence from Brougham is difficult to interpret at present because it is unclear to what extent the attitudes expressed in their burial rites are specific to this community or were more widely shared. The evidence at present would suggest they may be very community-specific, as certainly their burial ritual appears very unlike that practised at the same time by the garrison who occupied the fort to the south.[49] Some attitudes seem to be more widely shared such as the association of pork with high rank, but whether the taste for lamb was driven by ethnicity or funerary ritual is unknown. What the analysis did show was that various vessel types were regarded as age and gender specific. Analysis of more cemetery assemblages, where there is good information about the age and sex of the deceased, might prove to be very informative about dining practice.

CONCLUSIONS

The cases presented in this chapter have shown that deep-seated regional differences persisted well into Roman period and that even in the third century Britain was far from sharing a common cuisine or attitude to food. They have also shown that different events, be they secular or religious, could cut across normal eating habits providing people with

---

[48] See page 136 and fig. 15.2 no. 3.   [49] Lambert 1996.

the opportunity to taste different foods. Comparing the food associated with these 'special events' with that consumed by the community normally has the potential to cast light on wider attitudes to the world. Why, for example, is there a regular association of the consumption of young animals with religious events? Was it just that they were tastier, or did the gods demand unblemished beasts, and more widely perhaps, unblemished behaviour by their worshippers in certain matters?

CHAPTER 19

A different world

INTRODUCTION

The third century had been a difficult time for many parts of the empire. A succession of short-lived emperors had fought for control. There was pressure around its borders as barbarian tribes clamoured to be admitted, with incursions into areas where everyone had thought themselves safe for centuries. Britain had been peripheral to much of this turmoil, though Saxon raiding of the east and southern coasts was a problem. The political chaos of the third century was brought under a semblance of control by the reforms of Diocletian who came to power in AD 284. The empire that emerged from these in the fourth century was a very different place than that of the empire of the first and second centuries.

In continental scholarship there is a tradition of studying the world of late antiquity as a period that extends from the late third century into the seventh century. On this side of the Channel there is not this tradition as Roman Britain was long thought to end in AD 410 after the army had left Britain in AD 407.[1] What happened then is a very big question. It sometimes seems that there are as many answers as there are authors prepared to write books and papers on the end of Roman Britain, and they are legion. People tend to divide into two camps. There are those that consider the Roman way of life ended in the early fifth century, and what came after is somebody else's problem as it is certainly nothing to do with Roman Britain. Then there are those that think life continued and evolved, and that the AD 410 divide is an artificial construct. I belong to the latter tendency, and the reader should be aware that some of what they are now going to read would be disputed by those who take the other view.[2]

---

[1] For brief summary see Frere 1987: 357–8.   [2] See, for example, Esmonde Cleary 2000: 91.

Traditionally, major changes are attributed to the early fifth century including the sudden collapse of the pottery industries.[3] If that was indeed the case, it would have had major implications on how people cooked and ate. Pottery had become central to these processes even in many areas which had been aceramic prior to the Roman invasion. Understanding what happened to the vessel assemblages at the end of the fourth century is so central to the topic of this book, that much of this chapter will be taken up by a consideration of it, following a section on the dating problems we are faced with. Sites where we can study the eating habits of a community at the end of the fourth century, without the patterns being blurred by problems of residuality and redeposition, are rare, but the opportunity will be taken to explore one where this can be done. Finally the possible impact of Christianity on the diet of the population will be considered.

DATING PROBLEMS

As was outlined in Chapter 1, the foundations underpinning our ability to date most contexts derives from coinage. The understanding of the dates of pottery types depends on repeated associations in independently dated contexts and their stratigraphic relationships. Occasionally the dating is provided by dendrochronology or even, very rarely, by writing tablets where the date has been considerately included; but in essence pottery provides the backbone of dating.

Coinage was supplied by the state for two purposes: to pay the army and to provide a medium by which people could pay taxes. Gold and silver coins went to the army as pay, and returned to the state as taxes. Copper-alloy coinage was the small change that oiled the wheels of this circulation. With the withdrawal of the army in AD 407 there would have been no point in supplying either type of coinage to Britain. Site finds make it clear that the supply must have generally ceased in the AD 395–402 period, because coinage issued after that date is rare. This reflects the fact that the production of the western mints was much reduced after that date, and coins later than AD 402 are uncommon everywhere.[4] In some areas the supply seems to cease even before that. In the north-east, for example, it has been noted that coinage after AD 388 is rare.[5]

---

[3] Millett 1990: 225–6.   [4] Guest 2005: 28.   [5] Brigstock 2000: 35.

The consequence of this is that there is no independent yardstick against which to measure the date of a context or a new pottery type. Coins only ever provide a *terminus post quem*, and may often give too early a date but the dating of pottery and other types of items does not rely on a single coin; it will be a composite of many associations. These will highlight the anomolous early coins. From the end of the fourth century, this is no longer possible as no new coinage enters the coin pool. That the existing coinage continued to circulate, and presumably be used in transactions well into the fifth century, is suggested by at least two factors. The copper-alloy coinage of Theodosius (AD 375–95) often shows considerable wear,[6] and the edges of silver *siliquae* were carefully clipped to maintain the appearance of the coin whilst acquiring new bullion, to make new coins that imitated the existing ones.[7] So, contexts and associations that appear respectably late fourth century might well be several decades later. With this in mind we shall now explore vessel use in the fourth to fifth century.

VESSELS IN THE FOURTH CENTURY AND LATER

The best way to start to explore what sort of vessels people felt the need of is to compare assemblages of this period with those of the earlier centuries. Glass vessels show the changes that occurred particularly clearly. Table 19.1 shows dated assemblages that have been quantified according to form. Flasks and unguent bottles are not considered here as there is good evidence that many would have been connected with toilet regimes rather than being associated with eating and drinking.

In this table cups, bowls and jugs may be considered as tablewares whilst jars and bottles were more likely to have been used as containers. As can be seen, there are changes in the fourth-century assemblages. Jar forms are absent and the bottles form a lower proportion of the assemblage than they did earlier. Large tables of data like this can be a daunting prospect to interpret, and what the figures are telling us becomes much more obvious when the plots resulting from a correspondence analysis (CA) of the data are inspected (fig. 19.1). This is a very useful technique for dealing with this type of data, and for more details about it the reader is referred to the references given below.[8] Here all that is needed

---

[6] Brigstock 2000: 35.   [7] Guest 2005: 110–5.

[8] Treatments designed for archaeologists are Baxter 1994: 100–39; Shennan 1997: 308–41 and Baxter 2003: 136–46. See also Cool and Baxter 1999; 2002.

Table 19.1. *Glass-vessel assemblages of various dates (see column 1 for approximate date ranges) quantified according to form (EVE measures). The labelling used in fig.19.1 is shown italicised in brackets in Column 1.*

Site z	Cup	Bowl	Jug	Jar	Bottle	Total
London 75–90 (*1*)	7.60	4.20	3.64	0.20	2.52	18.16
Gloucester 71–100 (*1*)	3.40	2.40	1.40	0.36	4.55	12.11
Castleford 70–100 (*1*)	9.20	5.60	3.00	1.80	5.75	25.35
Carlisle 71–105 (*1*)	2.80	5.40	1.26	0.38	7.28	17.12
Chester 75–120 (*1*)	4.00	3.52	1.54	0.69	3.78	13.53
York 71–120 (*1*)	6.40	6.00	0.84	1.44	3.08	17.76
Colchester 65–150 (*1*)	9.20	5.60	3.00	1.80	5.75	25.35
Dorchester 75–150 (*1*)	3.60	1.20	1.42	1.43	2.52	10.17
Wroxeter 80–150 (*1*)	5.20	2.13	2.70	0.57	4.48	15.08
Verulamium 150–60 (*2*)	5.00	1.20	1.10	0.34	2.53	10.17
Pentre Farm 120–200 (*2*)	5.80	1.40	0.49	0	1.96	9.65
Catterick 150–250 (*2*)	5.40	0.54	0.56	0.20	3.64	10.34
Lincoln 160–230 (*2*)	4.20	0.40	1.37	0.40	2.31	8.68
York 175–250 (*2*)	4.20	1.40	1.12	0.36	2.31	9.39
York 160–280 (*2*)	7.20	0	0.28	0.34	1.68	9.50
Caister 300–400+ (*4*)	25.80	0.80	0.70	0	1.84	29.14
Colchester 300–400+ (*4*)	9.20	3.20	1.44	0	0.61	14.45
Dorchester 300–400+ (*4*)	5.00	2.80	0.84	0	1.36	10.00
Stanwick 300–400+ (*4*)	8.73	1.80	1.47	0	1.45	13.45
Towcester 300–400+ (*4*)	9.40	0	1.18	0	1.27	11.85
Winchester 300–400+ (*4*)	10.20	2.00	1.26	0	1.56	15.02
Wroxeter 300–400+ (*4*)	24.20	2.60	4.13	0	2.32	33.25
York 300–400+ (*4*)	10.00	3.00	0.70	0	0.98	14.68

is to explain that the technique produces, amongst other things, two plots, one describing the rows, the other the columns which can be shown separately or superimposed. The row plot shows the assemblages that have relatively similar proportions of forms in the same area of the plot. The column plot shows the relationship of the forms according to the proportions found in the different assemblages. The plots should be read in relation to the origin (the point where the axes cross). A group of sites in one area of the assemblage (row) plot will generally have a more than usually high proportion of the forms which are plotted in the same position, relative to the origin, on the form (column) plot.

Fig. 19.1 shows that the compositions of the assemblages change markedly with time. The first- to second-century assemblages are much more varied than the fourth-century ones, having a higher proportion of the container forms. The fourth-century assemblages are dominated by drinking vessels

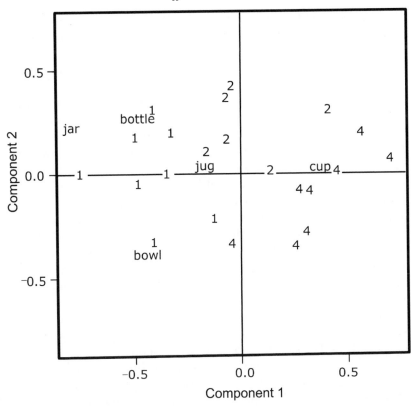

Figure 19.1. Correspondence analysis plot showing the change of glass-vessel assemblage compositions with time. (Date from Table 19.1: for explanation, see text.)

almost to the exclusion of everything else. It is clear that, by the fourth century in Britain, glass was regarded primarily as a medium appropriate to drink out of. Even glass flasks for toiletries become much less common. The interesting feature of fig. 19.1 is that the move towards glass being used primarily for drinking vessels starts early. The second- to third-century assemblages are positioned between the early and late ones, and at least one of these (York AD 160–280) has an assemblage very similar to a fourth-century one presumably reflecting the higher proportion of third-century material in it.

The study from which these assemblages have been extracted was able to show that the types of vessels in use also varied according to the type of site, its location and other factors, but the dominant influence was always the period it was derived from.[9] At different times people clearly had very different uses for glass vessels, and what happens in the later fourth to fifth century can clearly be seen as a continuum of this. It is possible to isolate a number of assemblages that appear to date to the very late fourth century and into the fifth century.[10] What can be seen in them is that the closed forms such as jugs and bottles become even scarcer than they were earlier in the century, and the concentration of forms that could be drunk out of is even more pronounced. In the light of this, the fact that the glass industries of the south-east of England were producing a very distinctive form of glass beaker in the later fifth and sixth centuries comes as no surprise.[11] This is normally seen as an Anglo-Saxon form, but were we in Britain to embrace the concept of the late antique, it would be seen as the natural development of the late Roman industries. Certainly the 'Anglo-Saxon' use of glass in the fifth and sixth centuries continues the pattern that had been developing in Britain from the third century, rather than that seen in the continental 'homelands'. It has been noted by the leading expert in the field that whereas bottles were a fairly common type in France and the Rhineland during the fifth and sixth centuries, they were not at all popular in England.[12] Viewed from the Roman side of the great divide of AD 410, this too comes as no surprise.

Why was there this change? The evidence at Brougham indicated that glass drinking vessels were reserved for adult males.[13] The association of glass drinking vessels and the elite is also seen beyond the frontiers of the province. In the later second and third centuries it is glass drinking cups rather than any other sort of glass vessel that are occasionally found on elite sites in the Highlands of Scotland, on the Shetland and Orkney Islands and even at Tara in Ireland.[14] Drinking out of glass may have served as a mark of distinction in the later Roman period in some communities. Perhaps what was important was the display element. The colour of the drink would be clearly visible, and might even have been enhanced by the glass. Fourth-century glass was a greenish colourless shade with many tiny bubbles, and vessels were thin-walled. The overall effect would have been a glass that shimmered, catching any light.

From the point of view of someone familiar with the patterns of use of glass vessels from the Roman to Anglo-Saxon periods, the normal model

---

[9] Cool and Baxter 1999.   [10] Cool 1995: 13.
[11] Kempston beakers – see Evison 2000: 62.   [12] Evison 2000: 65.
[13] See p. 219.   [14] Cool 2003: 142.

of the sudden collapse of the pottery industries in the early fifth century has always appeared curious. Did people really suddenly stop cooking and eating in the manner that had been habitual to them for generations? What sort of cataclysmic event could have triggered such an abrupt change? As discussed in earlier chapters, in some areas it took a century or more for people to change their habits in response to the greater availability of things that followed the conquest, and some never did. When the model of the transition from the Roman to the Anglo-Saxon world was one of marauding invaders raping and killing most people who they came into contact with and enslaving the others, the collapse of the pottery industries was explicable. Most people would not subscribe to such a model now, so where does the explanation lie? Some people have argued that the disappearance of the industries is because they were embedded in a monetised economy with the skill concentrated amongst a relatively small group of people. With the cessation of coinage use, they could no longer survive, and pots ceased to be made.[15] Pots to cook in, however, are not so many optional fripperies to be easily discarded. Whole new skills would have to be learnt. Did the change really happen so abruptly?

It is worth exploring whether the changes in pottery use had its origins at a much earlier period, as with the glass. There are hints that this may have been the case, as it has long been observed that the second half of the fourth century sees a decrease in the overall number of different pottery forms in use.[16] This can be seen very well when the pottery from York is examined. Occupation started there in the early 70s and continued well into the fifth century at least. Many excavations have been carried out both in the fort and *colonia* and the pottery from them is available in an estimable study.[17] As part of this a set of ceramic phases was developed together with a type series. Table 19.2 is derived from this and includes all the forms that had sufficient examples to allow a date range to be assigned to them. Samian pottery and mortaria were treated as special cases and cannot be tabulated in the same way and so are excluded. With the exception of the samian vessels, it probably includes all the main types that the inhabitants had a use for. It was explicitly commented that 'the overall number of mortaria used in York was very low',[18] so the absence of mortaria from the table is not important. They can be imagined as having a small but consistent presence throughout the period. The absence of

---

[15] Evans, J. 2000: 41. [16] Fulford 1979: 121.
[17] Monaghan 1997. [18] Monaghan 1997: 931.

Table 19.2. *The principal pottery vessel forms in use in Roman York excluding those made in samian pottery and mortaria.*

Date	Beaker	Cup	Flagon	Platter	Dish	Bowl	Jar	Lid	Total
1A – 71–100	1	1	4	1	—	2	4	—	13
1B – 100–120	4	1	3	—	—	4	4	1	17
2A – 120–60	4	1	4	2	3	7	4	3	28
2B – 160–200	7	3	6	3	4	6	10	4	43
3A – 200–225	9	2	4	1	3	3	7	2	31
3B – 225–80	7	2	1	1	4	2	6	—	23
4A – 280–360	2	—	2	—	3	1	7	—	15
4B – 360–410	1	—	2	1	3	5	5	—	17
4C – 410+	—	—	—	—	1	—	2	—	3
Total	35	10	26	9	21	30	49	10	190

samian vessels distorts the picture more. Were they to be included the numbers for the cup, platter, dish and bowl categories would have been increased by a small number in all ceramic phases up to about Ceramic Phase 3A.

The widest range of forms available was in the second and early third centuries. The figures for Ceramic Phase 2A are possibly lower than might be expected, as this period was a very quiet one at York with much of the garrison away. The decline in the range of forms available starts in the third century and, had it been possible to include the samian forms in the table, the decline would have been even more noticeable. It is not just that there would have been less choice within forms. Some, like lids and cups, just disappear, whilst others such as flagons and platters become much rarer. The disappearance of cups may be because glass was increasingly favoured for small-capacity drinking vessels,[19] but the decline in other types is not compensated by similar vessels in other materials. Glass and small-find assemblages, for example, do not show any balancing increase in fragments from jugs.

A correspondence analysis of the table (Fig. 19.2) again shows that the assemblage composition is very dependent on the period. One feature of CA is that it is possible sometimes to use it to recover chronological pattern, as the points frequently occur in a horseshoe pattern that can be read in order.[20] On the plot, the known chronological order is almost

---

[19] See p. 149.   [20] Baxter 1994: 118–23; 2003: 137–8.

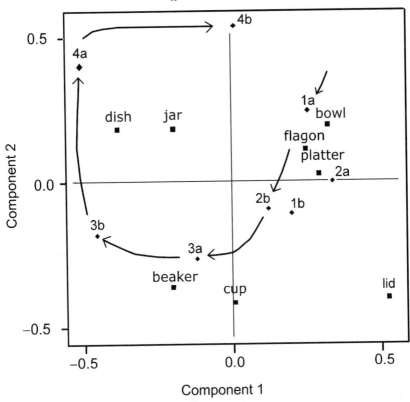

Figure 19.2. Correspondence analysis plot showing the changes in pottery vessels available at York with time. Note the phases plotting in sequence shown by the arrowed line. (Data from Table 19.2.)

precisely picked up by the changing proportions of the different forms present. Only the positions of the points for Ceramic Phases 1B and 2A are inverted. A comparison of the two plots makes it clear that whereas the early periods are characterised by tableware forms, the later ones are characterised by jars and dishes, and so are cooking orientated. As with the glass, change in the fifth century does not come suddenly to an unchanging suite of vessels, but could be looked on as having its origins much earlier.

The precise pattern of change is not the same in all areas,[21] but it is not just in the north that jars increasingly dominate the pottery assemblages

[21] Compare Evans 1993 and Millett 1979.

towards the end of the fourth century. At the Great Holts Farm villa near Chelmsford, a number of pottery assemblages of very late fourth- to fifth-century date were recovered.[22] In these (measured by EVEs) 60% of the assemblage consisted of jars followed by 24% dishes, 9% bowls and just over 1% mortaria. Beakers and flagons made up a mere 6% of the assemblage. It could be argued that this is a continuation of the rural patterns discussed in Chapters 17 and 18 where rural sites often seem to have a less varied and smaller tableware range. Finding late fourth-century urban assemblages where residuality is not a problem is difficult, but where it can be done a similar pattern often emerges. The case of Wroxeter will be discussed below, but the black earth deposits of the late fourth and fifth centuries at Canterbury also have a pottery assemblage where well over half of the, admittedly small, assemblage consists of jars with the rest divided between dishes and bowls.[23]

What is also noticeable is that the fourth century sees a reappearance of various handmade potting traditions in a variety of areas where wheel-made pottery had long been dominant. This can be observed both in the south and the north.[24] These handmade industries concentrated on cooking wares. The demise of the large industries that made the tablewares might have come about because there was no longer the demand for them, and that demand may have been in decline for some considerable time before the fifth century, as ways of serving food and drink changed.

Another factor that may possibly have been important is the appearance of the pottery. The large regional industries that came to dominate fourth-century pottery supply specialised in colour-coated wares often of glossy black or red shades.[25] These and other industries also produced white wares decorated by red painting. It is just possible that these were no longer to people's taste. This might seem a rather frivolous reason for the demise of these industries, but it might have been a contributory factor. A feature of very late fourth- to fifth-century small-find assemblages is a fascination with certain colours, and a deliberate seeking out of objects made of them.[26] Indeed I have often advised people, not entirely in jest, that if they want to find fifth century sites, they should look for ones where there are an unusually high preponderance of green, orange and

---

[22] Martin in Germany 2003: figs. 85–8.   [23] Pollard in Blockley *et al.* 1995: Table 16.
[24] Pollard 1988: 143, 151; Tyers 1996: 191–2; Monaghan 1997: 867.
[25] New Forest, Oxfordshire and the Nene Valley – see Tyers 1996.
[26] Cool 2000a: 54.

black objects. If this change of taste is affecting items such as jewellery, gaming equipment and textile equipment, why not pottery?

If we want to discover what happens at the end of the fourth century, a greater openness to looking at the pottery associated with sequences that clearly date from the fourth century into the sixth century would probably pay useful dividends. Normally this tends to be written off as clearly residual, occasionally with the grudging admission that if people had curated it carefully, it could still have been in use for a few decades into the fifth century. A sequence at the temple at Bath is a good example of this where there was clearly a tension between the excavators' view that occupation was continuing into the sixth century, and the pottery specialists' view that it ended in the early fifth century.[27] If all the later assemblages are fundamentally residual fourth-century material, then logically they should resemble an assemblage of that date appropriate for the type of site and region they are found in. In the case of small finds this is clearly not the case. The assemblages that can definitely be dated to the end of the fourth century and beyond can be shown to be very different to those of the early to mid-fourth century, despite being composed of 'fourth century' material.[28] Could the same be true of the pottery?

The Baths Basilica complex at Wroxeter ought to provide the ideal testing ground for exploring this. Over a thirty-five-year period starting in 1955, major campaigns of excavations were carried out that provide a sequence that stretches from the mid-first century to the seventh century. The two teams that carried out the work had very different priorities and interests, and this resulted in very different styles of excavation and publication. Despite three substantial monographs having been published reporting on the work, it is not easy to establish what the sequence of the material culture was over the period.[29] The team that concentrated their attention on the very late Roman to sub-Roman period took the view that as most of the very substantial amount of material recovered was from make-up layers, it did not relate to the occupation of the site. It was published in a summary form and resources concentrated on the structural narrative.[30] Whilst it is no doubt admirable that we have 2.5 kg of loose plans with the monograph itemising, it seems, the position of every cobble; it has meant that what is probably a key assemblage for understanding the fifth and sixth century languishes in an English Heritage store in dire need of a major research project to rescue it.

[27] Summarised in Tyers 1996: 79. [28] Cool 2000a.
[29] Barker *et al.* 1997: Ellis 2000; Webster 2002. [30] Barker *et al.* 1997: 12.

Even with the sadly curtailed data available in the publications, it is possible to show that the pottery should probably not be dismissed as residual make-up material of no interest. It may not be directly related to the Baths Basilica, but it does suggest that pottery was continuing to be used in Wroxeter a century or more after the proposed end of the Roman pottery industries. The late and sub-Roman occupation on the site was assigned a set of lettered Phases. Phase W extends from the late fourth century (post AD 367) to the end of the fifth century. Phase X was dated from the end of the fifth century to the mid-sixth century, Phase Y belonged to the mid-sixth century and Phase Z related to the great rebuilding seen on the site of the mid-sixth to the seventh century. Here Phases X and Y are treated as a single phase as they overlap. The pottery assemblages associated with these phases can also be compared to groups of pottery recovered from the other excavations on the site. These consist of the material used to infill the swimming pool (*natatio*) in the period *c.* AD 210–30, material deposited during the third century in the courtyard, and two groups from the portico. One of these dates to the early to mid-fourth century, the other contains very late fourth material. No suggestion was made that this indicated sustained occupation well into the fifth century, but the suspicion has to be that this is a very late group, contemporary with the material from Phase W in the other excavations. The pottery from these deposits is summarised in Table 19.3.

If the very late assemblages are just the redeposition of earlier material, then they should show no great difference in functional composition to the groups that definitely were deposited during the third and fourth centuries. As can be seen from the table, this is not the case. Flagons decrease with time, and jars increase. A correspondence analysis of the data (Fig. 19.3) shows clearly that there is a difference between the functional profiles of the third- and fourth-century assemblages and those of the late assemblages. The ordering of the groups along the first axis picks up the proposed chronology very closely. The earlier groups are characterised by the tablewares, the later by the cooking wares. This looks very much like the pattern that might be expected if the pottery was being derived from rubbish sources resulting from active use of the pottery in the fifth and sixth centuries, rather than just redeposition from earlier sources. Indeed it would be very difficult to explain the marked increase in riveted pottery seen in Phase Y (mid-sixth century)[31] other than by

---

[31] Barker *et al.* 1997: 218 Table 16.

Table 19.3. *Pottery from late Roman and sub-Roman contexts at the Baths Basilica, Wroxeter (EVEs).*

Phase	Date	Dish (%)	Bowl (%)	Jar (%)	Flagon (%)	Beaker (%)	Mortaria (%)	Total (EVE)
Natatio	210–30	11.5	23.8	29.8	20.8	9.9	4.3	84.6
Courtyard	3rd century	15.2	19.9	43.0	9.7	8.2	4.3	71.9
PorticoE	4th century	9.4	21.2	42.5	12.4	9.7	4.3	63.6
PorticoL	375+	7.2	24.6	53.8	4.3	3.5	6.7	97.6
W	367–500	11.4	19.3	54.3	4.3	8.0	2.6	126.8
X/Y	500–550	11.9	20.6	51.5	1.2	7.7	7.2	204.3
Z	550–700	12.8	21.4	50.6	2.4	6.1	6.7	314.8

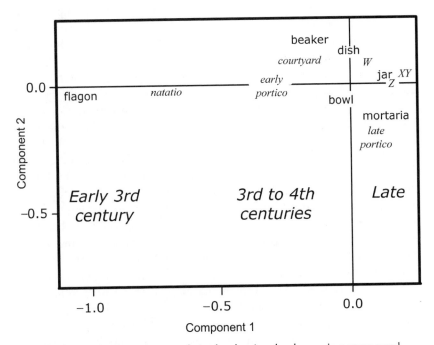

Figure 19.3. Correspondence analysis plot showing the changes in pottery-vessel assemblages at Wroxeter with time. (Data from Table 19.3.)

suggesting pottery was still an essential part of people's lives up to that point, and that it was only then that there started to be pressure on supplies that required careful repair and curation of existing vessels.

This data set, and the conclusions drawn from it, could be criticised on various grounds if one had a mind to. Given that it is derived from two different excavations, it might be that there were different collection and discard regimes in place. The fact that the broadly contemporary assemblages from the late Portico and Phase W plot on the same side of the graph suggests this may not be a major problem. It might be argued that various taphonomic processes were at work in the redeposited material favouring the more substantial vessels, the cooking wares, at the expense of the more thin-walled tablewares. The progressive decline of the flagons would seem to argue against this. Flagon rims are substantial and often break retaining the whole circumference which, when an assemblage is quantified by EVEs, can lead to an overestimate of the flagons in the assemblage in comparison to other forms. It could be expected that they would remain a substantial component in any redeposited group. As the pottery data currently exists, it does seem that there would have to be a great deal of special pleading to argue against continuing use well into the sub-Roman period.

The evidence suggests that the fourth and fifth centuries (and beyond), did see major changes in the way people served food, but possibly not so great a change in the cooking methods. Jar use seems to continue. We know that in Cornwall, potters serenely continued making the local Gabbroic pottery with its emphasis on cooking forms well into the post-Roman period.[32] There seems the distinct likelihood that other local industries specialising in cooking wares could also have survived for longer than is normally realised. After all, how do you date a form that functions well and has no need to develop typologically? Without the independent cross-checking that coinage can provide, it could as easily be late fifth century as earlier. Though it is true that many people in the fourth century would have purchased the products of the big industries working in Oxford, the Nene Valley etc., it should not be forgotten that more local industries continued to have a role to play. At Wroxeter itself, it has been calculated that 20% of the late Roman assemblage was locally produced with a further 14% of unknown origin that could equally have included local material.[33] Potting skills may not have been so centralised within the big industries as is sometimes assumed.

The change in how food and drink were being served is a fascinating one, but currently we do not have the data to explore what was happening

---

[32] Quinnell 2004: 109–11.   [33] Timby in Ellis 2000: Table 4.28.

in the very late assemblages. Tables 19.2 and 19.3 suggest an adoption of a jar – bowl assemblage, but were the bowls part of cooking equipment, for serving individual portions or for serving communal ones? A far greater emphasis on quantifying form, size, patterns of wear and colour of late Roman pottery would allow us to explore this in the future in much greater detail than is currently possible.

GUARDING THE NORTH YORKSHIRE COAST

The signal stations along the Yorkshire and Humberside coast date to the very end of the Roman period. These were tall masonry towers set within a courtyard defined by a wall and ditch. It is thought they were built as watchtowers to act as lookouts for pirate raiding and thus had a military function, though some have argued that they might have been strong places of refuge for the local inhabitants when the raiders came. The finds from them make it clear that both sexes were present, and generally they have a much more domestic rather than military flavour. The stations were certainly built and occupied in the later fourth century. When occupation commenced is a matter of some debate but the most likely date is in the last quarter of the century. How long they continued in occupation is also a matter of debate. If they were military establishments, then presumably not beyond the first decade of the fifth century. If they were places of refuge then a longer timespan would be possible.[34]

Their location makes them very susceptible to coastal erosion, and in the early 1990s the remaining part of the station at Filey was excavated because of this. Though a relatively small excavation, the full environmental sampling programme provides a very interesting snapshot of very late fourth- to fifth-century occupation.[35]

Given the patterns of vessel use discussed in the previous section it will come as no surprise that the relatively small pottery assemblage (23.41 EVEs, 29.24 kg) is dominated by jars. Measured by EVEs they make up 88% of the assemblage, followed by bowls (7.2%), flagons (3.3%) and dishes (1.7%). Drinking vessels are rare, represented by only ten sherds from pottery beakers and one fragment of a glass example. The jars were clearly used both as cooking vessels and water carriers. The sooting patterns make it clear that lids were used whilst cooking, though none were found in the pottery assemblage, possibly because they were made of wood. The rarity of anything to eat

[34] For general discussion see Ottaway 2001: 188–90; Wilson 1989.   [35] Ottaway 2001.

food out of in the assemblage might also suggest that wooden bowls were being favoured. An interesting feature is the strong presence (17% by weight) of what are described as very late handmade wares, primarily used to make jars but also the occasional dish and flagon. These are in addition to the other late fourth-century handmade calcite-gritted wares that make up nearly two thirds (by weight) of the assemblage. There are three different fabrics for this late material, which again might serve to suggest that potting skills might not have been as rare at the beginning of the fifth century as is sometimes suggested.[36]

The meat eaten came overwhelmingly from cattle, sheep and pigs.[37] The various measures of quantification when translated into meat weight suggested that there was no one dominant meat species. The bones present show that the meat was being supplied as dressed joints, and possibly in the case of the pigs and sheep in the form of cured hams. Several of the sheep scapulae show the hook damage typical of hanging up joints for curing.[38]

Game, as ever, played a minor role, though the presence of deer scapulae did indicate that venison was consumed. The amount of wild-bird bones recovered outnumbered those of the domestic fowl, but in part this probably reflected the natural deaths of seabirds on this cliff-top site, as opposed to them being elements in the food chain. Such birds were occasionally eaten as one guillemot definitely, and one cormorant possibly, showed cut marks from butchery. The amount of evidence for wild species being consumed is not large, but given the size of the assemblage (small) and given the normal pattern of game exploitation (vanishingly small), it looks more substantial than is often observed. Interestingly, this is a pattern that can be seen in other late military establishments in what might be thought of as marginal areas.[39] Does this indicate that there was stress on the supply chain, or that the possible taboos around eating game were losing their power? The provision of dressed carcases at Filey would suggest that the former was not the case.

With a military community there is always the possibility of individuals being present who do not share the dominant view of what can and cannot be eaten. The increase in game consumed at these sites might be reflecting the fact that some individuals did not share the same ethnicity

[36] Monaghan in Ottaway 2001: 140–47, for glass see also 130 no. 26.
[37] The discussion of the environmental evidence is derived from Dobney, Large, Carrott, Hall, Issitt and Large in Ottaway 2001: 148–82.
[38] See p. 89.   [39] See p. 113 Table 13.1

as their fellows. Equally though, the breaking down of taboos might be a factor. There are occasionally hints that more venison was consumed in the very late to sub-Roman period than was the case earlier. At Wroxeter red and roe deer were identified in all the very late phases and were most numerous in the mid-sixth- to seventh-century Phase Z. The total numbers were not large, but the occurrences seem more numerous than those recovered from contexts dating to the first to fourth centuries.[40] Caution has to be exercised in interpreting the figures as it is known that the animal bone from the early contexts was only selectively studied, contexts representing only 22% of the amount studied from the later ones. The earlier contexts produced 18 deer bones, the later 138. If the later contexts had produced deer bones at the same rate as the earlier ones, a figure of about 80 might have been expected. The pattern of a possible increase in game is not always observed. The late fourth- to early sixth-century occupation at Bath continues to show very low levels of venison consumption.[41] Though the picture is not uniform, there are sufficient hints in the record to suggest that investigating the exploitation of wild animals might be a useful way to explore the fifth century.

One dislike that the inhabitants of Filey shared with the inhabitants of much of the rest of the population relates to fish. Despite the sampling regime in place, fish were rare. A total of only sixty measured by NISP which may be compared to the figures for chicken which were eighty four. The amount consumed is even smaller when it is realised that some of the fish bones probably arrived through the action of seabirds roosting in the tower. If ever confirmation was needed that the Romano-British population did not have much of a taste for fish, this is the site that provides it. They lived by a sea full of fish for the taking and the sampling programme would have retrieved the bones had they been there in any quantity, and they were not. Shellfish were more acceptable though again not found in large quantities. Ones that could have been exploited locally and which were relatively numerous were limpets, winkles and mussels. The presence of three oyster shells is of some importance. These would not have been available locally and indicate that even at this very late date the oyster trade was still thriving.

Also of interest is the fact that amongst the charred grain assemblage, spelt wheat appears to be as common as barley, though neither is particularly

---

[40] Compare Armour-Chelu in Barker *et al.* 1997: 358–9 Table 47 with Meddens in Ellis 2000: 328, Table 4.3.
[41] Grant in Cunliffe and Davenport 1985: Mf 3/D2–4, Table 7.

common in the samples. Given that barley tends to be the dominant grain in the north, the presence of the spelt wheat together with the amount of pork and game eaten, might be marking out different eating habits. Whether they were different because of the very late date of the assemblage or because of the people who lived there is, at present, an open question. What is needed is the analysis of other very late assemblages to a similar high level as has been done for Filey. It would be of immense interest to know what the environmental evidence from the Wellington Row site in York is telling us. This was a very large excavation carried out in 1987–91 in the *colonia* area of the city, with the full panoply of sampling for which the archaeologists at York are famous. Only the pottery has been studied and published, but that makes it clear that occupation was going on well into the fifth century.[42] Publication of the site would provide a northern reference assemblage against which evidence such as that of Filey could be compared.

EATING AND CHRISTIANITY

We know that there was an organised Christian community in Britain in the fourth century, if not earlier. British bishops are recorded as attending both the Council of Arles in AD 314 and that of Ariminum in AD 359.[43] There is also an ever growing *corpus* of material with explicitly Christian symbols on it including the mid-fourth-century Water Newton treasure which seems to be the earliest group of Christian silver from the empire.[44] That group is comparatively modest in comparison to other finds of precious metal with Christian symbols such as those from Mildenhall and Hoxne.[45] Such finds, together with the evidence of places like the Lullingstone house church and the explicitly Christian mosaics at Hinton St Mary,[46] suggest that during the fourth century the religion was drawing adherents from the wealthy elite of the province as well as more humble members of the community. It was a time when the doctrines of the Church were still being fought over by rival sects, and it is clear that the British congregation was actively involved in these debates. Pelagius, whose works were declared heretical in AD 418, was British; and there were still many who followed his teachings rather than the orthodox Catholic ones in AD 429.[47] Against this background, it is worth

---

[42] Monaghan 1997: 1108–23.   [43] Frere 1987: 321–2.
[44] Painter 1977a.   [45] Painter 1977b; Bland and Johns 1993.
[46] Salway 1993: pls. facing 256 and 448.
[47] Salway 1993: 320–2.

considering what the growing influence of this religion would have been on the eating habits of the fourth century and later population.

During the millennia after the Roman period in Britain, the Catholic Church developed a vice-like control over the eating habits of its members with nearly half the year declared a fast.[48] The formalisation of this regime came later than the period with which we are concerned, but the Christian emphasis on fasting and the ascetic life had already started. Its development can be traced from the end of the second century, but the most rigorous propaganda for it came with Christianity's rise to power.[49] As the prospect of actual martyrdom receded after the Edict of Milan in 313, certain individuals looked around for other ways to distinguish themselves as part of the Christian elite, and asceticism was one way of doing this. There were always people who argued against this, pointing out that it was the sins of the body that were to be hated, not the body itself; but by the fourth century there were strong voices that 'demanded that the unresurrected living body, especially the female body, was to be hated and mortified'.[50]

It would be naive to think that a congregation that actively partook in the debates raging in the Church would not have been aware of these currents of thought, and there is a small amount of evidence that suggests it did have an effect on some people. One of the curious features of the demographic pattern of the Poundbury cemetery has always been the disproportionate number of young girls buried there. It is worth quoting what the report says about this:

At most ages from about seven years, girls greatly outnumbered the boys. The disproportion was especially marked between thirteen and fifteen when there were nearly four times as many girls as boys. While this ratio continues into the early twenties, the explanation cannot rest simply with death associated with childbearing, but must lie with the treatment accorded girls from an early age.[51]

The cause of death could not be ascertained, and the author went on to suggest that this treatment might have been the result of females being held in less esteem, and having less access to food and health care.

Given that it has been argued that the main cemeteries at Poundbury show many of the features to be expected in a Christian cemetery,[52] an alternative explanation might lie in the religious arena. It is appropriate here to point out that the identification of which cemeteries

---

[48] See p. 105.   [49] Grimm 1996: see especially 192–7.   [50] Grimm 1996: 178.
[51] Molleson in Farwell and Molleson 1993: 180.
[52] Woodward in Farwell and Molleson 1993: 236–7.

are and are not Christian in fourth century Roman-Britain is almost as contentious an area as what happens in the fifth century. The evidence for Christians at Poundbury though is very strong as one of the mausoleums was painted with a scene that includes the explicitly Christian symbol of the *Chi-Rho*.[53]

Within the western world, women seem particularly prone to take control of their lives by fasting. The comparison between medieval female fasting saints and modern anorexics has often been made,[54] and from at least the thirteenth century onwards there are records of holy Christian women choosing to fast to death. At that point the Church disapproved of such a course of action, but in the world of late antiquity there were some Church leaders who would appear to have thought this a good idea. Jerome in the fourth century was providing instructions for the preservation of virginity in women that 'bear a more than chance resemblance to the conditions that give rise to and are involved in anorexia nervosa'.[55] It is noticeable that his instructions for men are more moderate. The suggestion that the unusually high number of young female deaths might be the response to Christian teaching may not be as far-fetched as it might seem, as other aspects of this teaching do appear to be reflected in the material-culture record. The early Church Fathers were obsessed with what females did with their hair, and this may be the reason why the hairpin evidence indicates major changes in hair-dressing styles towards the end of the fourth century in Britain.[56]

Possibly by coincidence there is also evidence of nutritional stress seen in an individual buried at Shepton Mallet in the fourth century accompanied by a silver amulet with the *crux monogrammatica* motif.[57] This was a popular Christian symbol in the fourth century, and would seem to be strong evidence that the individual was Christian. The individual was an adult male probably of middle age. Not only did his teeth show enamel hypoplasia and his skull show cribra orbitalia, but he also had periostitis on his leg. The first two conditions can be interpreted as the result of nutritional stress in childhood, the last the same condition in adulthood.[58] He may just have been a particularly unfortunate individual, but then again he may have been from a particularly devout family.

It is clear from the tone of various of the early Church Fathers' writings on fasting that not everyone was convinced that this was the road to

---

[53] Green in Farwell and Molleson 1993: 135–9.   [54] Counihan 1999: 93–112.

[55] Grimm 1996: 170–1.   [56] Cool 2000b.

[57] For grave see Leach and Evans 2001: 35; for the amulet Johns in Leech and Evans 2001: 257–60; for the skeleton Pinter-Bellows in Leech and Evans 2001: 279, 281.

[58] See pp. 23–4 for a discussion of these conditions.

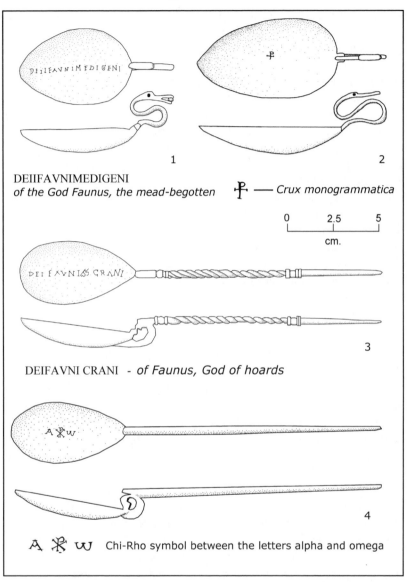

DEIIFAVNIMEDIGENI
of the God Faunus, the mead-begotten   ⳨ — *Crux monogrammatica*

DEIFAVNI CRANI - *of Faunus, God of hoards*

Ａ ⳩ ѡ Chi-Rho symbol between the letters alpha and omega

Figure 19.4. Fourth-century silver spoons used in both pagan (nos. 1 and 3) and Christian (nos. 2 and 4) worship. (After Johns and Potter 1983: nos. 56 and 74 (1 and 3); Johns and Potter 1985, no. 5 (2); Painter 1977a: 31 no. 11). Scale 1 : 2.

salvation in the fourth century. It is to be hoped that other Christians' experiences were more enjoyable. There is some evidence that food may have been as integral a part of worship for some Christian congregations as it was for their pagan contemporaries. The building thought to be a church at Butt Road, Colchester may provide some, though again the identification is contentious with some reviewers of the report happy to accept this interpretation and others not.[59] It was associated with an exceptional amount of chicken bones and immature pig bones, the classic meats of high-status feasting as has often been noted throughout this book.[60] Spoons also seem to be common to both Christian and pagan worship. Precisely the same types of spoons have religious inscriptions and symbols relating to both Christianity and devotion to other gods (see Fig. 19.4). Quite how these were used is unclear, but the ones with the short bird handles have bowls that are larger than the modern tablespoon and could be used for taking small quantities of presumably alcoholic beverages. Possibly the way some congregations celebrated was much the same whatever god was being worshipped.

CONCLUSIONS

It will be clear from the foregoing that there is a great deal we do not know about culinary habits at the end of the Roman period, however defined. What is clear is that things were changing but that this was not a sudden event, it had its roots a century or more earlier. Changes in what sort of vessels were wanted and how they were regarded start to become apparent in the third century. This did not happen in isolation. It is in the third century as well that we see the decline in the desire for amphora-borne commodities such as oil, whilst fish sauce may have gone even earlier.[61] It is in the third century that the nature of mortaria changes.[62] Tastes were altering in more ways than one. The late fourth and fifth centuries are often looked on as some sort of archaeological black hole. From a culinary point of view they don't look like that. New factors such as Christianity undoubtedly came into the equation, but they were acting on cultural changes that were already in play. A more rigorous attitude to fourth century assemblages and 'residual' material, might well enable us to tease out what those were.

---

[59] Compare for example Millett in *Archaeological Journal* 152 (1995) pp. 452–3 with Struck in *Britannia* 28 (1997) 498.
[60] Crummy *et al.* 1993: 178–80.   [61] See pp. 62–3.   [62] See p. 43.

CHAPTER 20

Digestif

What has emerged from our explorations of the foodways of Roman Britain?

The first thing is the range of eating habits and preferences in the different regions and how they altered through time. That this is so should surely not surprise us. Even today in a homogenised and globalised world, the different regions of Britain still retain local traditions and preferences. The Staffordshire oatcake is an entirely different beast to the traditional Scottish one. I have looked long and hard for something similar to Wiltshire lardy cakes in the various parts of Britain I have lived in since childhood, but to no avail. My partner remembers, with advantage, the season puddings his Yorkshire-bred mother would make to accompany roast chicken, but has never found their like elsewhere. These are just memories belonging to the second half of the twentieth century. The regional diversity of British cooking before that is well documented in such works as Dorothy Hartley's *Food in England*, which also shows the changes going on over the centuries before the impact of the Industrial Revolution changed British society so fundamentally. It should be expected that there would be differences observable in Roman Britain given that it covers a large geographical area and half a millennium of time. Equally we have seen that there was no one 'Roman' cuisine amongst the people who came to Britain after the conquest. Why should there be? They came from various areas of the empire with their own particular tastes and prejudices. Differences are to be expected.

It is worth bearing this in mind when considering the nature of Roman Britain more widely. There is a tendency to regard it as a single entity or at best a series of dichotomies – Roman–native, urban–rural, military–civilian. The reality was much more complex, and any consideration needs to include its regional and chronological diversity.

Allowing for this, it does seem reasonable to say that for the inhabitants of many parts of Britain, their culinary horizons would have expanded during the period under consideration. We could observe this starting to happen in the century or so before the conquest in parts of the south-east. In some areas the effects can only be seen a century or more after the conquest whilst in others many people wished to have nothing to do with new outlandish tastes and ways of eating. There are also signs that a differentiated cuisine of the type discussed in Chapter 5 was developing in places. Certainly some meats regularly seem to indicate elite dining, often appearing on sites that show a greater openness to a wider type of table-wares, a different choice of grain as a staple, etc.

Regularly observed patterns such as the combination of elite meats raise interesting questions about the nature of the Romano-British population. Why were chicken, pork and game seen as special? Various foods seem regularly to be distinguished by their absence or rarity. Did people not eat fish because they didn't like it? Is game so rare because the habitat for the animals was not available? Or in both cases are there more fundamental reasons that lie in the area of taboo? Young animals seem regularly to be a feature of temple assemblages. Is this because they were unblemished, and if so, what does this tell us about the relationship of the people with their gods? At present we are in the position of being able to identify patterns and ask questions, but not necessarily answer them. What is needed is for the patterns to be checked against new data sets to see if they do indeed recur regularly, and then for their other associations to be explored.

Methodologically these explorations have shown that though there is a great deal of good work going on in the excavation and analysis of sites, there is also work that falls short of best practice. The observant reader will have realised that from time to time I have been rather irritated by what I have found. I have seen good specialist work thoughtlessly consigned to the archive because the person writing the report does not know how to use it. I have seen similar work published but its implications totally ignored by the overall author when writing their discussions of the site. I have frequently thought that many people seem to have no idea what to do with all this information commissioned and produced at great expense. Equally, I have seen specialists so involved with their own area that their reports stand in splendid isolation, not integrated with the rest of the material and presented in such a way that it is impossible for anyone else to integrate them. Archaeology is expensive and to see resources squandered in any of these ways makes me not just irritated but really very angry. It ought to have the same effect on everyone. Yet, I have lost count of the number of reviews of excavation monographs I have read which end with a brief coda along the lines of 'there are lots of specialist reports but space does not allow me to comment on them'. These reports will often occupy half the book or more! It is not enough that they are there. They need to be integrated with each other and the stratigraphy, and if this is not done, it should be commented on. Only in this way will good practice drive out bad.

I would like to think that we excavate sites because we are curious about the past and the people who lived in it, rather than to keep us in employment and fill museum stores with boxes of finds. Various excavations have been referred to repeatedly in this book. That is because the authors of the reports have been curious and have used the data as a pathway into the past. As a result they have discovered much more from their data. These reports are a joy to read, not something that can be said about the majority of excavation reports. It is my hope that with time this attitude will become the rule rather than the exception. I could think of no better prospect than that in ten years time someone else will be writing a book exploring food and drink in Roman Britain because new data, thoughtfully produced, has rendered this one hopelessly out of date.

Appendix : data sources for tables

Table 3.1.   Bainesse – Evans, J. in Wilson 2002b: Table 12 (excluding
              prehistoric pottery); Leicester – Clark in Connor and Buckley
              1999: Tables 9, 12, 15, 22, 23, 28; Lincoln – Darling in Colyer
              et al. 1999: 52 and Table 32; Alchester – Booth *et al.* 2001:
              Appendix 4; Kingscote – Timby 1998: Table 7; Ivy Chimneys
              – Turner-Walker and Wallace in Turner 1999: Table 17;
              Asthall – Booth 1997: 133–4; Chignal – Wallace and
              Turner-Walker in Clarke 1998: Table 11.

Table 3.2.   Capacity derived from Tyers 1996: 87–104; weight range
              derived from Peacock and Williams 1986: Table 1; and
              Martin-Kilchner 1994: 354.

Table 4.1.   London East – Conheeney in Barber and Bowsher 2000, 286;
              Cirencester – Wells in McWhirr *et al.* 1982: Table 50; Dun-
              stable – Jones and Horne in Matthews 1981: 39; Poundbury –
              Molleson in Farwell and Molleson 1993: Table 28; Alington
              Avenue – Waldron in Davies *et al.* 2002: Table 29; Maiden
              Castle Road – Rogers in Smith *et al.* 1997: Table 33; Colchester
              – Pinter-Bellows in Crummy *et al.* 1993: Table 2.22; Bradley
              Hill – Everton in Leech 1981: Table 8.

Table 4.2.   London East – Conheeney in Barber and Bowsher 2000:
              285–6; Cirencester – Wells in McWhirr *et al.* 1982: Table
              70, 150, 186; Dunstable – Jones and Horne in Matthews
              1981: Table 6; Chignall – Stirland in Clarke 1998: 119–22;
              Poundbury – Molleson in Farwell and Molleson 1993: 183,
              185; Alington Avenue – Waldron in Davies *et al.* 2002:
              152–3; Colchester – Pinter-Bellows in Crummy *et al.* 1993:
              79, 88; Alchester – Boyle in Booth *et al.* 2001: Table 8.2–3.

Table 4.3.   Numbers of individuals taken from Molleson and Farwell 1993: Table 50.

Table 6.1.   Baldock – Stead and Rigby 1986: 297–378; Dalton Parlours – Sumpter in Wrathmell and Nicholson 1990: 135–46; West Yorkshire – Evans, J. in Roberts *et al.* 2001: 153–76; Warrington – Webster in Hinchliffe *et al.* 1992: 124–50; Segontium – Webster in Casey *et al.* 1993: 250–309; Menai Straits – Longley *et al.* 1998: 220–6; Caersws – Webster in Britnell 1989: 80–124.

Table 6.2.   Catterick Bridge – Evans, J. in Wilson 2002b: Tables 41– 2; Catterick Bainesse – Evans, J. in Wilson 2002b: Tables 18–19; Alchester Site B – Dickinson in Booth *et al.* 2001: Table 7.10; Alchester Site C – Dickinson in Booth *et al.* 2001: Table 7.11; Lincoln – Bird in Colyer *et al.* 1999: Table 29.

Table 7.1.   Kingsholm – Timby in Hurst 1985: Table 4; Exeter – Holbrook and Bidwell 1991: 14; 1992: Table 6; Wroxeter – Darling in Webster 2002: Table 5.15; London, Billingsgate – Green in Jones, 1980: 40–5; Wanborough – Keay in Anderson *et al.* 2001: Table 13; Carlisle – Taylor in McCarthy 1990: Tables 17 and 20; Gloucester – Timby in Hurst and Pitts 1986: Table 4 – Contexts A3.1. A4.2, A4.4; Wroxeter – Faiers in Ellis 2000: Table 4.22; Bainesse – Evans, J. in Wilson 2002b: Table 12 Phases 3–6; Carlisle – Taylor in McCarthy 1990: Table 23 – Building 8; South Shields – Bidwell and Speak 1994: Table 8.9 – Phases 3–5; Lincoln – Darling in Colyer *et al.* 1999: Table 33; Alchester – Booth *et al.* 2001: Appendix 4; London, New Fresh Wharf – Miller *et al.* 1986: fig. 76 Phases 4 and 5; London Shadwell – Lakin *et al.* 2002: Tables 7 and 9; Caister – Darling and Gurney 1993: Table 29; Newcastle Upon Tyne – Williams in Snape and Bidwell 2002: Table 15.7.

Table 7.2.   Longthorpe – Wilson in Frere 1974: 97; Peacock in Dannell and Wild 1987: Table VI; Nanstallon – Fox and Ravenhall 1972: 104 nos. 17–19; Castleford (fort) – Rush *et al.* 2000: Table 12; York – Monaghan 1993: Table 117 Periods 1 and 2; Segontium – Casey *et al.* 1993: 77; Canterbury – Green in Blockley *et al.* 1995: 638; London – Groves in Milne and Wardle 1996: 131; Dorchester – Williams in Woodward *et al.*

1993: Table 28 Period 6; Cirencester – Cooper in Holbrook 1998: Tables 20–21; Chelmsford – Going 1987: Table 9 ceramic phases 2–3; Towcester – Brown and Woodfield 1983: 77; Castleford (*vicus*) – Rush *et al.* 2000: Table 19; Wilcote – Hands 1993: 156; Williams in Hands 1998: 226; Cramond – Maxwell in Rae and Rae 1974: 206; Williams in Holmes 2003: 47; Greta Bridge – Croom and Bidwell in Casey and Hoffmann 1998: 178.

Table 7.3.   Castleford – Bastow in Abramson *et al.* 1999: Tables 8–13; Caerleon – Caseldine and Busby in Zienkiewicz 1993: 137; Vindolanda – Seaward in van Driel Murray *et al.* 1993: 105–107; Ribchester – Huntley in Buxton and Howard-Davis 2000: Table 32; Bearsden – Knights *et al.* 1983; Leicester – Monkton in Connor and Buckley 1999: 347 Phase 3; London – Willcox 1977: Table 1 – St Thomas Street; York – Kenward *et al.* 1986: Table 76; Dragonby – van der Veen in May 1996: Table 9.3; Bancroft – Peterson and Robinson in Williams and Zepvat 1994: 581; South Shields – van der Veen in Bidwell and Speak 1994: 260.

Table 9.1.   Castleford – Berg in Abramson *et al.* 1999: Fort Tables 26 and 27, *vicus* Table 30 Phases 2 and 3; Ribchester – Stallibrass and Nicholson in Buxton and Howard-Davis 2000: Table 48 Phase 1–4; Wroxeter – Meddens in Ellis 2000: Table 4.30 Period 1 and 2; Leicester – Gidney in Connor and Buckley 1999: Table 66, Phases 2a–h, k, l, 3a, b, e. Wilcote – Hamshaw-Thomas and Bermingham in Hands 1993: Tables 8 and 9.

Table 9.2.   The data in rows one and two are derived from Goldsworthy 1996: 292 Table 4. The Colchester bone weight data is derived from Luff 1993: Table 3.5a, Assemblages BKCJ3, CULA2, CULG4, GBSA7.
The calculation is as follows:

$$\text{Cattle:} \left(\frac{\text{bone weight}}{2} \right) \times 2.$$

$$\text{Sheep:} \left(\frac{\text{bone weight} \times 2.222}{100} \right) \times 55.$$

$$\text{Pig:} \left(\frac{\text{bone weight} \times 4}{100} \right) \times 75.$$

Table 11.1.   Colchester – Luff 1993: Table 5.1; Dorchester – Maltby in Woodward *et al.* 1993: 62 (Periods 5–10); Leicester – Gidney in Connor and Buckley 1999: Table 66; Southwark – Ainsley in Drummond *et al.* 2002: Table 125 (London Bridge).

Table 11.2.   Colchester – Luff 1993: Table 3.1 and 5.1; Fishbourne – Grant in Cunliffe 1971: 378 Table I, Eastham in Cunliffe 1971: 389. For comparability to the mammal-bone table, pre-palace deposits include the Period 2 construction assemblage.

Table 13.1.   Wroxeter (fort) – Noddle in Webster 2002: Table 7.1; Castleford – Berg in Abramson *et al.* 1999: Table 30 Phase I and II; Colchester – Luff 1993: Table 3.1 – Culver Street 2 and 3; Wroxeter (town) – Meddens in Ellis 2000: Table 4.30 Periods 1 and 2; Wilcote – Hamshaw-Thomas and Bermingham in Hands 1993: Table 6; Leicester – Gidney in Connor and Buckley 1999: Table 66; Caister – Harman in Darling and Gurney 1993: Table 40; Segontium – Noddle in Casey *et al.* 1993: Table 6.1.

Table 14.1.   Colchester – Murphy in Crummy 1992: 50 Table 8.14; [1] Pit C138, [2] Pit EF900. Gorhambury – Wainright in Neal *et al.* 1990: 28, 218. Southwark – Gray in Drummond-Murray *et al.* 2002: 244 OA14 {222}. Carlisle – McCarthy 2000: 21. Leicester – Monkton in Connor and Buckley 1999, Table 84 sample 775. Dorchester – Ede in Smith 1993: 73 MF 8–10; [1]Pit 27, [2]Pit 13. Bearsden – Knights *et al.* 1983. Stonea – van der Veen in Jackson and Potter 1996: Table 65; York – Greig in Buckland 1976: Table 2.

Table 15.1.   Kingsholm – Timby in Hurst 1985: Table 8 (the Dressel 28/30 have been attributed to Gaul following Holbrook and Bidwell 1991: 215). Exeter – Holbrook and Bidwell 1991: Table 14; 1992: Table 6. Wroxeter – Darling in Webster 2002: Table 5.15; Inchtuthil – Darling in Pitts and St Joseph 1985: Table XXIV.

Table 15.2.   Data from Davies *et al.* 1994: Appendix 5 Ceramic phases 1A and 2.

Table 15.3. The data set scanned is unfortunately too large for the references to be published here.

Table 16.1. Skeleton Green – Partridge 1981. Key Groups F52, F9, F23, F24, Ditch 1 F60, F50, F39 Ditch 2, F1, G22 Layers 7 and 9. Ermine Street – Witherington and Trow in Potter and Trow 1988: Tables 14–16 with additional information taken from the Arretine report (Hartley in Potter and Trow 1988: 94–6) and that on the Gallic imports (Rigby in Potter and Trow 1988: 110–14).

Table 16.2. Parminter in Neal *et al.* 1990, Tables 10–13. The Arretine cup was unstratified but can be dated to the pre-conquest period – Dannell in Neal *et al.* 1996: 198.

Table 16.3. Stead and Rigby 1989: Appendix 6. Formal burials belonging to Phases 1–3 and unphased. Tables based on the following deposits: 2, 3, 9–21, 23–7, 29–32, 34, 35, 37–40, 42–5, 47–50, 52–3, 55–9, 61, 66–77, 79–82, 84–6, 89–93, 95–9, 101, 102, 104, 106–12, 115, 117, 118, 120, 121, 123–5, 127–31, 133–44, 146–54, 156–89, 191–3, 196–205, 207, 208, 210–8, 221–4, 227, 229–42, 244, 248, 249, 251, 252, 255–60, 262–5, 267, 268, 270, 273–6, 278–83, 287–9, 293, 294, 296–303, 305, 307, 309–12, 314–17, 321, 322, 324, 325, 327, 328, 334–41, 343–76, 378–82, 384–91, 393, 395, 397–401, 408, 410, 412–17, 420–7, 434–41, 445, 447–50, 454–7, 449–65, 467, 469, 471, 472.

Table 16.4. Data set as Table 16.3.

Table 16.5. Data set as Table 16.3.

Table 17.1. Luff 1993: Table 3.5a. The Cattle total is a combination of COW and OXO, the sheep a combination of S/G and SMA – see Luff 1993: 24 for justification.

Table 17.2. Symmonds and Wade 1999: Tables 3.2, 3.4 and 3.6.

Table 17.3 Symmonds and Wade 1999: Tables 4.2, 4.4, 5.2, 5.9, 5.11, 5.14, 5.16, 5.18, 5.20, 5.25, 5.30, 5.36, 6.3, 6.6, 6.14, 6.16, 6.20, 6.26, 6.30, 6.32. PEG groups 3 and 4.

Table 17.4. Data taken from Cool and Price 1995: quantified by the methodology outlined in Cool and Baxter 1999.

Table 17.5. Pottery data taken from Groves in Milne and Wardle 1996: Tables 11 and 13. Glass data taken from Shepherd in Milne and Wardle 1996: 104–14 quantified by the methodology outlined in Cool and Baxter 1999.

Table 17.6. Data from Abramson *et al.* 1999: Tables 26, 36–8 (zone measures are missing for the sheep and pigs from Trenches 15/18 in tables 37 and 38). The notional meat measures are calculated using the minimum numbers of individuals and the average meat weights provided in Table 8.2.

Table 17.7. Data from Rush *et al.* 2000: Tables 2–4, 8–10, 21, 27.

Table 17.8. Data from Cool and Price in Cool and Philo 1998: 152–78 quantified by the methodology outlined in Cool and Baxter 1999.

Table 17.9. Data from Sykes in Miles *et al.* forthcoming and King, J. in Mackreth 1996: Mf 8: B13 Table 80.

Table 17.10. Data from Green and Booth in Miles *et al.* forthcoming and Perrin in Mackreth 1996: Tables 13–16 using EVE data provided in Mf 11: E12-3.

Table 17.11. Gage 1834, 1836, 1840; Gage Rokewode 1842. Vessels used to contain the cremated bone have been omitted.

Table 18.1. Pottery data from Clarke in Connor and Buckley 1999: Tables 12, 15 and 23. Glass data from Davies in Connor and Buckley 1999: 287–92 quantified by the methodology outlined in Cool and Baxter 1999.

Table 18.2. Data from Sykes in Miles *et al.* forthcoming; Cool in Miles *et al.* forthcoming; Evans in Roberts *et al.* 2001: 163–9.

Table 18.3. Data from Sykes in Miles *et al.* forthcoming and Richardson in Roberts *et al.* 2001: Table 39.

Table 18.4. Data from Levitan in Woodward and Leach 1993: Table 15. The quantification method used is number of identified bones. This counted epiphyses and non-repeatable characteristics for other skeletal parts. The aim was to avoid over-counting individual bones that may have been broken into several pieces. For discussion see Levitan in Woodward and Leach 1993: 258.

Table 18.5.   Data from Bond and Worley in Cool 2004b: Tables 7.18–20, 17.22. Deposits where only teeth were included have been excluded. Adults are individuals over the age of 18 who it is not possible to sex. The Male and Female categories are adults who it is possible to sex. Infants are aged 5 or less, immature individuals are aged between 5 and 18. Total deposit data from Cool 2004b: Table 6.9.

Table 19.1.   Data from Cool and Baxter 1999: Tables 1 and 2.

Table 19.2.   Data from Monaghan 1997: 977–1020.

Table 19.3.   Data from Symmonds in Barker *et al.* 1997: unnumbered tables on pp. 294–308 and Timby in Ellis 2000: Table 4.24. Material assigned to a bowl – jar category has been divided equally between jars and bowls. The beaker category includes cups for earlier assemblages.

References

ABBREVIATIONS

AY   Archaeology of York (published by the Council for British Archae-
            ology).
BAR BS   British Archaeological Report, British Series.
BAR IS   British Archaeological Report, International Series.
CAR   Colchester Archaeological Reports.
CBARR   Research Reports of the Council for British Archaeology.
EAA   East Anglian Archaeology.
RCHM   An Inventory of the Historical Monuments of the city of York.
York   Volume I *Eburacum* Roman York (London: Royal Commission on
            Historical Monuments England, 1962).
RIB   Collingwood, R. G. and Wright, R. P., 1965. *Roman Inscriptions
            of Britain*, Volume I. *Inscriptions on Stone*, (Oxford: Oxford
            University Press).
RIB II.1–8 Collingwood, R. G. and Wright, R. P., *The Roman Inscriptions of
            Britain Volume II. Instrumentum Domesticum (personal belongings
            and the like). Fascicules 1 to 8*, Frere, S. S. and Tomlin, R. S. O.
            (eds.) (Stroud: Alan Sutton, 1990–5).

ANCIENT SOURCES

Apicius *De Re Coquinaria* (Philip Reclam edition with German translation by
    R. Maier, 1991).
Caesar *De Bello Gallico* (Penguin edition. English translation by S. A. Handford,
    1951).
Cato *De Agricultura* (Prospect Books edition with English translation by
    A. Dalby, 1998).
Columella *De Re Rustica* (Loeb edition with English translation by E. S. Forster,
    and E. H. Heffner, revised edition 1968).
Dioscorides *Materia Medica* (Gunther, R. T. (ed), 1959. *The Greek Herbal of
    Dioscurides illustrated by a Byzantine AD 512, English edition by John Goodyer
    AD 1655* (New York reprint of 1933 publication)).

Martial *Epigrams* (Loeb edition with English translation by D. R. Shackleton Bailey, 1993).

Pliny *Natural History* (Loeb edition with English translation by various authors, 1938–63).

Tacitus *The Annals of Imperial Rome* (Penguin edition. English translation by K. Wellesley, revised editon 1971).

The Histories (Penguin edition. English translation by M. Grant, revised edition 1975).

Strabo *The Geographies* (Loeb edition with English translation by H. L. Jones, 1917–32).

Vegetius *Epitoma Rei Militaris* (Liverpool University Press edition with English translation by N. P. Milner, 2nd revised edition 1996).

MODERN WORKS

(Note: Where the actual year of a journal publication differs from the stated year for the volume, the reference is given in the form: author, actual year with the stated year given in brackets after the volume number.)

Abramson, P., Berg, D. S. and Fossick, M. R. 1999. *Roman Castleford. Excavations 1974–85 Volume II: the Structural and Environmental Evidence.* Wakefield: West Yorkshire Archaeological Services.

Alcock, J. 2001. *Food in Roman Britain.* Stroud: Tempus.

Allason-Jones, L. and McKay, B. 1988. *Coventina's Well.* Chesters: Trustees of the Clayton Collection.

Allen, J. R. L. and Fulford, M. G. 1996. 'The distribution of south-east Dorset black burnished category 1 pottery in south-west Britain'. *Britannia* 27: 223–81.

Alston, R. 1995. *Soldier and Society in Roman Egypt.* London: Routledge.

Anderson, A. S., Wacher, J. S. and Fitzpatrick, A. P. 2001. *The Romano-British 'Small Town' at Wanborough, Wiltshire.* London: Roman Society.

Anon. 1990. 'Verulamium', *Current Archaeology* 120: 410–17.

2002. *Portable Antiquities Annual Report 2000–2001.* London: Dept. Culture, Media and Sport.

2004. *Treasure Annual Report 2002.* London: Dept. Culture, Media and Sport.

Arthur, P. 1986. 'Roman amphorae from Canterbury'. *Britannia* 17: 239–58.

Bales, E. 2004. *A Roman Maltings at Beck Row, Mildenhall, Suffolk.* EAA Occasional Papers 20: Ipswich.

Banfield, W. T. 1937. *'Manna' A comprehensive treatise on bread manufacture.* London: MacLaren and Sons Ltd.

Barber, B. and Bowsher, D. 2000. *The Eastern Cemetery of Roman London Excavations 1983–1990.* London: Museum of London Archaeological Service.

Barker, P., White, R., Pretty, K., Bird, H. and Corbishley, M. 1997. *The Baths Basilica Wroxeter: Excavations 1966–90.* London: English Heritage.

Barnard, T. 2004. *Making the Grand Figure.* New Haven: Yale University Press.

Bateman, N. and Locker, A. 1982. 'The sauce of the Thames'. *The London Archaeologist* 4.8: 204–7.

Baxter, M. J. 1994. *Exploratory Multivariate Analysis in Archaeology.* Edinburgh: Edinburgh University Press.

2003. *Statistics in Archaeology.* London: Edward Arnold.

Bedwin, M. and Bedwin, O. 1999. *A Roman Malt House: Excavations at Stebbings Green, Essex 1988.* EAA Occasional Paper 6: Chelmsford.

Bestwick, J. D. 1975. 'Romano-British inland salting at Middlewich (Salinae), Cheshire', in De Brisay and Evans (eds.), pp.66–70.

Biddle, M. 1967. 'Two Flavian burials from Grange Road, Winchester', *Antiquaries Journal* 47: 224–50.

Biddulph, E. 2005. 'Samian wear'. *Current Archaeology* 196: 191–3.

Bidwell, P. T. 1985. *The Roman Fort of Vindolanda at Chesterholm, Northumberland.* London: English Heritage.

Bidwell, P. and Speak, S. 1994. *Excavations at South Shields Roman Fort Volume I.* Newcastle upon Tyne: Society of Antiquaries of Newcastle upon Tyne.

Bird, J. 1993. '3rd-century samian ware in Britain'. *Journal of Roman Pottery Studies* 6: 1–14.

Bird, J., Hassall, M. and Sheldon, H. (eds.) 1996. *Interpreting Roman London.* Oxford: Oxbow Books.

Birley, A. 1979. *The People of Roman Britain.* London: B.T. Batsford.

Birley, R. 1977. *Vindolanda.* London: Thames and Hudson.

Bland, R. and Johns, C. 1993. *The Hoxne Treasure.* London: British Museum Press.

Blockley, K., Blockley, M., Blockley, P., Frere, S. and Stow, S. 1995. *Excavations in the Marlowe Car Park and surrounding areas.* Canterbury: Canterbury Archaeological Trust.

Boon, G. C. 1961. 'Roman antiquities at Welshpool'. *Antiquaries Journal* 88: 13–31.

Booth, P. 1997. *Asthall, Oxfordshire: Excavations in a Roman 'Small Town'.* Oxford: Oxford Archaeological Unit.

Booth, P. and Evans, J. 2001. *Roman Alcester: Northern Extramural Area.* CBARR 127: York.

Booth, P., Evans, J. and Hiller, J. 2001. *Excavations in the Extramural Settlement of Roman Alchester, Oxfordshire, 1991.* Oxford: Oxford Archaeology.

Borgard, P. and Cavalier, M. 2003. 'The Lipari origin of the Richborough 527'. *Journal of Roman Pottery Studies* 10: 96–106.

Bouby, I. and Marinval, P. 2004. 'Fruits and seeds from Roman cremations in Limagne (Massif Central) and the spatial variability of plant offerings in France', *Journal of Archaeological Science* 31: 77–86.

Bourdieu, P. 1986. *Distinction.* London: Routledge.

Bowman, A. K. 1993. *Life and Letters on the Roman Frontier.* London: British Museum Press.

Bowman, A. K. and Thomas, J. D. 1994. *The Vindolanda Writing Tablets (Tabulae Vindolandenses II).* London: British Museum Press.

1996. 'New writing tablets from Vindolanda'. *Britannia* 27: 299–328.

2003. *The Vindolanda Writing Tablets (Tabulae Vindolandenses III)*. London: British Museum Press.

Bradley, R. 1975. 'Salt and settlement in the Hampshire Sussex Borderland' in De Brisay and Evans (eds.), pp.20–5.

Braun, T. 1995. 'Barley cakes and emmer bread' in Wilkins *et al.* (eds.), pp.25–37.

Braund, D. and Wilkins, J. (eds.) 2000. *Athenaeus and his World*. Exeter: University of Exeter Press.

Brigstock, R. J. 2000. 'Coin supply in the North in the late Roman period' in Wilmott and Wilson (eds.), pp.33–7.

Brillat-Savarin, J. E. 1826. *The Physiology of Taste*. New York: Liveright 1926.

Britnell, J. 1989. *Caersws Vicus, Powys: Excavations at the Old Primary School*. BAR BS 205: Oxford.

Brodribb, A. C. C., Hands, A. R. and Walker, D. R. 1971. *Excavations at Shakenoak Farm, near Wilcote, Oxfordshire 2*. Oxford: privately printed.

Brodribb, G. and Cleere, H. 1988. 'The *Classis Britannica* bath-house at Beauport Park, East Sussex', *Britannia* 19: 217–74.

Brown, A. E. and Woodfield, C. 1983. 'Excavations at Towcester, Northamptonshire: the Alchester Road Suburb'. *Northamptonshire Archaeology* 118: 43–140.

Brown, A. G. and Meadows, I. 2000. 'Roman vineyards in Britain: finds from the Nene Valley and new research'. *Antiquity* 74: 491–2.

Brown, F., Boyle, A., Howard-Davis, C. H. and Lupton, A. forthcoming. *A Road Through Time: Archaeological Investigations along the route of the A1(M) Darrington to Dishforth Road Scheme*.

Brown, N. R. 1999. *The Archaeology of Ardleigh, Essex, Excavations 1955–1980*. EAA 90: Chelmsford.

Brothwell, D. R. and Pollard, A. M. 2001. *Handbook of Archaeological Sciences*. Chichester: Wiley.

Bruce Mitford, R. 1972. *The Sutton Hoo Ship Burial: a Handbook*. London: British Museum Press.

Buckland, P. C. 1976. *The Environmental Evidence from the Church Street Roman Sewer System*. AY 14/1: London.

Buckland, P. C. and Magilton, J. R. 1986. *The Archaeology of Doncaster. Volume 1: The Roman Civil Settlement*. BAR BS 148: Oxford.

Buckland, P. C., Magilton, J. R. and Dolby, M. J. 1980. 'The Roman pottery industries of south Yorkshire: a review' *Britannia* 11: 145–64.

Burkeman, O. 2005. 'When the PM came to call'. *The Guardian G2 Supplement* 26 January 2005.

Bushe-Fox, J. P. 1949. *Fourth Report on the Excavations of the Roman Fort at Richborough, Kent*. Oxford: Society of Antiquaries of London.

Buxton, K. and Howard-Davis, C. 2000. *Bremetenacum: Excavations at Roman Ribchester 1980, 1989–1990*. Lancaster: Lancaster University Archaeological Unit.

Carreras Montfort, C. 2003. 'Haltern 70: a review'. *Journal of Roman Pottery Studies* 10: 85–91.

Carreras Montfort, C. and Williams, D. 2003. 'Spanish olive oil trade in late Roman Britain: Dressel 23 amphorae from Winchester'. *Journal of Roman Pottery Studies* 10: 64–8.

Caruana, I. D. 1992. 'Carlisle: excavation of a section of the annexe ditch of the first Flavian fort, 1990'. *Britannia* 23: 45–109.

Casey, P. J., Davies, J. L. and Evans, J. 1993. *Excavations at Segontium (Caernarfon) Roman Fort, 1975–1979*. CBARR 90: London.

Casey, P. J. and Hoffmann, B. 1998. 'Rescue excavations in the vicus of the fort at Greta Bridge, Co. Durham, 1972–4'. *Britannia* 29: 111–83.

Clark, P. 1983. *The English Alehouse: a Social History 1200–1830*. London: Longman.

Clarke, C. P. 1998. *Excavations to the south of Chignall Roman Villa, Essex 1977–81*. EAA 83: Chelmsford.

Clarke, G. 1979. *The Roman Cemetery at Lankhills*. Oxford: Clarendon Press.

Clauss, M. 2000. *The Roman Cult of Mithras*. (Translated by R. Gordon). Edinburgh: Edinburgh University Press.

Colyer, C., Gilmour, B. J. J. and Jones, M. J. 1999. *The Defences of the Lower City*. CBARR 114: York.

Connor, A. and Buckley, R. 1999. *Roman and Medieval Occupation in Causeway Lane, Leicester*. Leicester: University of Leicester Archaeological Service.

Cool, H. E. M. 1982. 'The artefact record: some possibilities', in Harden, D. W. (ed.), *Later Prehistoric Settlement in South-east Scotland*. Edinburgh: Dept. of Archaeology, University of Edinburgh, pp.92–100.

1995. 'Glass vessels of the fourth and early fifth century in Roman Britain', in Foy, D. (ed.), *Le Verre de l'Antiquité tardive et du Haut Moyen Age*. Cergy-Pontoise: Musée Archéologique Départemental du Val d'Oise, pp.11–23.

2000a. 'The parts left over: material culture into the fifth century', in Wilmott and Wilson (eds.), pp.47–65.

2000b. 'Hairstyles and lifestyles', *Roman Finds Group Newsletter* 19: 3–6.

2003. 'Local production and trade in glass vessels in the British Isles in the first to seventh centuries AD', in Foy, D. and Nenna M.-D. (eds.), *Échanges et commerce du verre dans le monde antique*. Montagnac: Éditions Monique Mergoil, pp.139–45.

2004a. 'Some notes on spoons and mortaria' in Croxford, B., Eckardt, H., Meake, J. and Weekes, J. (eds.), *TRAC 2003: Proceedings of the Thirteenth Annual Theoretical Roman Archaeology Conference Leicester 2003*. Oxford: Oxbow Books, pp.28–35

2004b. *The Roman Cemetery at Brougham, Cumbria: Excavations 1966–1967*. London: Roman Society.

2005. 'Roman stone mortars – a preliminary survey'. *Journal of Roman Pottery Studies* 12: 54–8.

Cool, H. E. M. and Baxter, M. J. 1999. 'Peeling the onion; an approach to comparing vessel glass assemblages'. *Journal of Roman Archaeology* 12: 72–100.

2002. 'Exploring Romano-British finds assemblages'. *Oxford Journal of Archaeology* 21: 365–80.

2005. 'Cemeteries and significance tests'. *Journal of Roman Archaeology* 18: 397–404.

Cool, H. E. M., Lloyd-Morgan, G. and Hooley, A. D. 1995. *Finds from the Fortress.* AY 17/10: York.

Cool, H. E. M. and Philo, C. (eds.) 1998. *Roman Castleford. Excavations 1974–85 Volume I: the Small Finds.* Wakefield: West Yorkshire Archaeological Services.

Cool, H. E. M. and Price, J. 1995. *Roman Vessel Glass from Excavations in Colchester 1971–85.* CAR 8: Colchester.

Copley, M. S., Berstan, R., Dudd, S. N., Straker, V., Payne, S. and Evershed, R. P. 2005. 'Dairying in Antiquity. I. Evidence from absorbed lipid residues dating to the British Iron Age'. *Journal of Archaeological Science* 32: 485–503.

Corcoran, J. X. W. P. 1952. 'Tankards and tankard handles of the British Early Iron Age'. *Proc. Prehistoric Society* 18: 85–101.

Counihan, C. M. 1999. *The Anthropology of Food and Body.* London: Routledge.

Cowell, R. W. and Philpott, R. A. 2000. *Prehistoric, Romano-British and Medieval Settlement in Lowland North-West England.* Liverpool: National Museums and Galleries on Merseyside.

Coy, J. 1989. 'The provision of fowls and fish for towns', in Serjeantson and Waldron (eds.), pp.25–40.

Cracknell, S. (ed.) 1996. *Roman Alcester: Defences and Defended Area.* CBARR 106: York.

Cracknell, S. and Mahany, C. (eds.) 1994. *Roman Alcester: Southern Extramural Area.* CBARR 97: York.

Cram, L. and Fulford, M. 1979. 'Silchester tile making – the faunal environment', in McWhirr, A. (ed.), *Roman Brick and Tile. Studies in Manufacture, Distribution and Use in the Western Empire.* BAR IS 68: Oxford, pp.201–9.

Creighton, J. 2000. *Coins and Power in Late Iron Age Britain.* Cambridge: Cambridge University Press.

Croom, A. T. 2001. 'Experiments in Roman military cooking methods'. *The Arbeia Journal 6–7* (1997–98): 34–47.

Crummy, N. 1983, *The Roman Small Finds from Excavations in Colchester 1971–9.* CAR 2: Colchester.

Crummy, N., Crummy, P. and Crossan, C. 1993. *Excavations of Roman and later Cemeteries, Churches and Monastic Sites in Colchester, 1971–88.* CAR 9: Colchester.

Crummy, P. 1984. *Excavations at Lion Walk, Balkerne Lane, and Middleborough, Colchester, Essex.* CAR 3: Colchester.

1992. *Excavations at Culver Street, the Gilberd School, and other sites in Colchester 1971–85.* CAR 6: Colchester.

1997. *City of Victory.* Colchester: Colchester Archaeological Trust.

Cubberley, A. L., Lloyd, J. A. and Roberts, P. C. 1988. 'Testa and clibani: the baking covers of classical Italy', *Papers of the British School at Rome* 56: 98–120.

Cunliffe, B. 1971. *Excavations at Fishbourne 1961–1969. Volume II: The Finds.* Leeds: Society of Antiquaries of London.

1984. *Danebury: an Iron Age Hillfort in Hampshire. Volume II. The Excavations 1969–1978: the Finds.* CBARR 52: London.

Cunliffe, B. (ed.) 1988. *The Temple of Sulis Minerva at Bath. Volume II. The Finds from the Sacred Spring.* Oxford: Oxford University Committee for Archaeology.

Cunliffe, B. 2005. *Iron Age Communities in Britain.* London: Routledge 4th edition.

Cunliffe, B. and Davenport, P. 1985. *The Temple of Sulis Minerva at Bath. Volume I. the Site.* Oxford: Oxford University Committee for Archaeology.

Cunliffe, B. and Poole, C. 1991. *Danebury: an Iron Age Hillfort in Hampshire. Volume V: the Excavations 1979–1988: the Finds* CBARR 73b: London.

Curle, J. 1932. 'An inventory of objects of Roman and provincial origin found on sites in Scotland not definitely associated with Roman constructions', *Proc. Soc. Antiquaries Scotland* 66: 277–397.

Curtis, R. I. 1991. *Garum and Salsamata.* Leiden: E. J. Brill.

Dalby, A. 1996. *Siren Feasts.* London: Routledge.

2000. *Empire of Pleasures.* London: Routledge.

Dalby, A., and Granger, S. 1996. *The Classical Cookbook.* London: British Museum Press.

Dannell, G. B. and Wild, J. P. 1987. *Longthorpe II: the Military Works-depot: an Episode in Landscape History.* London: Roman Society.

Dark, K. and Dark, P. 1997. *The Landscape of Roman Britain.* Stroud: Tempus.

Darling, M. J. and Gurney, D. 1993. *Caister-on-Sea. Excavations by Charles Green, 1951–55.* EAA 60: Dereham.

David, E. 1977. *English Bread and Yeast Cookery.* Harmondsworth: Penguin 1979 edition.

Davidson, A. 1999. *The Oxford Companion to Food.* Oxford: Oxford University Press.

Davies, B., Richardson, B. and Tomber, R. 1994. *A Dated Corpus of Early Roman Pottery from the City of London.* CBARR 98: York.

Davies, R. W. 1971. 'The Roman military diet'. *Britannia* 2: 122–42.

Davies, S. M., Bellamy, P. S., Heaton, M. J. and Woodward, P. J. 2002. *Excavations at Alington Avenue, Fordington, Dorchester, Dorset, 1984–87.* Dorchester: Dorset Natural History and Archaeological Society.

Dearne, M. J. and Branigan, K. 1995. 'The use of coal in Roman Britain'. *Antiquaries Journal* 75: 71–105.

De Brisay, K. W. and Evans, K. A. (eds.) 1975. *Salt: the Study of an Ancient Industry.* Colchester: Colchester Archaeological Group.

den Boesterd, M. H. P. 1956. *Description of the Collections in the Rijksmuseum G.M. Kam at Nijmegen V: The Bronze Vessels.* Nijmegen: Dept. of Education Arts and Sciences.

Dickson, C. and Dickson, J. H. 2000. *Plants and People in Ancient Scotland.* Stroud: Tempus.

Dobney, K. M., Jaques, S. D. and Irving, B. G. 1995. *Of Butchers and Breeds. Report on Vertebrate Remains from Various Sites in the City of Lincoln.* Lincoln: City of Lincoln Archaeology Unit.

Douglas, M. 1966. *Purity and Danger*. London: Routledge.

Down, A. 1989. *Chichester Excavations 6*. Chichester: Phillimore.

Draper, J. 1985. *Excavations by Mr H. P. Cooper on the Roman Site at Hill Farm, Gestingthorpe, Essex* EAA 25: Chelmsford.

Drummond, J. C. and Wilbraham, A. 1957. *The Englishman's Food*. London: Pimlico. 1991 reprint of revised edition.

Drummond-Murray, J., Thompson, P. and Cowan, C. 2002. *Settlement in Roman Southwark*. London: Museum of London Archaeological Service.

Drysdale, J. 1983. *Classic Game Cookery*. London: MacMillan.

Durrani, N. 2004. 'Luxury Bath'. *Current Archaeology* 195: 105.

Eckardt, H. 2002. *Illuminating Roman Britain*. Montagnac: Éditions Monique Mergoil.

Edwards, J. 1984. *The Roman Cookery of Apicius*. London: Rider.

Ellis, P. (ed.) 2000. *The Roman Baths and Macellum at Wroxeter*. London: English Heritage.

Esmonde Cleary, S. 2000. 'Summing up', in Wilmott and Wilson (eds.), pp.89–94.

Evans, A. J. 1892. 'On a Late Celtic urn-field at Aylesford, Kent'. *Archaeologia* 52: 316–81.

Evans, D. R. and Metcalf, V. M. 1992. *Roman Gates Caerleon*. Oxford: Oxbow Books.

Evans, E. 2000. *The Caerleon Canabae: Excavations in the Civil Settlement 1984–90*. London: Roman Society.

Evans, J. 1987. 'Graffiti and the evidence of literacy and pottery use in Roman Britain'. *Archaeological Journal* 144: 191–204.

  1993. 'Pottery function and finewares in the Roman north'. *Journal of Roman Pottery Studies* 6: 95–118.

  1995. 'Later Iron Age and 'native' pottery in the north-east', in Vyner, B. (ed.) *Moorland Monuments: Studies in the Archaeology of north-east Yorkshire in honour of Raymond Hayes and Don Spratt*. CBARR 101: York, pp.46–68.

  2000. 'The end of Roman pottery in the north', in Wilmott and Wilson (eds.), pp.39–41.

Evershed, R. P., Dudd, S. N., Lockheart, M. J. and Jim, S. 2001. 'Lipids in Archaeology', in Brothwell and Pollard (eds.), pp.331–49.

Evison, V. I. 2000. 'Glass vessels in England AD 400–1100' in Price, J. (ed.), *Glass in Britain and Ireland AD 350–1100*. British Museum Occasional Paper 127: London, pp.47–104.

Farrar, R. A. H. 1975. 'Prehistoric and Roman saltworks in Dorset' in De Brisay and Evans (eds.), pp.14–20.

Farwell, D. E. and Molleson, T. I. 1993. *Poundbury Volume II: the Cemeteries*. Dorchester: Dorset Natural History and Archaeological Society.

Fitzpatrick, A. P. 2003. 'Roman amphorae in Iron Age Britain'. *Journal of Roman Pottery Studies* 10: 10–25.

Fitzpatrick, A. P. and Morris, E. L. (eds.) 1994. *The Iron Age in Wessex: Recent Work*. Salisbury: Trust for Wessex Archaeology.

Fitzpatrick, A. P. and Timby, J. 2002. 'Roman pottery in Iron Age Britain', in Woodward and Hill (eds.), pp.161–72.

Flemming, R. 2000. 'The physicians at the feast. The place of knowledge at Athenaeus' dinner-table' in Braund and Wilkins (eds.), pp.476–82.

Fox, A. and Ravenhall, W. 1972. 'The Roman fort at Nanstallon, Cornwall'. *Britannia* 3: 56–111.

France, N. E. and Gobel, B. M. 1985. *The Romano-British Temple at Harlow.* Gloucester: Alan Sutting Publishing.

Frere, S. S. 1972. *Verulamium Excavations Volume I.* Oxford: Society of Antiquaries of London.

1974. 'The Roman fortress at Longthorpe'. *Britannia* 5: 1–129.

1987. *Britannia.* London: Routledge. 3rd revised edition.

1991. 'Roman Britain in 1990: sites explored'. *Britannia* 22: 222–92.

Fulford, M. 1975. *New Forest Roman Pottery* BAR BS 17: Oxford.

1979. 'Pottery production and trade at the end of Roman Britain: the case against continuity', in Casey, P. (ed.) *The End of Roman Britain* BAR BS 71: Oxford, pp.120–32.

2001. 'Links with the past: pervasive 'ritual' behaviour in Roman Britain'. *Britannia* 32: 199–218.

Fulford, M., Rippon, S., Ford, S., Timby, J. and Williams, B. 1997. 'Silchester: excavations at the north gate, on the north walls, and in the northern suburbs 1988 and 1991–3'. *Britannia* 28: 87–168.

Gade, D. W. 2000. 'Horse' in Kiple and Ornelas (eds.), pp.542–5.

Gage, J. 1834: 'A plan of barrows called the Bartlow Hills, in the parish of Ashdon, in Essex, with an account of Roman sepulchral relics recently discovered in the lesser barrows'. *Archaeologia* 25: 1–23.

1836: 'The recent discovery of Roman sepulchral relics in one of the greater barrows at Bartlow, in the parish of Ashdon, in Essex'. *Archaeologia* 26: 300–17.

1840: 'An account of further discoveries of Roman sepulchral relics in one of the Bartlow Hills'. *Archaeologia* 28: 1–6.

Gage Rokewode, J. 1842: 'An account of the final excavations made at the Bartlow Hills'. *Archaeologia* 29: 1–4.

Gardner, W. and Savory, H. N. 1964. *Dinorben.* Cardiff: National Museum of Wales.

Garnsey, P. 1999. *Food and Society in Classical Antiquity.* Cambridge: Cambridge University Press.

Germany, M. 2003. *Excavations at Great Holts Farm, Boreham, Essex, 1992–94.* EAA 105: Chelmsford.

Gillam, J. P. and MacIvor, I. 1954. 'The temple of Mithras at Rudchester'. *Archaeologia Aeliana* 4th series 32: 176–219.

Going, C. J. 1987. *The Mansio and other Sites in the South-Eastern Sector of Caesaromagus: the Roman Pottery.* CBARR 62: London.

Going, C. J. and Hunn, J. R. 1999. *Excavations at Boxfield Farm, Chells, Stevenage, Hertfordshire.* Hertford: Hertfordshire Archaeological Trust.

Goldsworthy, A. K. 1998. *The Roman Army At War, 100 BC – 200 AD*. Oxford: Clarendon Press.

Goody, J. 1982. *Cooking Cuisine and Class*. Cambridge: Cambridge University Press.

Gowers, E. 1993. *The Loaded Table*. Oxford: Clarendon Press.

Gozzini Giacosa, I. 1992. *A Taste of Ancient Rome*. (translated by Anna Herklotz). Chicago: University of Chicago Press.

Grant, A. 1981. 'The significance of deer remains at occupation sites of the Iron Age to Anglo-Saxon periods', in Jones and Dimbleby (eds.), pp.205–13.

Grant, M. 1996. *Antithimus: On the Observance of Food*. (Totnes: Prospect Books.)

Graser, E. R. 1940. 'The Edict of Diocletian on maximum prices' in Frank, T. *An Economic Survey of Ancient Rome. Volume V: Rome and Italy of the Empire*. Baltimore: John Hopkins Press, pp.305–421.

Green, C. S. 1987. *Excavations at Poundbury. Volume I: the Settlements*. Dorchester: Dorset Natural History and Archaeological Society.

Green, F. J. 1981. 'Iron Age, Roman and Saxon crops: the archaeological evidence from Wessex', in Jones and Dimbleby (eds.), pp.129–53.

Green, K. 1979. *Report on the Excavations at Usk 1965–1976. The Pre-Flavian Fine Wares*. Cardiff: University of Wales Press.

Green, M. J. 1998. 'Vessels of death: sacred cauldrons in archaeology and myth', *Antiquaries Journal* 78: 63–84.

Greig, J. 1982. 'Garderobes, sewers, cesspits and latrines', *Current Archaeology* 85: 49–52.

Grimes, W. F. 1930. *Holt Denbighshire* Y Cymmrodor 41: London.

Grimm, V. E. 1996. *From Fasting to Feasting: the Evolution of a Sin*. London: Routledge.

Guest, P. S. W. 2005. *The Late Roman Gold and Silver Coins from the Hoxne Treasure*. London: British Museum Press.

Günther, R. T. 1897. 'The oyster culture of the ancient Romans', *Journal Marine Biological Assoc.* 4: 360–5.

Gurney, D. 1986. *Settlement, Religion and Industry on the Roman Fen-edge, Norfolk* EAA 31: Dereham.

Halbaek, H. 1964. 'The Isca grain, a Roman plant introduction in Britain' *New Phytologist* 63: 158–164.

Hall, A. R. and Kenward, H. K. 1990. *Environmental Evidence from the Colonia*. AY 14/6: London.

Hall, A. R., Kenward, H. K. and Williams, D. 1980. *Environmental Evidence from Roman Deposits in Skeldergate*. AY 14/3: London.

Hands, A. R. 1993. *The Romano-British Roadside Settlement at Wilcote, Oxfordshire I Excavations 1990–92*. BAR BS 232: Oxford.

1998. *The Romano-British Roadside Settlement at Wilcote, Oxfordshire II Excavations 1993–96*. BAR BS 265: Oxford.

Harden, D. B. 1960. 'The Wint Hill hunting bowl and related glasses'. *Journal of Glass Studies* 2: 45–81.

Hartley, D. 1954. *Food in England*. London: Little, Brown. 1999 reprint.

Hartley, K. F. 1973. 'The marketing and distribution of mortaria', in Detsicas, A. (ed.), *Current Research in Romano-British Coarse Pottery.* CBARR 10: London, pp.39–51.

Hartley, K. 1998. 'The incidence of stamped mortaria in the Roman Empire, with special reference to imports to Britain', in Bird, J. (ed.), *Form and Fabric.* Oxford: Oxbow Books, pp.199–217.

Hassall, M. W. C. and Tomlin, R. S. O. 1986. 'Roman Britain in 1985 II: Inscriptions'. *Britannia* 17: 428–54.

Havis, R. and Brooks, H. 2004. *Excavations at Stansted Airport, 1986–91. Volume 1: Prehistoric and Romano-British.* EAA 107: Chelmsford.

Hawkes, C. F. C. and Hull, M. R. 1947. *Camulodunum. First Report on the Excavations at Colchester 1930–1939.* Oxford: Society of Antiquaries of London.

Henig, M. 1984. *Religion in Roman Britain.* London: BT Batsford.

1995. *The Art of Roman Britain.* London: BT Batsford.

Heslop, D. H. 1987. *The Excavation of an Iron Age Settlement at Thorpe Thewles, Cleveland, 1980–1982.* CBARR 65: London.

Hill, J. D. 1989. 'Re-thinking the Iron Age'. *Scottish Archaeological Review* 6: 16–24.

2002. 'Just about the potter's wheel? Using, making and depositing Middle and Later Iron Age pots in East Anglia', in Woodward and Hill (eds.), pp.143–60.

Hillman, G. 1981. 'Reconstruction crop husbandry practices from charred remains of crops', in Mercer, R. (ed.) *Farming Practice in British Prehistory.* Edinburgh: Edinburgh University Press, pp.123–62.

Hinchliffe, J., Williams, J. H. and Williams, F. 1992. *Roman Warrington: Excavations at Wilderspool 1966–9 and 1976.* Manchester: Department of Archaeology, Manchester University.

Hingley, R. 2000. *Roman Officers and English Gentlemen.* London: Routledge.

Hinton, P. (ed.) 1988. *Excavations in Southwark 1973–76 Lambeth 1973–79.* London: London and Middlesex and Surrey Archaeological Societies.

Hodder, I. 1982. *Symbols in Action.* Cambridge: Cambridge University Press.

Holbrook, N. (ed.) 1998. *Cirencester: the Roman Town Defences, Public Buildings and Shops.* Cirencester: Cotswold Archaeological Trust.

Holbrook, N. and Bidwell, P. T. 1991. *Roman Finds from Exeter.* Exeter: Exeter City Council and University of Exeter.

1992. 'Roman pottery from Exeter 1980–1990'. *Journal of Roman Pottery Studies* 5: 35–80.

Holden, T. G. 1995. 'The last meals of the Lindow bog men', in Turner, R. C. and Scaife, R. G. (eds.) *New Discoveries and Perspectives.* London: British Museum Press, pp.76–82.

Holland, T. 2003. *Rubicon.* London: Little, Brown.

Hollingsworth, M. 2004. *The Cardinal's Hat.* London: Profile Books.

Holmes, N. 2003. *Excavations of Roman Sites at Cramond Edinburgh.* Edinburgh: Society of Antiquaries of Scotland.

Houlston, M. 1999. 'Excavations at the Mount Roman villa, Maidstone, 1994'. *Archaeologia Cantiana* 109: 71–172.

Huntley, J. P. 2000. 'Late Roman transition in the north: the palynological evidence', in Wilmott and Wilson (eds.), pp.67–71.

Hurst, H. R. 1985. *Kingsholm*. Cambridge: Gloucester Archaeological Publications.

Hurst, H. R. and Pitts, L. F. 1986. *Gloucester, the Roman and Later Defences*. Cambridge: Gloucester Archaeological Publications.

Jackson, R. P. J. and Potter, T. W. 1996. *Excavations at Stonea, Cambridgeshire 1980–85*. London: British Museum Press.

James, S. 2003. 'Writing the legions: the development and future of Roman military studies in Britain'. *Archaeological Journal* 159 (2002): 1–58.

Jansen, W. 2001. 'French bread and Algerian wine: conflicting identities in French Algeria' in Scholliers, P. (ed.), *Food, Drink and Identity* (Oxford: Berg), pp.195–218.

Jarrett, M. G. and Wrathmell, S. 1981. *Whitton: an Iron Age and Roman Farm-stead in South Glamorgan*. Cardiff: University of Wales Press.

Jessup, R. F. 1954. 'Excavation of a Roman Barrow at Holborough, Snodland'. *Archaeologia Cantiana* 68: 1–61.

Johns, C. M. 1981. 'The Risley silver lanx: a lost antiquity from Roman Britain'. *Antiquaries Journal* 61: 53–72.

Johns, C. M. and Potter, T. W. 1983. *The Thetford Treasure*. London: British Museum Publications.

  1985. 'The Canterbury late Roman treasure'. *Antiquaries Journal* 65: 321–52.

Johnson, A. P. 1983. *Roman Forts*. London: A. & C. Black.

Johnston, R. F. 2000. 'Pigeons', in Kiple and Ornelas (eds.), pp.561–4.

Jones, D. M. (ed.), 1980. *Excavations at Billingsgate Buildings 'Triangle', Lower Thames Street, London, 1974*. London: London and Middlesex Archaeo-logical Society.

Jones, M. 1981. 'The developments of crop husbandry', in Jones and Dimbleby (eds.), pp.95–127.

Jones, M. and Dimbleby, G. 1981. *The Environment of Man. The Iron Age to the Anglo-Saxon Period*. BAR BS 87: Oxford.

Keevil, G. D. 1992. 'A frying pan from Great Lea, Binfield, Berkshire'. *Britannia* 22: 231–33.

Kenward, H. K., Hall, A. R. and Jones, A. K. G. 1986. *Environmental Evidence from a Roman Well and Anglian Pits in the Legionary Fortress*. AY 14/5: London.

Kenward, H. K. and Williams, D. 1979. *Biological Evidence from the Roman Warehouses in Coney Street*. AY 14/2: London.

Keppie, L. J. F. and Arnold, B. J. 1984. *Corpus Signorum Imperii Romani. Great Britain Volume I Fascicule 4 Scotland*. Oxford: Oxford University Press.

King, A. 1978. 'A comparative survey of bone assemblages from Roman sites in Britain', *Institute of Archaeology Bulletin* 15: 207–32.

  1999. 'Meat diet in the Roman world: a regional inter-site comparison'. *Journal of Roman Archaeology* 12: 168–202.

2005. 'Animal remains from temples in Roman Britain'. *Britannia* 36: 329–69.

King, D. 1987. 'Petrology, dating and distribution of querns and millstones. The results of research in Bedfordshire, Buckinghamshire, Hertfordshire and Middlesex'. *Bulletin of the Institute of Archaeology* 23 (1986): 65–126.

Kiple, K. F. and Ornelas, K. C. (eds.), 2000. *The Cambridge World History of Food*. Cambridge: Cambridge University Press.

Knight, D. 2002. 'A regional ceramic sequence: pottery of the first millennium BC between the Humber and the Nene', in Woodward and Hill (eds.), pp.119–42.

Knights, B. A., Dickson, C. A., Dickson, J. H. and Breeze, D. J. 1983. 'Evidence concerning the Roman military diet at Bearsden, Scotland, in the 2nd century AD'. *Journal of Archaeological Science* 10: 139–52.

Koster, A. 1997. *Description of the Collections in the Provincial Museum G. M. Kam at Nijmegen 13: The Bronze Vessels 2. Acquisitions 1954–1996 (including vessels of pewter and iron)*. Nijmegen: Provincie Gelderlan.

Kurlansky, M. 1998. *Cod*. London: Jonathan Cape.

2002. *Salt: a World History*. London: Jonathan Cape.

Lakin, D., Seeley, F., Bird, J., Rielly, K. and Ainsley, C. 2002. *The Roman Tower at Shadwell, London: a Reappraisal*. London: Museum of London Archaeological Service.

Lambert, J. 1996. *Transect through Time. The Archaeological Landscape of the Shell North-Western Ethylene Pipeline*. Lancaster: Lancaster University Archaeological Unit.

Leach, P. 1982. *Ilchester. Volume 1: Excavations 1974–5*. Bristol: Western Archaeological Trust.

Leach, P. and Evans, C. J. 2001. *Fosse Lane, Shepton Mallet 1990*. London: Roman Society.

Leech, R. 1981. 'The excavation of a Romano-British Farmstead and Cemetery on Bradley Hill, Somerton, Somerset'. *Britannia* 12: 177–252.

1982. *Excavations at Catsgore 1970–1973*. Bristol: Western Archaeological Trust.

Lentacker, A., Ervynck, A. and Van Neer, W. 2004. 'The symbolic meaning of the cock: the animal remains from the *mithraeum* at Tienen', in Martens, M. and De Boe, G. (eds.), *Roman Mithraism: the Evidence of the Small Finds*. Brussels: Instituut voor het Archeologisch Patrimonium, pp.57–80.

Leon, E. F. 1943. 'Cato's cakes'. *The Classical Journal* 38: 213–21.

Lethbridge, T. C. 1953. 'Burial of an Iron Age warrior at Snailwell'. *Proc. Cambridge Antiquarian Society* 46 (1952): 25–37.

Longley, D., Johnstone, N. and Evans, J. 1998. 'Excavations on two farms of the Romano-British period at Bryn Eryr and Bush Farm, Gwynedd'. *Britannia* 29: 185–246.

Luard, E. 1986. *European Peasant Cookery*. London: Corgi edition 1988.

Luff, R. 1993. *Animal Bones from Excavations in Colchester, 1971–85*. CAR 12: Colchester.

Mackreth, D. F. 1996. *Orton Hall Farm: a Roman and Early Anglo-Saxon Farmstead*. EAA 76: Manchester.

McCarthy, M. R. 1990. *A Roman, Anglian and Medieval site at Blackfriars Street, Carlisle Excavations 1977–9.* Kendall: Cumberland and Westmorland Antiquarian and Archaeological Society.

1991. *Roman Waterlogged Remains and Later Features at Castle St., Carlisle.* Kendal: Cumberland and Westmorland Antiquarian and Archaeological Society.

2000. *Roman and Medieval Carlisle: the Southern Lanes.* Carlisle: Dept of Archaeological Sciences, University of Bradford.

MacGregor, A. 1976. *Finds from a Roman Sewer System and an Adjacent Building in Church Street.* AY 17/1: London.

MacGregor, M. 1976. *Early Celtic Art in North Britain.* Leicester: Leicester University Press.

MacKinder, A. 2000. *A Romano-British Cemetery on Watling Street.* London: Museum of London Archaeological Service.

McKinley, J. I. 2000. 'Phoenix rising: aspects of cremation in Roman Britain', in Pearce *et al.* pp.38–44.

McWhirr, A., Viner, L. and Wells, C. 1982. *Romano-British Cemeteries at Cirencester.* Cirencester: Cirencester Excavation Committee.

Malcolmson, R. and Mastoris, S. 1998. *The English Pig.* London: Hambledon Press.

Maltby, M. 1981. 'Iron Age, Romano-British and Anglo-Saxon animal husbandry – a review of the faunal evidence', in Jones and Dimbleby, pp.155–203.

1985. 'Assessing variations in Iron Age and Roman butchery practices: the need for quantification', in Fieller, N. R. J., Gilbertson, D. D. and Ralph, N. G. A. (eds.), *Paleaobiological investigations: research design methods and data analysis.* BAR IS 266 : Oxford, pp.19–30.

1994. 'Animal exploitation in Iron Age Wessex', in Fitzpatrick and Morris (eds.), pp.9–10.

1997. 'Domestic fowl on Romano-British sites: inter-site comparisons of abundance'. *International Journal of Osteoarchaeology* 7: 402–14.

Manning, W. H. 1983. 'The cauldron chain of Iron Age and Roman Britain', in Hartley, B. and Wacher, J. (eds.), *Rome and her Northern Provinces.* Gloucester: Alan Sutton, pp.132–54.

1985. *Catalogue of the Romano-British Iron Tools, Fittings and Weapons in the British Museum.* London: British Museum Press.

Marsh, G. D. 1978. 'Early second century fine wares in the London area', in Arthur, P. R. and Marsh, G. D. (eds.), *Early Fine Wares in Roman Britain.* BAR BS 57: Oxford, pp.119–223.

Martin-Kilcher, S. 1994. *Die römischen Amphoren aus Augst und Kaiseraugst: ein Beitrag zur römischen Handels- und Kulturgeschichte. 2: die Amphoren für Wein, Fischsauce, Süfrücte (Gruppen 2–24) und Gesamtaswertung.* Basel: Römermuseum Augst.

2003. 'Fish-sauce amphorae from the Iberian peninsula: the forms and observations on trade with the north-west provinces'. *Journal of Roman Pottery Studies* 10: 69–84.

Matthews, C. L. 1981. *A Romano-British inhumation cemetery at Dunstable* (=*Bedfordshire Archaeological Journal* 15).

Mattingly, D. J. (ed.) 1997. *Dialogues in Roman Imperialism* Journal of Roman Archaeology Supplementary Series 23: Portsmouth, Rhode Island.

May, J. 1996. *Dragonby.* Oxford: Oxbow Books.

Mays, S. 1998. *The Archaeology of Human Bones.* London: Routledge.

Meadows, I. 1996. 'Wollaston: The Nene Valley, a British Moselle?' *Current Archaeology* 150: 212–5.

Merrifield, R. 1987. *The Archaeology of Ritual and Magic.* London: BT Batsford.

Miles, A. 1975. 'Salt-panning in Romano-British Kent', in De Brisay and Evans (eds.), pp.26–31.

Miles, D., Palmer, S., Smith, A. and Edgeley Long, G. forthcoming. *Iron Age and Roman settlement in the Upper Thames Valley: excavations at Claydon Pike and other sites within the Cotswold Water Park.* Oxford: Oxford Archaeology.

Miller, J. I. 1969. *The Spice Trade of the Roman Empire.* Oxford: Clarendon Press.

Miller, L., Schofield, J. and Rhodes, M. 1986. *The Roman Quay at St Magnus House, London.* London: London and Middlesex Archaeological Society.

Millett, M. 1979. 'An approach to the functional interpretation of pottery', in Millett, M. (ed.) *Pottery and the Archaeologist.* London: Institute of Archaeology, pp.35–47.

1987. 'An early Roman burial tradition in central southern England'. *Oxford Journal of Archaeology* 6: 63–8.

1990. *The Romanization of Britain.* Cambridge: Cambridge University Press.

1999. '*Coloniae* and Romano-British studies' in Hurst, H. (ed.) *The Coloniae of Roman Britain: New Studies and a Review.* Portsmouth Rhode Island: Journal of Roman Archaeology Supplementary Series 36, pp.191–6.

1996. 'Characterising Roman London' in Bird *et al.* (eds.), pp.33–7.

Milne, G. and Wardle, A. 1996. 'Early Roman development at Leadenhall Court, London and related research'. *Trans. London and Middlesex Archaeological Soc.,* 44 (1993): 23–169.

Monaghan, J. 1993. *Roman Pottery from the Fortress.* AY 16/7: York.

1997. *Roman Pottery from York.* AY 16/8: York.

Moreno Garcia, M., Orton C. R. and Rackham, D. J. 1996. 'A new statistical tool for comparing animal bone assemblages'. *Journal of Archaeological Science* 23: 437–53.

Morris, E. 1994. 'Production and distribution of pottery and salt in Iron Age Britain: a review'. *Proc. Prehistoric Soc.* 60: 371–94.

Muir, E. 1954. *An Autobiography.* London: Methuen revised edition.

Neal, D. S. 1974. *The Excavation of the Roman Villa in Gadebridge Park, Hemel Hempstead 1963–8.* London: Society of Antiquaries of London.

1996. *Excavations on the Roman Villa at Beadlam, Yorkshire.* Leeds: Yorkshire Archaeological Society.

Neal, D. S., Wardle, A. and Hunn, J. 1990. *Excavation of the Iron Age, Roman and Medieval Settlement at Gorhambury, St. Albans.* London: English Heritage.

Nevell, M. 2005. 'Salt making in Cheshire: the Iron Age Background', in Nevell and Fielding (eds.), pp.9–14.

Nevell, M. and Fielding, A. P. (eds.) 2005. *Brine on Britannia.* (= *Archaeology North West* 7 (Issue 17 for 2004–2005).

Niblett, R. 1985. *Sheepen: an Early Roman Industrial Site at Camulodunum.* CBARR 57: London.

1999. *The Excavation of a Ceremonial Site at Folly Lane, Verulamium.* London: Roman Society.

Nuber, H-U. 1972. 'Kanne und Griffschale. Ihr Gebrauch im täglichen Leben und die Beigabe in Gräbern der römischen Kaiserzeit', *Bericht der Römisch-germanischen Kommission* 53: 1–232.

O'Connor, T. 1988. *Bones from the General Accident site, Tanner Row.* AY 15/2: London.

1989. '"What shall we have for dinner?" Food remains from urban sites', in Serjeantson and Waldron (eds), pp.13–23.

2000. *The Archaeology of Animal Bones.* Stroud: Sutton Publishing.

2001. 'Animal bone quantification', in Brothwell and Pollard (eds.), pp.703–10.

Orton, C. 1993. 'How many pots make five? An historical review of pottery quantification'. *Archaeometry* 35: 169–84.

1996. 'Dem dry bones' in Bird *et al.* (eds.), pp.199–208.

Oswald, F. 1943. 'The mortaria of Margidunum and their development from AD 50 to 400'. *Antiquaries Journal* 22: 45–63.

Ottaway, P. 2001. 'Excavations on the site of the Roman signal station at Carr Naze, Filey, 1993–94'. *Archaeological Journal* 157 (2000): 79–199.

Painter, K. S. 1977a. *The Mildenhall Treasure.* London: British Museum Press.

1977b. *The Water Newton Early Christian Silver.* London: British Museum Press.

2001. *The Insula of the Menander at Pompeii. Volume IV: the Silver Treasure.* Oxford: Clarendon Press.

Parker, A. J. 1988. 'The birds of Roman Britain'. *Oxford Journal of Archaeology* 7: 197–226.

Parrington, M. 1978. *The Excavation of an Iron Age Settlement, Bronze Age Ring-ditches and Roman Features at Ashville Trading Estate, Abingdon, (Oxford-shire), 1974–76.* CBARR 28: London.

Partridge, C. 1981. *Skeleton Green, a Late Iron Age and Romano-British site.* London: Roman Society.

Peacock, D. P. S. 1977. 'Pompeian red ware' in Peacock, D. P. S. (ed.), *Pottery and Early Commerce. Characterization and Trade in Roman and Later Ceramics.* London: Academic Press, pp.147–62.

Peacock, D. P. S. and Williams, D. F. 1986. *Amphorae and the Roman Economy.* London: Longman.

Pearce, J. 2002. 'Food as substance and symbol in the Roman army: a case study from Vindolanda', in Freeman, P., Bennett, J., Fiema, Z. T. and Hoffmann, B. (eds.), *Limes XVIII. Proceedings for the XVIIIth International Congress of Roman Studies held in Amman, Jordan (September 2000).* BAR IS 1084: Oxford, pp.931–44.

Pearce, J., Millett, M. and Struck, M. (eds.) 2000. *Burial, Society and Context in the Roman World*. Oxford: Oxbow Books.

Penney, S. and Shotter, D. C. A. 1996. 'An inscribed Roman salt-pan from Shavinton, Cheshire'. *Britannia* 27: 360–5.

Perrin, J. R. 1981. *Roman Pottery from the Colonia: Skeldergate and Bishophill*. AY 16/2: London.

1990. *Roman Pottery from the Colonia 2: General Accident and Rougier Street*. AY 16/4: London.

Perring, D. 2003. ' "Gnosticism" in fourth-century Britain: the Frampton mosaics reconsidered'. *Britannia* 34: 97–127.

Philpott, R. 1991. *Burial Practices in Roman Britain*. BAR BS 219: Oxford.

Piggott, S. 1952–53. 'Three metal-work hoards of the Roman period from southern Scotland'. *Proc. Soc. Antiquaries of Scotland* 87: 1–50.

Pitts, L. and St Joseph, J. K. 1985. *Inchtuthil: the Roman Legionary Fortress Excavations 1952–65*. London: Roman Society.

Pollard, R. J. 1988. *The Roman Pottery of Kent*. Maidstone: Kent Archaeological Society.

Porter, R. and Rousseau, G. S. 1998. *Gout: the Patrician Malady*. New Haven: Yale University Press.

Potter, T. W. and Trow, S. D. 1988. *Puckeridge-Braughing, Hertfordshire: the Ermine Street Excavations 1971–72* (= *Hertfordshire Archaeology* 10).

Price, E. 2000. *Frocester. Volume 1: the Site*. Stonehouse: Gloucester and District Archaeological Research Group.

Price, J. 1996. 'A ribbed bowl from a late Iron Age burial at Hertford Heath, Hertfordshire', *Annales du 13e Congrès de l'Association Internationale pour l'Histoire du Verre*. Lochem: AIHV, pp.47–54.

Price, J., Brooks, I. P. and Maynard, D. J. 1997. *The Archaeology of the St. Neots to Duxford Gas Pipeline*. BAR BS 255: Oxford.

Protz, R. 1995. *The Ultimate Encyclopaedia of Beer*. London: Carlton Books.

Purcell, N. 1995. 'Eating Fish: the paradoxes of seafood', in Wilkins *et al.* (eds.), pp.132–49.

Quinnell, H. 2004. *Trethurgy*. Truro: Cornwall County Council.

Rae, A. and Rae, V. 1974. 'The Roman fort at Cramond, Edinburgh, excavations 1954–1966'. *Britannia* 5: 163–224.

Rahtz, P. and Watts, L. 2004. *Wharram. A Study of Settlement on the Yorkshire Wolds, IX. The North Manor Area and North-west Enclosure*. York: York University Archaeological Publications.

Richards, M. P., Hedges, R. E. M., Molleson, T. I. and Vogel, J. C. 1998. 'Stable isotope analysis reveals variations in human diet at the Poundbury Camp cemetery site'. *Journal of Archaeological Science* 25: 1247–52.

Richmond, I. A. and Gillam, J. P. 1951. 'The temple of Mithras at Carrawburgh'. *Archaeologia Aeliana* Series 4 29: 1–92.

Rickett, R. 1995. *The Anglo-Saxon Cemetery at Spong Hill, North Elmham, Part VII: the Iron Age, Roman and early Saxon settlement*. EAA 73: Dereham.

Rivet, A. L. F. and Smith, C. 1979. *The Place-names of Roman Britain*. London: BT Batsford.

Roberts, C. and Manchester, K. 1995. *The Archaeology of Disease*. Stroud: Sutton Publishing 2nd edition.

Roberts, I. (ed.), 2005. *Ferrybridge Henge: the Ritual Landscape*. Wakefield: West Yorkshire Archaeological Services.

Roberts, I., Burgess, A. and Berg, D. 2001. *A New Link to the Past. The Archaeological Landscape of the M1-A1 Link Road*. Wakefield: West Yorkshire Archaeological Services.

Rodwell, K. 1988. *The Prehistoric and Roman Settlement at Kelvedon, Essex*. CBARR 63: London.

Rogerson, A. 1977. 'Excavations at Scole, 1973'. EAA 5: 97–224.

Roth, J. P. 1999. *The Logistics of the Roman Army at War (264 BC – AD 235)*. Leiden: Brill.

Rule, M. and Monaghan, J. 1993. *A Gallo-Roman Trading Vessel from Guernsey*. Guernsey: Guernsey Museum.

Rush, P., Dickinson, B., Hartley, B. and Hartley, K. F. 2000. *Roman Castleford. Excavations 1974–85 Volume III: the Pottery*. Wakefield: West Yorkshire Archaeological Services.

Salway, P. 1993. *The Oxford Illustrated History of Roman Britain*. Oxford: Oxford University Press.

Sanquer, R. and Galliou, P. 1972. 'Garum, sel et salaisons en Armorique Gallo-Romaine', *Gallia* 30: 199–223.

Saunders, C. 1978. 'The iron firedog from Welwyn, Hertfordshire, reconsidered'. *Hertfordshire Archaeology* 5 (1977): 13–21.

Savory, H. N. 1971. *Excavations at Dinorben, 1965–9*. Cardiff: National Museum of Wales.

Scarborough, J. 1995. 'The opium poppy in Hellenistic and Roman medicine' in Porter, R. and Teich, M. (eds.) *Drugs and Narcotics in History*. Cambridge: Cambridge University Press, pp.4–23.

Sealey, P. R. 1985. *Amphoras from the 1970 Excavations at Colchester Sheepen*. BAR BS 142: Oxford.

Sealey, P. R. and Davies, G. M. R. 1984. 'Falernian wine at Roman Colchester'. *Britannia* 15: 250–4.

Sealey, P. R. and Tyers, P. A. 1989. 'Olives from Roman Spain: a unique amphora find in British waters'. *Antiquaries Journal* 69: 53–72.

Serjeantson, D. and Waldron, T. (eds.), 1989. *Diet and Craft in Towns*. BAR BS 199: Oxford.

Sharples, N. F. 1991. *Maiden Castle: Excavation and Field Survey 1985–6*. London: English Heritage.

Shennan, S. 1997. *Quantifying Archaeology*. Edinburgh: Edinburgh University Press. 2nd edition.

Shepherd, J. 1998. *The Temple of Mithras London*. London: English Heritage.

Shotter, D. 2005. 'Salt proprietors in Cheshire. Realities and possibilities', in Nevell and Fielding (eds.), pp.41–6.

Smith, R. A. 1912. 'On Late-Celtic antiquities discovered at Welwyn, Herts'. *Archaeologia* 63: 1–30.

Smith, R. J. C. 1993. *Excavations at County Hall, Dorchester, Dorset, 1988.* Salisbury: Wessex Archaeology.

Smith, R. J. C., Healy, F., Allen, M. J., Morris, E. L., Barnes, I. and Woodward, P. J. 1997. *Excavations along the Route of the Dorchester By-pass, Dorset, 1986–8.* Salisbury: Wessex Archaeology.

Snape, M. and Bidwell, P. 2002. 'Excavation at Castle Garth. Newcastle upon Tyne, 1976–92 and 1995–6: the Excavation of the Roman fort'. *Archaeologia Aeliana 5th Series* 31: 1–249.

Sparey-Green, C. 2002. *Excavations on the south-eastern Defences and Extramural Settlement of Little Chester, Derby* (= *Derbyshire Archaeological Journal* 122).

Stead, I. M. 1967. 'A La Tène Burial at Welwyn Garden City'. *Archaeologia* 101: 1–62.

Stead, I. M. and Rigby, V. 1986. *Baldock. The Excavation of a Roman and pre-Roman Settlement, 1968–72.* London: Roman Society.

1989. *Verulamium. The King Harry Lane Site.* London: English Heritage.

Stefani, G. (ed.) 2005. *Cibi e Sapori a Pompei e Dintorni.* Pompei: Soprendenza Archeologica di Pompei.

Steingarten, J. 1998. *The Man who ate Everything.* London: Headline Book Publishing.

Steures, D. C. 2002. 'Late Roman thirst: how dark coloured drinking sets from Trier were used'. *Bulletin Antieke Beschaving* 77: 175–9.

Stirland, A. and Waldron, T. 1990. 'The earliest cases of tuberculosis in Britain'. *Journal of Archaeological Science* 17: 221–30.

Stokes, P. 1996. 'Debris from Roman butchery: a new interpretation'. *Petits Propos Culinaire* 52: 38–47.

Strong, D. E. 1966. *Greek and Roman Gold and Silver Plate.* London: Methuen.

Symonds, R. P. 2003. 'Romano-British amphorae'. *Journal of Roman Pottery Studies* 10: 50–9.

Symonds, R. P. and Wade, S. 1999. *Roman Pottery from Excavations in Colchester, 1971–86.* Colchester: CAR 10: Colchester.

Swan, V. G. 1992. 'Legion VI and its men: African legionaries in Britain'. *Journal of Roman Pottery Studies* 5: 1–33.

Tassinari, S. 1993. *Il Vasellame Bronzeo di Pompei.* Rome: 'L'Erma' di Bretschneider.

Tchernia, A. 1986. *Le Vin de l'Italie Romaine.* Rome: École Française de Rome.

Tchernia, A. and Brun, J.-P. 1999. *Le Vin Romain Antique.* Grenoble: Glénat.

Thompson, D. 2002. *Thai Food.* London: Pavilion Books.

Timby, J. R. 1998. *Excavations at Kingscote and Wycomb, Gloucestershire.* Cirencester: Cotswold Archaeology.

Tomalin, D. 1989. 'A Roman symmetrical flanged bronze strainer found in Surrey and its counterparts in Highland Britain'. *Surrey Archaeological Collections* 79: 53–65.

Tomlin, R. S. O. 1992. 'The Roman 'carrot' amphora and its Egyptian provenance'. *Journal Egyptian Archaeology* 78: 307–12.

1996. 'A five-acre wood in Roman Kent' in Bird *et al.* (eds.), pp.209–15.

1998. 'Roman manuscripts from Carlisle: the ink-written tablets', *Britannia* 29: 31–84.

Toynbee, J. M. C. 1971. *Death and Burial in the Roman World*. Baltimore: Johns Hopkins. 1996 reprint.

Tuffreau-Libre, M. 1992. *La Céramique Commune Gallo-Romaine dans le Nord de la France*. Paris: Errance.

Turner, R. 1999. *Excavations of an Iron Age settlement and Roman Religious Complex at Ivy Chimneys, Witham, Essex 1978–83*. EAA 88: Chelmsford.

Tyers, P. 1984. 'An assemblage of Roman ceramics from London'. *The London Archaeologist* 4.14: 367–74.

1996. *Roman Pottery in Britain*. London: Routledge.

van der Veen, M. 1985. 'Evidence for crop plants from north-east England: an interim overview with discussion of new results' in Fieller, N. R. J., Gilbertson, D. D. and Ralph, N. G. A. (eds.) *Palaeobiological Investigation Research Design; Methods and Data Analysis* Oxford: BAR IS 266, pp.197–219.

1991. 'Charred grain assemblages from Roman-period corn driers in Britain'. *Archaeological Journal* 146 (1989): 302–19.

van Driel Murray, C., Wild, J. P., Seaward, M. and Hillam, J. 1993. *Preliminary Reports on the Leather, Textiles, Environmental Evidence and Dendrochronology*. Hexham: Roman Army Museum Publications.

Vaughan, J. G. and Geissler, C. A. 1997. *The New Oxford Book of Food Plants*. Oxford: Oxford University Press.

Vernon, K. 2000. 'Milk and dairy products' in Kiple and Ornelas (eds.), pp.692–702.

Wacher, J. 1995. *The Towns of Roman Britain*. London: BT Batsford, revised edition.

Waldron, T. 1989. 'The effects of urbanisation on human health' in Serjeantson and Waldron (eds.), pp.55–73.

Ward, S. 1988. *Excavations at Chester. 12 Watergate Street 1985: Roman Headquarters Building to Medieval Row*. Chester: Chester City Council.

Webster, G. 1980. *The Roman Invasion of Britain*. London: BT Batsford.

2002. *The Legionary Fortress at Wroxeter*. London: English Heritage.

Wenham, L. P. 1968. *The Romano-British Cemetery at Trentholme Drive, York*. London: HMSO.

Wenham, L. P. and Heywood, B. 1997. *The 1968 to 1970 Excavations in the Vicus at Malton, North Yorkshire*. Leeds: Yorkshire Archaeological Society.

White, K. D. 1995. 'Cereals, bread and milling in the Roman world' in Wilkins *et al.* (eds.), pp.38–43.

Whitwell, J. B. 1976. *The Church Street Sewer and an Adjacent Building*. AY3/1: London.

Wilkins, J., Harvey, D. and Dobson, M. 1995. *Food in Antiquity*. Exeter: University of Exeter Press.

Willcox, G. H. 1977. 'Exotic plants from Roman waterlogged sites in London'. *Journal of Archaeological Science* 4: 269–82.

Williams, D. and Carreras, C. 1995. 'North African amphorae in Roman Britain: a re-appraisal'. *Britannia* 26: 231–52.

Williams, D. and Evans, J. 1991. 'A fragment from a probable Roman *Clibanus* from Catterick, North Yorkshire'. *Journal of Roman Pottery Studies* 4: 51–3.

Williams, D. F. and Peacock, D. P. S. 1983. 'The importation of olive oil into Iron Age and Roman Britain' in Blázquez Martínez, J. M. and Remesal Rodríguez, J. (eds.) *Produccion y comercio del aceite en la Antiquedad 2° congreso internacional*. Madrid: Universidad Computense, pp.263–80.

1994. 'Roman amphorae in Iron Age Wessex' in Fitzpatrick and Morris (eds.), pp.29–32.

Williams, R. J. and Zepvat, R. J. 1994. *Bancroft: a late Bronze Age/Iron Age Settlement, Roman Villa and Temple Complex*. Aylesbury: Buckinghamshire Archaeological Society.

Williams-Thorpe, O. and Thorpe, R. S. 1988. 'The provenance of donkey mills from Roman Britain'. *Archaeometry* 30: 275–89.

Willis, S. 1996. 'The Romanization of pottery assemblages in the east and north-east of England during the 1st century AD: a comparative analysis'. *Britannia* 27: 179–221.

2002. 'A date with the past: late Bronze and Iron Age pottery and chronology', in Woodward and Hill (eds.), pp.4–21.

Wilmott, T. 1997. *Birdoswald*. London: English Heritage.

Wilmott, T and Wilson, P. (eds.), 2000. *The Late Roman Transition in the North*. BAR BS 299: Oxford.

Wilson, P. R. 1989. 'Aspects of the Yorkshire signal stations', in Maxfield, V. A. and Dobson, M. J. (eds.), *Roman Frontier Studies 1989. Proceedings 15th International Congress of Roman Frontier Studies*. Exeter: Exeter University Press, pp.142–7.

2002a. Cataractonium *Roman Catterick and its Hinterland. Excavations and Research, 1958–1997. Part II*. CBARR 128: York.

2002b. Cataractonium *Roman Catterick and its Hinterland. Excavations and Research, 1958–1997. Part I*. CBARR 129: York.

Winder, J. M. 1992. A Study in the Variation of Oyster Shells from Archaeological Sites and a Discussion of Oyster Exploitation. PhD thesis, University of Southampton.

Woodiwiss, S. (ed.) 1992. *Iron Age and Roman salt production and the medieval town of Droitwich: Excavations at the Old Bowling Green and Friar Street*. CBARR 81: London.

Woodward, A. and Hill, J. D. (eds.), 2002. *Prehistoric Britain: the Ceramic Basis*. Oxford: Prehistoric Ceramics Research Group.

Woodward, A. and Leach, P. 1993 *The Uley Shrines. Excavation of a Ritual Complex on West Hill, Uley, Gloucestershire: 1977–9*. London: English Heritage.

Woodward, P. J., Davies, S. M. and Graham, A. H. 1993. *Excavations at the Old Methodist Chapel and Greyhound Yard, Dorchester, 1981–1984*. Dorchester: Dorset Natural History and Archaeological Society.

Woolf, G. 1998. *Becoming Roman.* Cambridge: Cambridge University Press.

Wrathmell, S. and Nicholson, A. (eds.), 1990. *Dalton Parlours: Iron Age Settlement and Roman Villa.* Wakefield: West Yorkshire Archaeological Service.

Young, C. J. 1977. *The Roman Pottery Industry of the Oxford Region.* Oxford: BAR BS 43.

Zienkiewicz, J. D. 1986. *The Legionary Fortress Baths at Caerleon: II the Finds.* Cardiff: National Museum of Wales.

    1992. 'Pottery from excavations on the site of the Roman Legionary Museum, Caerleon 1983–5'. *Journal of Roman Pottery Studies* 5: 81–109.

    1993. 'Excavations in the *Scamnum Tribunorum* at Caerleon: the Legionary Museum Site, 1983–5'. *Britannia* 24: 27–140.

Index